H. D. LEWIS

OUR EXPERIENCE
OF GOD

9780006421511

COLLINS
The Fontana Library of Theology and Philosophy

First published by George Allen and Unwin Ltd., 1959

First issued in the Fontana Library, 1970

*Also available in a cloth-bound edition
published by George Allen and Unwin Ltd.*

© *George Allen and Unwin Ltd., 1959*

*Printed in Great Britain
Collins Clear-Type Press, London and Glasgow*

Our Experience
of God

H. D. Lewis is Professor of the History and Philosophy of Religion at King's College, London. He has also held the Chair of Philosophy at University College, Bangor. He was at Oxford from 1954-55 as a Leverhulme Fellow and has been invited to several American universities including Bryn Mawr and Yale, at both of which he was visiting Professor, and Harvard Divinity School where he was visiting Lecturer.

He is currently Editor of the journal *Religious Studies* and Chairman of the Council of the Royal Institute of Philosophy, having previously held office as President of the Mind Association, the Aristotelian Society and the Society for the Study of Theology.

Other publications by H. D. Lewis include *Morals and the New Theology*, *Morals and Revelation*, *Freedom and History* and *Dreaming and Experience* (from the Hobhouse Memorial Lecture). Two series of Gifford Lectures given by him from 1966-67 and 1967-68 are to be published shortly in the Muirhead Library of Philosophy of which he is Editor.

To My Wife
and
to the Memory of My Parents

CONTENTS

PREFACE

In his recent book, *My Philosophical Development*, Bertrand Russell tells us that one of the two sources of his original interest in philosophy was his anxiety 'to discover whether philosophy would provide any defence for anything that could be called religious belief, however vague'. He soon concluded that philosophy could not do this and, as he also tells us, 'came to disbelieve first in free will, then in immortality, and finally in God'. My own experience, if I may compare my own case with that of an eminent philosopher, has been almost entirely the reverse. Religion had very little to do with my initial interest in philosophy. I was attracted to the subject at first by the clarity and neatness with which philosophical positions and arguments were presented to me by my first teachers in the subject, in whom I was singularly fortunate. Never have I listened to lectures which impressed me more by their elegance and clarity than those which the late Professor James Gibson delivered to his classes at Bangor, and I should like to take this opportunity of paying my tribute to the memory of that most learned and courteous gentleman.

In course of time, however, as I reached more advanced stages in the study of philosophy and became in turn a teacher of the subject myself, the bearing it had on my religious beliefs became more apparent and of more absorbing interest to me; and I am sure that I could not hold the faith which I now profess with the same firmness had I not had the good fortune to become a philosopher.

This is not at all because I found in philosophy a new and independent way of establishing religious truths, an alternative route to the one I had traversed before. It will be a major theme of this book that we cannot construct a religion for ourselves out of merely philosophical elements, and that the attempt to provide some philosophical or similar substitute for religion, as it normally presents itself, is misconceived. Perhaps Bertrand Russell and others have made the mistake of expecting philosophy to help in the way I disavow, and possibly much of their agnosticism may be traced to this source.

The place of philosophy in religion is not to provide proofs or supports for beliefs which are otherwise held on inadequate grounds, but to make more explicit for us what is the nature and status of the beliefs we do hold and commend to others. It cannot thus be said that philosophy is ever indispensable for religion any more than it is for art or morality. But the more sophisticated and self-consciously reflective we become, the more we are aided by holding our beliefs against the light of a philosophical study of their nature.

A philosophical study of this sort induces, among other things, a more judicious attitude towards erroneous beliefs, or beliefs which seem so to us. At more rudimentary levels of religion erroneous beliefs find some corrective in the solidarity they have with the religious life as a whole, and the mischief they may perpetrate is lessened in the same way. But when beliefs are detached more completely from the total experience by which they were shaped, and for which they ought to provide a focus, those elements in them which offend us appear more stark and monstrous. There are, I believe, many intelligent persons who have turned away from religion, or failed to consider it seriously, because they have not understood how to place or interpret certain features of religion, and especially doctrines, which seem to them objectionable. But they might not have been alienated so easily if they had understood better how religious beliefs are formed and how to disentangle the elements of truth and falsity in them.

Since I have referred to Bertrand Russell, I may perhaps be allowed to take him again as my example. I do not believe that Russell, who can write with such penetration and wisdom about certain problems, could have dealt so cavalierly with Christian claims as he does in *Why I am not a Christian* had he brought any profound understanding of religion to his assessment of its claims. This goes for many who are influenced by his writings, and for other truth-loving persons whose agnosticism has taken a very similar course. They have taken the shadows, sometimes at many removes, for the substance.

This, in turn, is due to an even more insidious mistake that may be made about religion, a mistake that has a great deal to do with current disbelief; it is the assumption that religious beliefs are to be established, if at all, in the same way as we learn other things. Men look for God as they would look for some other peculiar entity, something not perhaps obviously discernible but to be found, if at all, as we find other things in the world or, as in science, we learn strange facts about its structure. But nothing we can identify with God is found in this way, we only learn more and more about the world. God is not a constituent of the world, one among many; He is somehow altogether beyond it. But many people, not finding God as they would find other things, despair, not unnaturally, of finding Him at all. How can we get altogether outside what we experience? Some do indeed make this desperate attempt, and they find themselves peering into a void in which they see nothing at all. Others suppose that religion depends on cultivating strange experiences or odd states of mind, and they find they have no taste for this or much aptitude for it; and even if they had, would they not still be discovering further new things about themselves and their environment? Is not the seeker for God in the hopeless position of seeking for something he could not possibly identify?

Despair, or indifference, engendered in this way is accentuated by social conditions inimical to firm belief and by the absence of the sort of environment most conducive to religious insight. This is the situation so well described by Simone Weil in *The Need for Roots*. It owes much to the extraordinary changes that have come about in the material conditions of existence in recent years, coupled with the upheavals of two world wars. Periods of transition and disturbance favour more the attitudes of scepticism than of sustained beliefs such as men have in religion. This is not a new problem, although it is perhaps sharper than at any time today. To deal with it is a task in itself, more especially as it would be vain as well as absurd to oppose the provision of amenities and the new understanding of nature which science brings. But I mention these matters here solely to acknowledge the bearing they have on my theme and to add that I shall only be dealing with them incidentally in this book. If, however, I meet with success in my more frontal attack on scepticism the way will be clearer for dealing with the more social side of the question of belief, for the two are very closely connected.

The limited aim which I set myself is to try to show how we are to deal with the dilemma which presents itself in religion, namely that we seem to say something about a reality too elusive or beyond our grasp for us to say anything sensible about it at all. Many philosophers and theologians have dealt expressly with this issue of late, some in a more sceptical vein, others in support of belief, and we have now at least this advantage that the problem has been very sharply defined for us in recent controversy. It is by no means a new problem, and perhaps some of our sceptics are a little too prone to overlook the consciousness of the present dilemma which shrewd religious persons have always had. Nonetheless, recent sceptical criticism of religion, and the widespread popular scepticism to which the former gives shape and expression, bring home very clearly to us the task which confronts the apologist. Much close and clear-sighted thinking, on both sides of the fence, has ensured this important advance.

I shall not however review closely the course which recent controversy about religion has taken. This may seem remiss, but there are already available excellent introductions to this subject,[1] and I have myself had opportunities to provide fairly elaborate surveys[2] of recent work in the philosophy of religion. It would be tedious to go over ground that has already been much trodden, and I have thus kept for the most part to the course which I wish to take on my own account. I do, however, provide in the first two chapters an indication of current solutions to the problem of religious belief which do not seem to me satisfactory, but I do this without detailed investigation and solely as a means of bringing the reader as easily as possible to the point where more constructive work may begin. These two chapters are of a preliminary or introductory character and I do not wish in the least to give the impression that the

[1] For example. *Faith and Logic*, Ed. B. Mitchell; *New Essays in Philosophical Theology*, Ed. A. Flew and A. MacIntyre; *Foolishness to the Greeks*, T. R. Milford; *Words and Images*, E. L. Mascall; *The Modern Predicament*, H. J. Paton, pp. 1-58; *Essay in Christian Philosophy*, I. Trethowan, pp. 103-20; 'God and Logical Analysis' by the same author and L. Williams, *Downside Review*, Summer 1956; *Theological Language* and 'Empiricism and Religion', *The Christian Scholar*, June 1956, I. T. Ramsey; 'On the Logic of Creeds', Harald Eklund, *Theoria*, Vol. XXII.

[2] 'Survey of Recent Work in the Philosophy of Religion', *Philosophical Quarterly*, April and July 1954; 'Recent Empiricism and Religion', *Philosophy*, July 1957; 'The Cognitive Factor in Religious Experience', *Proceedings of the Aristotelian Society*, Supplementary Volume XXIX.

positions I reject are not worthy of close examination—
were this book the proper place for it!

I have also been more concerned with the question
'How are particular religious assertions justified?' than
with that of the 'being' or existence of God. This is
partly because the first of these questions has been somewhat overshadowed by the second in recent controversy
and the peculiar conditions attaching to it not sufficiently
grasped. But I am also aware that what I have to say
about the second question, which is of course logically
the initial one, is not very new and does not add much to
what recent writers like E. L. Mascall and C. A. Campbell, in somewhat different ways, have said about it. I
have tried to put the main point here in my own way,
and I hope that may not prove unhelpful, but, if I were
to go further into this topic, it would be by critical
discussion of traditional ways of treating the subject,
such as the famous theistic arguments. My intention at
first was in fact to include a detailed discussion of the
alleged proofs or arguments. But that is one of many
things which I have discarded in order to keep my book
within reasonable proportions and sketch my main view
fairly boldly.

A philosopher, more I imagine than any other writer,
has the embarrassment that any topic he raises merges
into others. This is one reason why so many notable
philosophers have left so little behind them. Their work
never seemed final enough to let it go. Plato, it will be
remembered, was always talking about the 'long and
toilsome route' to be taken, and he meant by this that
you had to get to the bottom of all the main questions
before you could be happy about any one of them. He
took to the dialogue form as a partial solution to the
problem. It is possible to be unduly awed by this difficulty
and never attempt a task of a fairly comprehensive kind,
and that may have much to do with the present distrust
of metaphysics and the partiality for statements in the

more provisional form of papers rather than books. One must however take some chances, and I have been fairly bold in taking some topics in my stride in this book, especially those like 'moral freedom' or 'ethical objectivity' on which I have expressed my views more fully elsewhere. I have also held over for the present the application of my main theses to specific theological and doctrinal questions, although the way I view this task and my slant on its problems will be reasonably evident in passages like the last sections of chapter XVIII.

To venture on a very bold comparison, this book has been 'ripened and plucked from me' in its present form, like Hobbes's *De Cive*, by the exigencies of the times. I cannot disguise the fact that I feel there to be a very urgent need to deal with the questions raised in this book. This is due in part to the conviction that the growing point in philosophy today is to be found where controversies centre on such questions as 'Why is there anything at all?' But I am also much affected, as are many others, by concern at the spread of religious indifference and the secularism which springs largely from despair of obtaining any light on the main questions which religion raises and of being religious without sacrifice of intellectual integrity. The light one may shed on such questions may be dim, but where the need is great that light should not be hidden. For these reasons I have confined myself to a fairly general outline of the view of religion I commend and have not weighted my book with more detail and technicalities than the minimum needed to give a fairly comprehensive picture of religion as I see it; and I have also as far as possible written my book as a continuous essay, although divided for convenience into chapters, hoping in these ways to win the attention of readers other than professional students of philosophy and theologians.

I have, finally, to thank many persons for their very generous help. Indication has been given in earlier books of my deep indebtedness to the work and friendship of Professor C. A. Campbell. He has put me further in his debt by reading the whole of this book in typescript, and a similar kindness has been done to me by Dr A. C. Ewing and Professor W. G. Maclagan. The first two chapters were read for me by Professor H. H. Price and I have also benefited much from conversations with him about the subjects discussed in this work. Professor J. N. Findlay read two chapters when they were presented as a paper to a philosophical club in London and allowed me to make use of his comments upon them. Dr D. A. Rees put his wisdom and wide experience at my disposal by correcting the proofs, and I was also assisted in this tedious task by my wife.

The publishers must be thanked for much kindness, including the permission to reproduce, in chapters III and IV, some material from my contribution to *Contemporary British Philosophy*, Third Series. It is also a pleasure to thank the trustees of the Leverhulme Trust for a fellowship which enabled me to spend a whole session free from departmental duties.

December 1958   H. D. LEWIS

CHAPTER I

RELIGION AND BELIEF

The claim that a religion is true appears to be a fundamental one which the advocate of a particular religion
would find it hard to avoid. There are no doubt many
other important things to be said about religions, and
some of them would be of considerable interest even to
the out-and-out sceptic. No one could deny that religion
has been a social phenomenon of the greatest importance,
and to understand how it functioned in the past is at
any rate part of the study of history or sociology. But a
religion could not be kept alive by interest of this kind.
Even if we felt that it would be a good thing for religion
to continue as a useful illusion, it does not seem in the
least likely that we could put much heart into the work
of encouraging it once the mask had unmistakably fallen
from our own eyes.

Fiction can of course be fascinating, and a great deal
with which we divert ourselves and enrich our minds is
fiction known to be such. There are readers, I am told,
who lose interest in a story the moment they learn that it
is not true. But that is not, happily for ourselves and the
writers of plays and novels, the case with most of us.
We take delight in fiction as well as in fact, and the
extent to which spice is added to a story by knowing
that it is true must, I imagine, vary a great deal from one
individual to another. Whether all this presupposes that
there is some sense in which fiction is also true need not
be considered here. It might be argued that fiction shows

us something which is true about ourselves or the world, although it cannot by its nature be literally true. But whether or not the value of fiction turns on some subtle truths it succeeds in conveying, it is certain that religion would lose its hold upon us if we had to regard it as fiction. If someone invented a religion, however colourful its rites and attractive the ideas to be entertained within it, we could not take it seriously unless we were also convinced of its truth. We cannot just divert ourselves with a religion or play at it. We must believe and take the belief to heart.

I am writing here in terms of the greatest generality and I do this deliberately. For what sort of belief it is that counts in religion is one of the things to be considered in this book. There are many beliefs and many ways of holding and expressing them, and I offer no hope of exhausting the study of this subject in the field of religion or of even noting all its main features. But I do wish to begin with the insistence that the question of belief and truth is a fundamental one, and that anyone who allied himself to a religion for the lure which the practice of it had independently of any belief associated with that religion, would not be treating it seriously as religion. He might find certain practices aesthetically pleasing or soothing. But that is not how we normally think of religion, and a person who took part in the practices we usually find in religion in a spirit of complete disillusionment about the truth of that religion would either be branded as a hypocrite or be thought to be making a fool of himself. If he were attracted solely by the beauty, let us say, of some religious ceremony or merely wished to listen to its music, he would do so with clear reservations and not as a votary properly participating.

It does not follow that agnostics and sceptics should be discouraged from witnessing the practices of religious people. For how can any practice be properly known except by taking due note of it? This is part of the dilemma involved in commending a religion, for on the one hand it will be argued that the religion cannot be properly understood by those who merely consider it from a distance or from 'outside', and on the other hand no one wishes to put himself in the false position of coming 'inside' unless he is first convinced. Religious persons are sometimes apt to trade on this by putting it to the doubter that an uncritical commitment is the only way. The position in fact calls for much restraint and patience on both sides. It is very hard indeed for the unbeliever to view religion fairly, as in slighter measure it is hard for members of different religious persuasions to be just to one another. The ceremonial side of religion in particular will appear strange, and sometimes ridiculous, to those who view it from outside. It may of course be ridiculous, and the belief which inspires it. But how hard it is to know this when we are not devotees ourselves.

In practice there are many ways of coping with this problem. A religion could not properly claim our interest unless there were at any rate some initial case to be made for it—least of all if the disciplines it might impose were difficult and costing ones. But there is a case to be put— *contra gentiles* as it were; and much that I shall try to say in this book will be part of it. Then, again, the outsider may not have been always or wholly outside; there may be something to build on. And, even more important at the moment, we may allow for the difference between the point of view of the observer and that of the participator. I believe there are matters here which call for more ingenuity and resourcefulness on the part of Church leaders than they have hitherto seen to be needed. Many earnest seekers are put off by the fear—a very estimable one—of being in a false position. But my concern at the moment is not with the strategy of evangelism on its practical side. There are people more experienced and better placed than I to cope with that, and I must be content to drop my present reflection among them in the passing.

A point more germane to my present purpose is that any interest the religious apologist hopes to enlist must be directed to the expectation that his religion may be found to be true, and by this I do not mean that it must be true in the sense of being a genuine form of religion, in the way we sometimes have in mind in speaking of a true poet or a true work of art. I mean that true religion in the latter sense must also be true in the sense that its beliefs are not false or meaningless. That will not be all that it involves. As the Epistle of James reminds us: 'Pure religion and undefiled before God and the Father is this, To visit the fatherless and widows in their affliction, and to keep himself unspotted from the world.' But it is certainly not just that. There is also something to be believed, in the spirit of which the 'works' are to be performed. A religion must stand the test of truth and falsity in the normal sense, and I do not think we could find any religion of which this is not the case.

I must stress further that I am not at the moment concerned with overt professions of faith or the formulation of creeds and doctrines. That is a subject to which I shall come in due course. All that I am anxious to maintain at the moment is that there must be at the core of a religion something significant to which the distinction of true and false in the normal or literal sense applies, however elusive or metaphorical its form.

This seems to apply to all religions, but it has more prominence in some. There are also religions which allow a very wide latitude in matters of belief, most forms of Hinduism for example. It has even been said that one could believe anything and be a Hindu. But that is certainly mistaken, and it is one of the reasons why Hinduism has never been able to absorb the Moslem religion. A person who declared that the sacred Hindu scriptures were not to be venerated or that there could be no kind of rebirth could hardly call himself a Hindu. In the Christian religion belief is very prominent and it would be altogether absurd for anyone to call himself a Christian and also profess himself indifferent to certain fundamental Christian beliefs.

Consider, in the light of this, the recent decline of religion. There is little doubt that religion is rapidly losing its hold on the minds of men in many parts of the world, not least in our own society. There are several reasons for this, including the devastation wrought by the upheavals of two world wars. But have not factors of this sort operated largely by inducing a despondent attitude towards the possibility of our knowing that religious beliefs were true, or could ever be rendered probable? If these were firmly thought to be true, or even if it were only a reasonably likely possibility that they were true, it seems hard to think that they could be unheeded and thought to be of little account.

For the sort of things which religious people usually maintain appear to be of the most momentous nature, and if sound and acceptable they could hardly fail to make an overwhelming difference to our outlook. Take, for example, a fairly straightforward belief in our survival of bodily death. I know that the religious idea of immortality includes more than this. Some of my philosophical friends have even gone to the length of affirming that the Christian idea of 'Resurrection' does not even include survival. But that is certainly carrying things too far, and if pressed would be wellnigh unintelligible. Consider then this prospect of survival. Suppose it were announced that irrefutable evidence had been obtained, in some scientific manner such as by psychical research, that we do survive. We need not consider now whether physical investigations or any branch of science could ever achieve this result. All we need suppose is that it had somehow been established, with the sort of certainty by which it is held that there is no life, let us say, on the moon, that we do survive. Then it seems to me that there is no doubt whatsoever that this would elicit the profoundest interest and continue to determine our attitude and behaviour in a great many ways.

If it were further shown that those who did survive might enjoy considerable happiness, and that one condition of entering upon this agreeable state and removing the present spectre of the painful termination of life at the close of its brief span was that we should fulfil certain conditions now, then it seems highly unlikely that all this would not be heeded with at least the same care with which men make provision for their old age and the well-being of their children, or look after their health. We consult doctors at need and attend to what they say, because we have reasonable grounds for believing that, with the advance of medical science, we are likely to derive considerable benefit from medical and surgical treatment when our health is imperilled. If the chances were remote, we might of course still turn in desperation now and again to a doctor, or we might take an apparently incurable and frightening complaint to a quack with an alleged secret remedy. But doctors would not make an honourable living out of us and have their work organized as one of the major professions unless, with all allowance for their fallibility, we assumed that they usually knew what they were about.

I submit that if ordinary persons had the same confidence as this in the truths of religion they would heed them in the same way. And when we consider that a religion like Christianity offers us the fellowship of a Supreme Being who is our creator and sustainer and who has appeared as a man amongst men to ensure our eternal salvation, then this, much more than some fairly crude belief in survival, could not fail to be a dominant fact in our lives—if we fully believed it to be true.

Allowance must of course be made for the facility we seem to have for believing certain things in a somewhat remote and unimaginative way. Newman taught us much about this in a book which is not, unhappily, as well known as it should be today, namely *The Grammar of Assent*. He distinguished between 'real' and 'notional' beliefs. The latter are beliefs we certainly do hold but which have not made a very deep impression upon us because they do not touch us personally or have never been made very vivid for us. I may not doubt at all the truth of a report of a railway disaster of which I read in the papers, but the horror of the incident does not overwhelm me as it might if someone I loved were involved in it—or if I were given an exceptionally harrowing description of the scene of suffering and death. We may bring to mind here the shrewd observation of Thomas Hobbes, that although 'the power of spirits invisible' is greater than the power of men, the latter is usually much more feared. This, I believe, reflects much more than Hobbes's religious scepticism, but when every allowance has been made for the need to enliven our beliefs and bring out, as prophets and preachers should, the implications of what we profess, the assertions made in the name of religion are so overwhelming and, in the case of a religion such as Christianity, so closely related to social and ethical matters, that no one could easily be indifferent to them once assured of their truth.

Lapses and disloyalty are of course another matter. The saints may betray their faith, and they have often confessed themselves 'the prince of sinners', but they have not been able to view their betrayal with an easy indifference. The realization of it is, on the contrary, a torment and source of profound despair.

There seems therefore every reason for regarding the question of truth as a fundamental one for religion. And if this may seem a somewhat trite and obvious observation with which to embark on a study of religion, the substantial excuse may be pleaded that writers about religion, and especially those who have concerned themselves expressly with religious experience, have in point of fact been much more occupied with descriptions of 'the varieties of religious experience', to borrow the title of William James's famous book, in other words with the phenomenology of the subject, than with the properly epistemological question of how anything comes to be known as true in religion—what sort of certainty we have, and what its guarantee is.

The psychology of religious experience no doubt affords scope for highly arresting and colourful accounts of religion, such as have been most skilfully and helpfully provided by writers like William James or Ronald Knox. But to scrutinize the credentials of alleged religious experience and consider how it may take its place as a source of knowledge and illumination is also in its way no less exciting and, if I am right in the hints I have just been dropping, at least of equal practical importance with any other investigation of religion.

Perhaps I may also be allowed to protest against the practice of many writers on religion of seeming to address themselves firmly to the properly epistemological questions and then, when the difficulties begin to mount, diverting their attention to matters of a more descriptive character on the edges of the epistemological question, such as an account of conditions to be observed by those who would arrive at the truth in religion, or sheltering behind mysterious formulae to be made available to the apologist *in extremis*. If we are to arouse interest in religion today, we must not burke the really hard issues or give an impression of not having the courage of our convictions intellectually when it comes to the point.

At the same time, no one should turn to a study of religion with the expectation that all the difficulties will be slickly disposed of. He will certainly be doomed to disappointment if he takes up this book in that spirit. For one of the things I shall be most concerned to exhibit is the elusive character of religious awareness and the subtlety of the processes which it involves. This does not mean in the least that religion must become today a matter for sophisticated intellectuals. Far from it. But it does mean, as I shall be at pains to stress, that there is no simple mechanical way of laying hold once and for all on religious truths and happily disposing of their difficulties. Plato spoke often of the long and toilsome route the philosopher must follow. I have tried not to make this book very long or very toilsome to read. But I must, at the outset, disclaim any intention of displaying the nature of religious insight itself as anything other than a blessing to be enjoyed by those who are prepared to pay an exacting price.

At this point it will be well to make some reference to the course which has recently been taken by the philosophical study of religion. There has of late been a lively renewal of interest in religious questions among philosophers, after a period of considerable apathy and indeed aversion to religion. And this has come about in a way, and taken a form, that is very significant.

It is well known that the dominant trend in philosophy today, in English-speaking countries at least, is a rigorously empiricist one. For the empiricist the meaning of assertions and the test for truth must be found in experience, and experience in this context is generally understood in terms of our impressions of the external world and our subjective sensations. Even the most liberal form of empiricism has to restrict itself to our experience in the 'here and now' of the present world. The consequences of this seem fatal for religion and it is hard, in that sphere at least, for the empiricist to avoid anything short of total scepticism.

To a generally sceptical line in philosophy roughly following the course laid down by Hume, recent philosophers have added a special technique for disposing of statements which appear to be sensible and yet go beyond the sort of limits which empiricism can admit. This is known as linguistic analysis, and the feature of it which most concerns us now is the attempt to represent any statements which do not conform to the accepted empiricist criteria as confusions engendered by forms of speech. It is possible to make assertions which have a perfectly correct and normal grammatical form, and which may indeed seem very important and profound, but which in fact have no meaning at all. A common example is the question : 'Does gravity run faster than virtue?' Perhaps no one would be taken in by this, but many similar atrocities have from time to time been perpetrated, and their authors, no less than others, have been taken in by them.

There is therefore much to be said for those who warn us not to be misled by language and urge that we should look more carefully at the structure of language in order to avoid confusion and error. Two serious examples from philosophical and religious thinking may be noted. Not so very long ago it used to be common to refer to the State or to Society (with a capital S) as if these were some mysterious sort of entity or superstructure over and above the lives and personalities of their individual members. I do not think the philosophers who encouraged this, and perhaps were mainly responsible for it, were merely deluded by words. They had impressive arguments which went astray at some point. But their errors were no doubt aided by rather vague metaphorical expressions and a somewhat loose use of terms. A similar hypostatization of an abstraction may be found in much that theologians from time to time have said about a mythical 'Man' whose fallen state they deplore and who is somehow all of us at the same time. This is the sort of view I have ventured to criticize on more than one occasion in discussions of the familiar doctrines of universal sin. Again I should be far from ascribing the errors I deplore solely to linguistic confusion, but such confusion has no doubt had some part in making some sinister notions plausible.

The perils which beset us in this way have not gone undetected in the past. Plato and Aristotle seem to have been acutely conscious of the deceptiveness of language and were always pressing for careful analysis to ensure that we were not misled or arguing at cross purposes. They also appreciated well how easy it is to suppose that something profound and original has been said by the mere use of novel or impressive terms. But other philosophers, of all schools, have followed Plato and Aristotle in putting us on our guard against the deceptiveness of words. It was not a 'linguistic philosopher', in the sense that this word has acquired in contemporary philosophy, who showed most devastatingly what little, if any, explanatory value a term like 'instinct' had in itself.[1] We notice that birds build their nests without training or conscious anticipation of the purpose of the nest, that they migrate and return to build under the same roof another year. It is very hard to understand how this, and many similar activities, come about. But whatever we are to say about it, the more use of a label, like 'instinct', does not advance the subject except to the extent of a convenient grouping. Much the same may be said of abuses of a word like 'telepathy'. Some persons appear able to communicate with each other without the ordinary media of speech or the observation of behaviour. We might perhaps explain this in terms of some notion of a universal mind, although I do not think this very plausible. But merely to label these extraordinary occurrences 'telepathy' does not take us very far. Nor does one need to be of a particular philosophical persuasion to appreciate that.

Many linguistic philosophers, however, have maintained that all the assertions we make which are not in accord with strictly empiricist principles must be attributed to fundamental confusions due largely at least to the language we use. The confusion does not always

[1] G. C. Field: 'Faculty Psychology and Instinct Psychology', *Mind*, July 1921.

display its irrational character at once, for in the play of thought which is confused in these ways there may be considerable exercise of reason. It is as if someone were to tell a story about a square circle, that it was invented at a certain time by a person whose character and prodigious efforts might be described, that it was lost and disappeared for a long period and then turned up unexpectedly, that various quarrels broke out about it leading to terrible wars. The historian would be asked to reckon with the square circle; and some might tell the story much more correctly than others, some would tell it more eloquently and colourfully, and others would display more ingenuity in tracing its ramifications with other interests. But at the heart of this activity, whatever the elegance or sense disclosed at the perimeter, there would be sheer nonsense.

This is very largely how many of our contemporaries view the beliefs that have usually been held in religion about the soul, immortality and God; and the impact of this on religious philosophy has naturally been considerable. Several writers have recently reviewed the course that has been taken by attempts to cope with the so-called challenge of positivism and linguistic philosophy to religion, and I have myself attempted more than one survey of this kind.[2] I shall therefore confine myself to the observations that bear most closely on my own theme.

Let me note then some of the main ways in which recent empiricism has affected thought about religion. The first is the one we should most naturally expect. It is this. If philosophers and others have been induced, in venturing beyond the limits of empiricism, to fall into irretrievable confusion, then religion appears to be the sphere *par excellence* where this would happen; and if it is a major part of the task of the philosopher to expose such confusions and debunk pretentious nonsensical beliefs, then religion seems to afford a peculiarly inviting

[2] See the Preface.

field for the exercise of the new techniques. Some writers have entered into the task with gusto and have had an enjoyable time casting down, for good as it seemed to them, the idols that had imposed on men for so long.

An ingenious and, in some ways, impressive and instructive attempt to rebut the normal form of religious belief is that whereby Professor J. N. Findlay practically reverses the traditional ontological argument for the existence of God by producing an ontological *disproof* of the existence of God. He observes that necessary existence is indispensable to the idea of God and pre-supposed in the attitude of worship, and he then notes that it is an accepted principle of contemporary philo-sophy that all statements about existence are contingent. The reply has been made to this—very properly to my mind—that the idea of God falls outside the conditions which govern our thought about finite things, it is unique; and this is a beginning on the right road to understanding and wisdom in religion. The soundness displayed by Findlay in presenting what the attitude of worship involves has also been acclaimed. But the sub-stance of his argument as it stands is that the belief in God as a real being or entity is radically confused, and that we must substitute something else for it—in Findlay's case an ever-receding ideal which our attainments will never overtake.

Others have stressed the seeming unintelligibility of Christian doctrines of the 'Trinity' and the 'Incarnation'; and yet others have taxed the Christian with the diffi-culty of reconciling various forms of evil with the belief in an omnipotent God of Love, the seeming plausibility of the belief being ascribed at some point to confusions which the study of language dispels.

Professor Antony Flew, for example, argues in this way. He refers[3] to the belief that God is 'all-good' and 'all-

[3] *New Essays in Philosophical Theology*, edited Antony Flew and Alasdair MacIntyre, p. 144 *et seq.*

powerful', a belief which is obviously difficult to reconcile with the existence of evil. One of the commonest ways of seeking to escape from the dilemma engendered in this way has been to urge that evil has come about through the abuse by men of the freedom of will which God had to bestow upon them in order to make moral attainment possible for men. I believe that this solution of the problem of evil is quite adequate as far as it goes. My own complaint about it would be that there is much evil which it does not cover. But Professor Flew is not content with that, he thinks there is no force at all in the 'free-will defence', and that even in its application to moral evil and its consequences the 'defence' can be shown to be 'broken-backed'.

He attempts to show this by claiming that 'God might have made people so that they always in fact *freely* chose the right'.[4] This seems on the face of it a contradiction, for how could we be free if God had already guaranteed that we always did what was right? Professor Flew, however, thinks the contradiction is only apparent and that the difficulty can be met if we consider 'the paradigm case of acting freely'. For do we not often say that a person has elected to do something of his own free will when it is certain that we consider him bound to act in that way and predict confidently what he will do? I am writing at my desk at the moment, and I do so of my own accord; I am not working under any threat or compulsion. But a friend who knew my habits or who had been told how I proposed to spend the day would have the strongest grounds for predicting that I should spend the morning working at home.

Professor Flew's example is that of two persons who announce their engagement and thus make it known that they intend to get married long before they do so. No one would suggest in this case that they were not getting

4 *Op. cit.*, p. 149.

married of their own accord. We may be certain, knowing the persons concerned, that they will get married. But this does not imply in the least that they are to be married under some pressure or compulsion.

The plausibility of this 'short way' with the libertarian is however only superficial. For what most advocates of free will today would hold is that there are *some* occasions when our conduct is not determined. To hold that our actions are never in any measure predictable would be absurd. We cannot deny the obvious continuity of most of our conduct; but the question remains whether there may not be exceptions to this; and that question is not settled by noting that there is *one* very common use of the terms 'free will', 'our own accord' and so forth, which is quite consistent with our actions being predictable. The word 'freedom' has, in short, many applications, and one of the things which the preoccupation with language ought to have made plain is that we cannot settle philosophical problems by making one use of a term paramount and exclusive.

There are many further matters raised in Professor Flew's ingenious paper. But I refer to his central contention here merely as an illustration of one form which the concern with language has taken in some recent sceptical approaches to the philosophy of religion.

A fairly downright destructive line of this kind has not, however, been the only one to be followed by those who have fallen under the spell of some form of the current empiricism. Many have been deeply disquieted by the seemingly sceptical implication of their philosophical views. Owing certain religious allegiances already, by upbringing for example, and finding that the importance of religion for them abides, they have sought to force a reconciliation of their sceptical philosophy with their religion. Exceptional ingenuity and persistence have been displayed in this forlorn attempt. Some have sought to exclude the factor of belief altogether from their 'faith'.

Religion becomes thus a matter of a certain attitude towards the world or our present existence, or the cultivation and satisfaction of certain alleged 'religious emotions', though what might signalize these as religious is not made very plain. Sometimes we are told to 'believe in', not 'believe that', as if we could 'believe in' God without also believing that He exists. Others severely reduce the scope of religious assertions and then reinterpret the beliefs which were thought to be centred on some supreme or transcendent object in terms of the world and our finite life as we know it now. That God created the world has been held to mean that 'everything which we call "material" can be used in such a way that it contributes to the well-being of men'.[5] That is in fact not even a corollary of the belief in Creation, but it shows the straits to which the empiricist is reduced in seeking to make room for religion. The latest, as well as the most impressively presented, of these desperate expedients is that of Professor Braithwaite who has argued that, in substance, religion is no more than a moral policy and that whatever there seems to be over and above this are mere stories. The stories need not be true in any sense. It is not, as religious writers sometimes maintain, that a myth like the creation stories in Genesis points to something beyond itself or expresses metaphorically what is not literally true. There is, for Braithwaite, no beyond to refer to, and the function of the stories is simply to inspire us to adhere to the proper moral policy. It does not matter whether they are in any sense true, or taken to be true. All that is needed is that we should entertain them assiduously enough to be stimulated by them. But this is a very far cry indeed from any normal form of the Christian religion, and it has been subjected to much severe criticism.[6] The

[5] David Cox, *Mind*, April 1950, p. 216.

[6] For example by Dr A. C. Ewing in 'Religious Assertions in the Light of Contemporary Philosophy', *Philosophy*, July 1957.

centrality of ethical ideas for a religion like Christianity is evident, and since there appear to be theological writers who query this, we cannot but welcome Professor Braithwaite's insistence on the essential moral factors in Christianity. But it is very hard to believe that the Christian religion, to which Professor Braithwaite adheres, does not require these moral matters to be related to something which the founder of this religion, and his followers generally, considered to be much more fundamental.

It does not follow, however, that there is nothing to be gained for the understanding and deepening of religion from the cautious approach to its problems which prevails today and from the scrutiny of religious language. For, in the first place, religious persons, like others, are apt to fall into confusion, and they have often had recourse to utterances notable for little besides obscurity; and they have sometimes used arguments which paid little heed to good sense and consistency. To be forced into the open, to be induced to be as explicit in apologetics as the case allows, is an excellent discipline, and one could not easily find a better example of this than some of the comments made by Professor Flew, in the paper to which I have already referred, on some very cavalier treatments of the problem of suffering. I also believe that, with the exception of one fundamental matter to be noted very shortly, religious assertions must be supported by evidence of some kind. Religious writers have often neglected this requirement or evaded its implications, and so much is this a besetting sin of religious apologists that many of those who seem to have been most concerned with the analysis of religious language have themselves sometimes suggested that little is required to silence the sceptic or agnostic besides the exhibition of the peculiarity or alleged special logic of religious language. The logic of statements about the Resurrection, it is urged, is not the same as the logic of statements about survival of death, much less of anticipation of ordinary finite events.

But while there is substance in the last suggestion, making it necessary for us to guard against too close an assimilation of religious assertions to the assertions we make in other contexts, it does not provide us with an easy solvent of all our difficulties. There yet remains some need to exhibit how religious statements are to be justified, how we decide between the claims of different religions and accept some religious beliefs while rejecting others. This is a necessity which the concern for verification and the more downright forms of the sceptical linguistic challenge have accentuated. Even if 'clarity is not enough' we certainly need all the clarity possible for us, and we must be as precise as our case allows. The pages which follow owe a great deal to a conviction which I share with many sceptical colleagues, namely, that some indication must be given, by those who adhere to religion, of how specific religious assertions are warranted, and, since many have been helped to appreciate this by the recent preoccupation with the meaning of religious beliefs and the method of justifying them, I should much regret it if there appeared from the same philosophical quarter an evasion of the original challenge more subtle and insidious, and more inescapably dogmatic, than the obscurities the 'challenge' was meant to expose.

At the same time it is not without some justification that religious apologists have fallen back, under pressure, on the peculiarities of religious statements. And there are here two respects in which the course taken by the philosophy of linguistic analysis seems helpful. The first is the emphasis upon the open texture of language and the variety of types of statements and beliefs. This is a significant feature of the sort of preoccupation with language which seems to have superseded the more downright positivism which held the field at first. It should make us more accommodating when confronted with a further notion which arises more directly from the challenge presented by the more uncompromising empiricist; and this brings us to an aspect of recent controversy which is exceptionally important and instructive for our purpose.

In most matters, the line which is taken by opponents of empiricism is to argue directly in support of the notions the empiricist rejects, the idea of the self as an abiding entity of some kind or the belief in moral principles not to be accounted for in terms of some reaction of our own. And this seems to me the course to be adopted, heeding well the shrewd observation of Dr Mascall that 'the one thing we must not do (with the positivist) is to try to prove our conclusions from his premises'.[7] But when we turn to religious questions, however unplausible or fantastic the religious writer may find some of the expedients desperately adopted by the empiricist to be, he is also uneasily aware of a sneaking sympathy with him. Somehow or other the positivist also appears to be on the right lines, and there is something oddly attractive to the religious thinker in what he says. One writer[8] has detected a close affinity, for example, between the ideas of Otto in *The Idea of the Holy* and those of the pioneer of modern positivism, Wittgenstein, as we find him in the *Tractatus*.

This is because, in religion, we are dealing with matters which seem bound to be incomprehensible; by their very nature, and not merely through present limitations of our minds, they seem to pass beyond the sphere in which intelligent discourse is possible. They concern a reality which is altogether 'beyond' us or transcendent, and the doctrines which come thus to be propounded, speaking for example of Three Persons in One or of God as being also a man, appear openly to flout the ordinary

[7] *Existence and Analogy*, p. 84.
[8] T. McPherson, 'Religion as the Inexpressible', *New Essays in Philosophical Theology*.

criteria of good sense and consistency. If, as some allege, God is 'wholly other', if He is altogether outside the sphere within which normal explanations are possible, we appear to be confronted with an overwhelming and irreducible mystery and there seems to be no reason why beliefs, if they are possible at all, should conform to ordinary standards. The linguistic philosopher occasionally presents this by saying that religious language is different from ordinary language, and that savours not a little of evasions of really difficult problems; for we have still to ask to what these languages refer. But there is no doubt that the question of the meaning and status of religious assertions is a vital one. In some regards at least there is something very queer about them, and, while shrewd thinkers in the past have often had a very full appreciation of this, we owe a debt to our linguistic and sceptical contemporaries for making this point peculiarly evident to us again.

The need was greater because of the severely rationalist character of a great deal of the thinking which immediately preceded the rise of recent empiricism. Much as the sponsors of the philosophy of linguistic analysis today assume with the most serene confidence that the so-called 'revolution in philosophy' has come to stay, so, at the close of the last century and the beginning of the present one, it was held very generally and with equally unruffled confidence that the sort of idealist philosophy initiated by Hegel would remain the philosophy of the future, admitting only of modifications of detail and applications to new fields. Since our philosophical memories appear to be so very short, it may be well to be reminded of this at present. But the beginning of the end for idealism of the more rationalistic sort came when it was made increasingly evident that the expectation that all things would admit eventually of an exhaustive rational explanation, came up against some stubborn facts which appeared to be just 'given' and could not be reduced altogether to their relations to one another. There is some 'given' element of this sort in perception, there seem to be ultimate ethical principles which we must accept without giving any further reason for them, and there are pain and moral evil. The need to take our rational explanations as far as we can remains, and this is one reason why the neglect of idealist philosophy is so much to be deplored. But the attempt to present everything in our experience as part of an all-inclusive system of such a nature that everything within it could be seen to be what it is by a rational necessity inherent in the whole, appears far too optimistic and doomed to failure.

Nor does this come about merely because there is much in the world as we find it which remains baffling. There appear to be unavoidable limits to rational explanation, and this is where the topic impinges most closely on religion. For our dilemma appears to be this, that on the one hand we feel impelled to look for rational explanations as far as we can, but, on the other, we find that this very process points beyond itself to some 'explanation' in a very strange sense which is not the normal one of showing how things fit together or affect one another. A possible way out of this dilemma is just to lop off one horn of it, and that is of course the procedure adopted by many professional thinkers and laymen today. We must, they say, just accept the world as we find it; where it makes sense, that should be welcomed, and, where we come up against ultimate questions of why anything should be as it is or what happens at the point where normal explanation ends, there is nothing to be done but to shrug our shoulders and turn our minds from questions which seem bound to be unreal or confused, since there is *ex hypothesi* no answer to them. What is it to ask a question when we do not even know what sort of answer could satisfy it—and when any conceivable answer appears to be ruled out from the start?

This is however just the point where the enquirer must

not let himself be browbeaten by the sceptic. Nor must he give way to unreason. Under cover of the fact that we seem to be confronted in religion with some mystery which passes our understanding, some religious writers, including some very well-known and influential theologians of the present day, have taken the liberty of setting ordinary standards of truth and consistency at nought and have multiplied doctrines, some of them highly mischievous ones, almost as they pleased or as the requirements of an accepted tradition seemed to dictate. Others put themselves beyond all criticism by merely affirming that there are certain things 'given to be believed', and thus, while tantalizing and alienating the honest seeker, come perilously close to aligning themselves with the reactionary authoritarian dogmatism which is the major menace of our civilization. Merely to say that religion is a mystery is not enough, least of all if we take licence from this to make an unnecessary mystery of matters capable of being rationally treated. How, if religion is a mere mystery, do we choose what religion to adopt, and what form of that religion is best? Rational criticism there must be somewhere if we are not simply to put one uncompromising dogma against another in hopeless antagonism.

At the same time the element of mystery remains, an irreducible mystery. It is not that there is something *we* cannot understand, and may never be able to, as higher mathematics is a mystery to most men and may provide problems which no one is clever enough to solve. Our present 'mystery' is not that of the detective story where we have not yet got the clue but know that there is one. It is 'mystery' rather in the sense of not admitting of explanation, and it is highly significant how the sceptical down-to-earth trend in contemporary philosophy is curving round on itself in a puzzled preoccupation with such questions as 'Why is there anything at all?'[9] 'Could the

[9] See J. J. C. Smart in *New Essays in Philosophical Theology*, edited Antony Flew and Alasdair MacIntyre, p. 46.

world come to be out of nothing?' For these are the really germinative questions with which we come to the beginning of wisdom in religion.

Let me put the point this way.[10] Whenever we provide an explanation of something, it is always possible to ask why this explanation holds. The pistol goes off because we fire it; how does this happen? Because of the nature of sparks and gunpowder and so forth. But why should this product explode when fired? Because of its chemical composition. But why should the ingredients composing it behave as they do? Because of the way atoms, molecules and so forth behave. The physicist comes to the rescue of the chemist. But why should things behave as the physicist finds that they do? However complete and comprehensive our explanations, it always seems possible, like a persistent child, to ask 'Why?' And even if we had reason to believe that all profitable questions had been raised and answered, which appears most exceptionally unlikely, there would still remain the question, not only in physics, but everywhere, of why the world should be the kind of world it happens to be; and the more we persist in this the more evident does it become that the question 'why' is changing its character and that we are coming to confront ourselves with a demand which we feel to be inevitable, but which by its very nature cannot be met or properly formulated. We can only speak vaguely of the universe making sense or of 'reality being a whole' and yet 'making sense' or being a 'whole' in some way quite other than that in which things normally do so.

The temptation to throw in one's hand at this point is naturally great. For not only is it hard to express what we feel to be the case about the universe here, but it may also be asked what reason we have for believing that the seemingly radical incompleteness of explanations, as we offer them, is somehow countered and that we are not

[10] Cf. C. A. Campbell, *Scepticism and Construction*, p. 15.

living in a universe which just happens to be and which has some random element at the very heart of it.

This is a very hard objection to meet. For from the very nature of the case there are no reasons or arguments to be offered here, and that is why so many critically minded persons stumble, especially if they also pride themselves on being tough-minded. At the same time there appears to me to be nothing more certain than that the universe is a 'whole' or 'system' in the highly elusive sense to be given to the words in this context, and I may put this very simply by saying that I just cannot accept it that things merely happen to be as they are—in the last analysis. Nor is this just because it is uncomfortable or intellectually unsatisfying to have to confess defeat or live in a world which has this random character to it. The inability in question is an intellectual one. It seems plain to my mind that the world cannot be an ultimately random one and that it must have some completeness or explanation which goes beyond anything which mind or 'explanation' normally provides.

One is not however wholly at a loss in conveying this conviction to others or inducing it where it is absent. I have already been making a fairly hard effort to that end, and there are ways of supplementing this and bringing out the sort of mystery by which our existence is surrounded, mystery not in the merely negative sense but in the positive sense of there being something incomprehensible to 'account' for things being what they are, even though words like 'account', and any other we may substitute for it, are bound to be inadequate here.

One course open to us, for example, is to draw attention to the peculiar problems which confront us when we think about space or time. I am not thinking of the staggering immensities of space as the physical cosmologist and astronomer describe them today, but of aspects of space or time which are evident even before the astounding discoveries of modern science are considered at all. It is impossible to think of a furthest point of space, wherever we place it there could always be something beyond that; and I am not in the very least daunted in saying this by theories of relativity and receding constellations. The question is not about the limits of what we can find about space, nor about the conceptions, like that of a 'curved space', which the physicist and mathematician may find helpful for their rather special purposes. I submit that space as we all of us find it in experience is something to which no limit is conceivable. On the other hand, we cannot just let the matter rest there. For the notion of space going on and on *ad infinitum* is equally bewildering, and, while I obviously cannot argue this further, I can invite others to continue reflecting on the matter in the expectation of inducing them to see it as I do. And if they do so they seem to be at the point where the universe displays some unity of a 'supra-rational' character whose mystery we can never reduce.

In the case of time this strategy is even more successful. For while philosophers, especially recent philosophers of the school of Analysis, have shown how confused and misleading our ideas about time are apt to be, there remains something quite fundamentally bewildering about the notions of either a first moment of time or of time that has always been going on. This is not at all in the class of the paradoxes which sometimes present themselves to sophisticated thought, like 'Achilles and the tortoise'. It is not something we expect some clever logician to dispel, but another aspect of the irreducible but positive mystery in which the world as we find it is somehow rooted.

Recourse may also be had here to the traditional arguments for the existence of God; and with this allusion to the traditional arguments we may take the discussion to a further stage and begin a new chapter.

CHAPTER 2

BELIEF AND MYSTERY

The objections to the main arguments for the existence of God are well known. But it seems to me that what these arguments tried to express, most of all in the cases of the cosmological and ontological ones, is the conviction of the self-subsistent supra-rational source of the world as we find it. Where the arguments fail is in trying to break into a series of steps what is in fact one insight, and also in seeking to start from purely finite factors and reason to conclusions about the infinite. The attractiveness of such procedure is evident, for if it could be shown that features of the ordinary finite experiences, which none of us would deny, can be made the basis of arguments similar in substance to those we generally accept, then the religious apologist would be in a very strong position *vis-à-vis* the sceptic; he would be in a good position to compel acquiescence from those who are prepared to give the subject honest attention, and he could make his appeal universal. But the sort of insight which lies at the heart of our belief in God is none the less sadly misrepresented in this way.

It is true that we do proceed from finite facts, and from any such facts you please, to some reality 'beyond' or 'other than' these. But the movement of thought which proceeds in this way is unique and has no strict analogy elsewhere. That is just what the usual form of the arguments overlooks. If, for example, we appeal to

the traditional 'first cause' argument, we invite the
rejoinder that, on our premiss that everything must have
a cause, the alleged 'first cause' must have a cause as
well. In all probability we shall also import into our
argument many unwarranted assumptions designed to
fortify the unavoidable weakness of our case. This is
seen particularly plainly in the work of Descartes. His
intention was to ensure for religious assertions, or at
least for the basic ones, the sort of certainty which seems
least shakable in other matters, and to this end he thought
he could provide arguments which no clear-headed
person could possibly dispute from premises which were
equally certain parts of our common human heritage.
This is how it happens that he makes those strange
assertions about a cause applying to the objective as
well as to the formal reality of an idea and containing
within itself all the reality of the effect. The latter notion,
together with many other questionable features of Descartes's formulation of the principle of causation, would
not, I submit, occur to us if we thought simply about
cause and effect. But Descartes, or those from whom he
unwittingly took his cue, was thinking of the causal
principle already in the context of our religious thought,
and he thus came to import into it matters which have
only significance in terms of the very peculiar and absolute dependence of all things on God. In other words,
Descartes's arguments could not be given plausibility
without loading the seemingly finite matters with which
they began with something of the trans-finite reference
of the conclusion; and what is, in this regard, peculiarly
and instructively evident in the case of Descartes may
be detected also in the form which such arguments take
in the work of other thinkers, before and after Descartes.

The benefit we derive from the study of the traditional
arguments is thus two-fold; we appreciate in the first
instance how they fail as arguments, and in the second
place we acquire an insight into the movement of

thought which lies behind them and makes them plausible. The cosmological and the ontological arguments in particular converge on the requirement that the conditioned and incomplete realities we directly encounter should have some source which is not limited in that way. To begin with the general principle that existence can be some kind of quality or predicate, as the ontological argument usually does, is obviously to invite trouble and expose ourselves to rejoinders like those of Kant. On the other hand, if we make it plain that we are only thinking of some compulsion which affects our thought about God and insist that in *this* case existence has some inevitability which we do not find elsewhere, then we seem to be on firmer ground and come in effect to the same position as lies behind the cosmological argument, namely that there has to be some supreme unconditioned Being.

The argument from design has much less to be said for it and tends to proceed on the assumption that the relation of God to the world is in essentials the same as that of other agents to their artefacts. We are thus invited to find God, *in the first instance*, in the design or harmony we may detect in the world we inhabit; but it has often been pointed out that this argument could not get under way at all unless we presuppose at the start that explanation is needed or that the world is in some way made or created. The most that it could in any case provide would be a finite God (or gods), another being whose power far surpasses our own but whose agency is in principle the same as ours. Harmony and structure and worth we do no doubt discover in the world, in impressive if also imperfect ways, and if we consider these in the light of our prior or independent conviction that the world is a dependent one, in the sense indicated hitherto, we can ascribe to them the highest importance in our religious view. But we do not begin with them.

My own feeling is that those who find the 'argument from design' impressive, and they include some very great names as well as numerous ordinary folk, are combining with it the initial insight into the inevitability of there being some complete and unconditioned source of the sort of realities we actually meet; and to this extent it also converges on the insight which lies behind the other arguments.

These are matters which other writers have brought out well of late, in particular some Neo-Thomist philosophers like Dr Mascall and Dom Illtyd Trethowan. The former, commenting on St Thomas's First Way, declares : 'The point is not really that we cannot have an infinite regress in the order of nature, but that such an infinite regress in the series of moved movers would necessitate an unmoved First Mover not *in* the order of nature but *above* it'.[1] To Trethowan we owe the shrewd advice to go on looking 'at what being stands for until it breaks into finite and infinite'. It is this one leap of thought in which finite and infinite are equally present, and which cannot be broken up into steps which we may negotiate one by one, that brings us to the ultimate mystery of which I spoke earlier.

Philosophers may be further aided here if they reflect on one of their own most intractable problems, namely that of 'the grounds of induction'. On the one hand it seems very hard to provide rational grounds for proceeding in what seems a rational way : for as soon as we attempt this we appear to be moving in a circle. On the other hand it is felt that some ground or justification there must ultimately be. Is not the answer here also in terms of the conviction we have that the intelligibility of the world has its warrant in some source that goes beyond itself and of which any further account is by the nature of the case unobtainable?

A consequence of what has been hitherto maintained

[1] *He who is*, p. 44.

is that to understand the meaning of the reference to the mysterious source of our existence is also to appreciate the inevitability by which it must also be. The problem of meaning becomes thus, as our positivist critics have helped us to understand, a paramount one at this crucial point in the philosophy of religion. It is not as with other concepts of which we may have a perfectly clear understanding while remaining uncertain whether anything exists corresponding to them. I can understand quite well what is meant by 'dragon' and there is nothing in the idea itself to preclude there being extraordinary fire-breathing creatures of this sort somewhere—or many-headed beasts. I can also think of creatures with powers far exceeding our present ones. But whether in fact there are such beings is a further question to be settled by evidence of some kind; we have to discover them, or traces of them, and cannot deduce their existence from our conceptions of them. But at the very heart of religion lies this quite unique notion of something of which we cannot conceive at all without seeing at the same time that it must be.

To put this in more expressly religious terms, there is substance in the view that the sceptic and agnostic do not so much find themselves unconvinced that in fact there is a God as fail to see what is meant by 'God'; and we cannot first tell them what we mean and then proceed to show that God is also real. If they can be induced to see what we mean when we speak of God they will at one and the same time be convinced of His existence; and this is not without considerable importance for religious propaganda in all its forms.

Much of the recent philosophical criticism of religious notions owes its apparent strength to neglect of the distinctiveness of the insight which lies at the core of them, and the consequent assimilation of religious assertions to other beliefs whose nature, and the criteria to which they must conform, are very different. Supporters of religion have done themselves an injustice by the same oversight. It is one apprehension, one 'leap of thought' in the words I have used earlier, which reveals to us what the infinite means in the way we can grasp it and also exhibits the inevitability of its being, as peculiarly involved in the being of anything.

A further term which suggests itself here, in designation of the insight I am now discussing, is 'intuition'. This seems to me on the whole an appropriate term and one which it is convenient to use in the absence of a better. But it has some disadvantages, and, as I propose to put this term from time to time to its present use, it will be well to note its limitations. The major one is that the words 'intuition of God' have not infrequently been used to designate a view very completely at variance with what I wish to maintain in the present context and later. That view is that finite beings may have some direct contact with the infinite as it is in itself, much as some writers have held that we have some wholly unmediated awareness of one another's minds or 'acquaintance' with them. That we can so transcend the limitations of creaturely nature and enter, in the more explicit language of religion itself, directly into the 'mind' or being of God seems to me a preposterous supposition, not because of the special limitations under which we labour in our present status, but because it wholly misrepresents the absolutism and finality of the ultimate source of our existence which I have been seeking to display and which is so fundamental to the way we apprehend that source. I find it hard indeed to make much of any suggestion that one mind can be literally one with any other mind or have acquaintance with it. The suggestion seems to do violence to the essential nature of thought and consciousness. But quite independently of any difficulties that attend the notions of direct acquaintance or of the merging of minds in the present sense at the finite level, the supposition that we could be strictly part of the

infinite, rather than dependent upon it, conflicts altogether with the unity and completeness the infinite must
have in itself.

Mystical experience is frequently represented as if it
involved a literal union with God or absorption into His
being, and it is understandable that this should happen.
For, in the first place, in becoming aware of our dependence on God it is a natural error to empty our independent existence of any substance and represent all that we
are and do as the express activity of God. The clearest
example of this mistake, and the most interesting, seems
to me to be the form which Islamic theology has sometimes taken. For here theological thinking has circled
round into almost complete contradiction of itself. Beginning with the orthodox Islamic insistence on the transcendence of God and thus on the absolute difference
between God and man, it has allowed this very conviction to slide into the insistence that our dependence on
God implies that our lives and activities are themselves
the activities of God. This, as is well known, led in some
cases to highly presumptuous heresies and to claims by
seers and religious teachers to be themselves divine.

Orthodox Islamic teaching would not endorse this form
of mystical philosophy, but there seems to me to be a
case to be made for the view that by assimilating its
insight into the transcendence of God too readily to
the display of superior power at the natural level, and
making God's supremacy all too creaturely in this and
in other ways, Islamic theology, by contrast with the
Biblical notion of Creation, lent itself all too easily to
the deviation into what proves in due course the opposite
of its initial contention.

The merit of the Hebrew and Christian doctrine of
creation is that it preserves our dependence on a mysterious source which is complete and ultimate in itself while
also allowing us our distinct creaturely existence, and
even the freedom of rebellious wills—a possibility which

Islam, except in a few and extremely unorthodox forms, could not seriously countenance. The Bible does not formulate the notion in question in abstract or philosophical terms, but I do not think that what the Bible presents in more vivid and familiar language, reflective of less sophisticated experience, can nowadays be seriously thought to be other than the convictions to which I have just referred.

A further way in which the belief in a literal union of ourselves with God comes about is through the exceptionally intimate sense of the presence of God which some persons have enjoyed. I shall consider in due course how this can be understood without any suggestion of the diminution of the essentially mediated character of the experience of God enjoyed in such cases. But this is not a topic that can be profitably investigated at this stage. I shall wish to make every allowance for the exceptional closeness of the union with God which is possible to us, and which saintly persons have attained. But at the moment it must suffice to enter a warning against taking the language which expresses this mystical union and the blessedness of it too readily at its face value. In the main, the mystics who impress us most have been the keenest to make this point themselves.

By 'intuition of God' then I do not mean to refer to a direct or unmediated union with God. Nor do I wish the term 'intuition' to be understood in accordance with another common usage, namely that which refers to swift and subtle reasoning where the observations or other items it involves are not displayed as openly as usual, for example a sailor's intuition about the weather based on long experience and subtle observation, or the shrewd insight which some statesmen and others are believed to have into other people's characters, or the alleged 'woman's intuition'. Least of all am I thinking of the sinister delusions of a Hitler, also sometimes called intuitions. Nor am I thinking of any genuine occult or paranormal powers men may have. In its more technical use in philosophy, the word 'intuition' refers to modes of knowledge (or belief if there are fallible intuitions) which do not admit of further support or reason, like the distinct steps in an argument or the insight we have in ethics into the worth of certain things in themselves. At some points in our thinking it seems that there must be intuitions of this sort. But whether there are or not, or whether the usual account of them as intuitions is sound or not, we must not assimilate the intuition of ultimate being, which I have been discussing, too closely even to the properly technical applications of the term elsewhere in philosophy. For these refer to apprehensions of some feature of finite experience and have there their explicit and determinate content. There is, in short, no very close analogy to our apprehension of the inevitability of there being one ultimate and complete or unconditioned reality of which, or of the relation of dependence of other beings on it, no account is possible other than the divination of its inevitability in the ways of which I have already given the only sort of indication of which the case allows.

It must be stressed, however, that the elusive insight or intuition in question has the same compelling character as the apprehensions we have in logic or mathematics. It presents what we feel must be the case, and its elusiveness in other regards does not affect the certainty which it brings. Admittedly not all have this insight, it is not psychologically necessary, but it is an intuition of something necessary in a way not substantially different from the sense in which truths in mathematics or logic are necessary. It is at the other extreme to wishful thinking or to the strange psychological necessity by which, on some views, we are bound to adopt certain beliefs for consolation or to sustain ourselves in some other way. Its necessity, in short, is in the way it is seen to be true.

Nor must it be supposed that the apprehension of the

world breaking, as Trethowan put it, into finite and infinite is elusive in the sense of being rare or difficult to evoke. I believe it comes to most people sooner or later. They may not recognize it in abstract formulations, and these, as I have been at pains to insist, may easily be misleading. Nor is the form of religion with which a person is familiar, or his understanding of it, always likely to induce a receptive attitude of mind to this initial religious insight. In finding some forms of religion distasteful, or certain religious beliefs and practices without warrant, we may close our minds to anything we remotely associate with religion. And this I believe accounts for much atheism and agnosticism today. It is not the only explanation of current unbelief. There is also the rush and excessive superficial liveliness of modern life, together with other conditions not conducive to a contemplative attitude. Not that all must here be put to the debit side of modern conditions. Beyond their certainties and the routine of petty preoccupations and culturally numbing distractions, there present themselves the major uncertainties and menaces which, if they do not drive men to despair and drowsy escapism, cannot fail to stir at some level the deepest reflection, of which there is probably more than finds its way to professional and sophisticated thought. But whatever the causes and extent of modern scepticism, my impression is that there are few people whose minds do not open at some stage to the sense of the infinite and the mystery which surrounds existence, provided they are not inhibited by false and misleading preconceptions. They may not come with us the rest of the way a religious person wishes to go. But that is another matter of which more will be said later. We certainly do an ill service to religion if we smother or alienate or underestimate the vague and inarticulate and much bewildered sense of something elusively and irretrievably 'beyond' which is also intertwined with present reality, the sense of ultimate but sustaining mystery in which all religion begins, as I shall much stress later. On the contrary this should have much prominence in our commendation of religion and we should welcome the intimations and confessions of it which come, sometimes unwittingly, even from most unexpected quarters. That there may also be complete and unrelieved scepticism seems to me likewise true, although the chances of making an inroad upon it are greatly enhanced if we heed the matters to which I have just alluded and combine sense and understanding with our exhortations.

But having got thus far we appear to be faced with a major obstacle. For, it will be argued, suppose we admit that the world can be viewed as dependent, in the way suggested, on some irreducibly mysterious source which has to be in some radical way different from the world itself, just what does this give you? What importance or interest for us has this 'something we know not what' when from the nature of the case its mysteriousness is bound to remain impenetrable; and, in any case, if nothing further is maintained have you not more in common with the agnostic than with the adherent of a particular religion as he normally appears? Religion seems to present some very definite beliefs; these affirm, for example, that God can be thought of in personal terms and that this is the only way to think of Him properly, that His will towards us may be known, that He may be described as a God of love and grace, that He is active in the world, that His presence can be felt, that we can communicate with Him, pray and expect our prayers to be answered. This seems a very far cry from an irreducible mystery.

It is with this question that we come face to face with the problem to be mainly discussed in this book. A great deal has been written lately in line with the thesis I have hitherto advanced. I have referred already to some recent Neo-Thomist writers. Others have converged on a similar position to theirs, in respect of the point at issue now, in the form of Transcendental Theology, stressing the absolute difference of God and man, of finite creaturely being and Creator Lord. And some have felt uneasy, not without justification, at this seemingly unbridgeable gulf between the human and the divine. They feel that we are being either reduced in religion to a vague and bodiless piety or invited to make our religion determinate in as random a way as you please; and the latter suspicion has much to deepen it in the misuse of their insight whereby transcendentalist theologians like Barth and Brunner lapse into unreason and bring our ordinary understanding of present reality, especially in moral matters, into complete contempt.

But if we are not to take some sinister course of this kind, and if we are to be resolute in not reducing the ultimate character of the mystery with which we have to deal, can we give any specific content to religion and affirm certain determinate beliefs to be true, and others false? Is not the positivist, at this point at any rate, lurking in ambush for us with the deadliest weapons from which there is no escape? Must we not for ever be silent or immediately contradict the insight which gives us a silence to be broken at all? On the one hand there is the challenge to come into the open with our beliefs and not let them be eroded, as Professor Flew put it, to vanishing point; and on the other there seems to be the difficulty, that once we try to bring the irreducible mystery with which our existence is surrounded into 'the atmosphere', as it were, of our own experience, it disintegrates altogether.

Some religions are less embarrassed by this than others, not merely because they allow more latitude to their adherents and attach less importance to dogma, but also because they concern themselves with highly general and vaguely specified ways in which union with some supreme reality may be obtained. In some cases this has also carried with it an attitude of negation or passivity towards the present world, salvation being thought to be attained by passing altogether beyond the ills and limitations of finite existence. Such religions seem to me to be in error, both in their conception of the one supreme reality and in their understanding of finitude, and the ill consequences for our social and moral outlooks of the notion that nothing counts besides the absorption of ourselves into some reality other than ourselves and differently constituted are well known. In any case it has not been possible to retain this rarefied attitude consistently, and the most daringly otherworldly religions have had at some point to relate themselves to the conditions of present existence, yielding, for the rank and file of their votaries especially, various views about the significance the 'beyond' seems to have for life here and now, views which conspicuously lack the benefit of integration into the proper functioning of our distinctive faculties. Some of the leaders of world-negating religions have become newly sensitive to these difficulties of late and are importing into their religions, in their more attractive forms, a dynamic this-worldly element as a corrective to the forswearing, in theory and in some respects in practice, of present reality. Such is the highly influential teaching of Sri Aurobindo in modern Hinduism, and this holds much promise of fruitful interaction between religions and cultures which are otherwise most antipathetic.

It might be urged also that there are religions which evade the present dilemma by being altogether this-worldly. But I doubt very much whether we can properly say that there are such religions, and I shall have more to say on this head in the next chapter.

For the most part, religions have presented determinate beliefs of the utmost importance for our practice now. This seems altogether desirable, it is what we have come in the West specially to expect, and in the Christian religion we have bold and extensive beliefs about a personal God and His dealings with us such as those listed already. Some theologians of today will perhaps take exception to the words 'knowledge *about*'. They insist that we do not have 'knowledge about' God, but an encounter with Him. It is easy to see the attractiveness of this notion for those who are perplexed by the uncertainties of Biblical and kindred studies, the more so since it is most essential to insist that our relation with God must take the form of personal encounter and meeting. One of the major themes of this book will be the need for enlivened personal apprehension of God and the guide and corrective which this supplies to beliefs and attitudes which become false by being stagnant. We owe much to the recent existentialist emphases. But among the many aberrations of this extremely one-sided and often obscure approach to religion, few seem to be more strange and misleading than the notion that there can ever be encounter of the kind in question (or any other) independently of some 'knowledge about'.

Admittedly there is a genuine distinction to be drawn between knowing about persons and meeting them. We all know a great deal about persons whom we have never 'met' or 'known', as these words are normally used. I should perpetrate a deliberate falsehood if I said that I had met President Eisenhower. I know what most intelligent citizens know about him without special study; I have heard his voice on the radio and could have seen him on television, as I have in news-reels at the cinema. But to know him I should be expected to have come much closer to him personally. His colleagues, friends, relatives and so on are the people who know him. At the same time it is of some importance to stress here that the distinction we draw in this way is very fluid and by no means as sharp as some theologians suppose, and that it varies much according to the context in which we speak. Suppose, for example, I attended a meeting addressed by the Prime Minister. It would still be misleading to say that I had met him, and it would remain so if I had made bold to put questions to the speaker and been answered. But suppose I had been taken round at the end to the platform and shaken hands with Mr Macmillan, and perhaps put my question to him there. I do not think I could be accused of not playing the game at all if I then said I had met the Prime Minister. But is there all that difference in substance between the latter case and the earlier ones? Suppose furthermore that I made a habit of attending all the Prime Minister's meetings and asking questions, might there not then be grounds for saying that I knew or had got to know him quite well; and might not he also say, as soon as I appeared among his audience, 'I know that fellow, he will be putting questions or making a nuisance of himself any minute'? At what point, in short, do we say seriously that we know people? Is not this one of the cases where we should take much to heart the warning so clamorously and insistently made recently not to be unduly and uncritically influenced by words?

These trivial examples may seem a far cry from high theological debate. But they serve well to illustrate the fact that having encounter with people or things[2] still requires some knowledge about them obtained in some fashion. Such knowledge may be fuller and more intimate and obtained in a more subtle way than our knowledge about those with whom we have at best impersonal dealings. But it is knowledge, or belief, all the same. I love my friends and relatives, or have acute dislike of others, on the basis of what my intimate relationships with them disclose to me about them, often without my giving the matter very deliberate attention.

[2] Martin Buber and some of his followers do speak, rather oddly, of having encounter with things or meeting them. It is in this vein that Buber sometimes writes of an I-Thou relation with a tree.

Such knowledge is at least an essential ingredient in my knowing or meeting people, and in their coming to count for me. It is not dispensable even in the most intimate relationships, such as those we have within our families; and dramatic accounts of moments of encounter, as when a prisoner in the dock becomes, as we say, a real person to the judge or the judge to him, alter this no whit, however impressive and important in themselves.

Nor, it appears to me, is encounter with God any different in the present respect. I do not know what it would mean at all to encounter God independently of what I believe His character and activity to be or what He requires of me in some situation. And therefore, however suggestive the notion of encounter may be, it does not relieve us in any way of the hard epistemological problems of the nature of the cognitive factor in religious experience. We cannot just cry 'encounter' any more than we can just cry 'mystery'. And thus we are left with the exceedingly trying dilemma that there are some quite determinate things we believe to be true about God, both in a general way and, for some religions at least, in relation to ourselves as individuals, while at the same time needing to respect the mysterious incomprehensible character which any reality must have if it is to be God, unconditioned, the Creator and Lord of all Life. Mention of 'encounter' and 'meeting', if anything, accentuates this, for here the beyond is an exceedingly 'present' and familiar reality as well. How is this possible, as the Christian religion in particular affirms it to be?

To make bold and aggressively paradoxical play with the alleged scepticism which is inseparable from genuine religion, as some of our contemporaries have also done in desperation, is likewise of no avail. For whatever the scepticism in question may involve (and it could be understood in various ways), it still does not relieve us of the problem provided by the element of positive belief which seems indispensable in religion.

One answer to our problem, though only a partial one, has had a long history and has deservedly earned much respect by the skill and care with which it has been presented, recently and long ago. It is the doctrine of analogy, the substance of which is to educe out of the insight into there being one ultimate necessary being the relation in which this must stand in general to dependent beings. This is not done in the way idealists sought a clue to the nature of the absolute by presenting it as a rational system similar in principle to the rationality we discover in our experience. The infinite is apprehended better as eluding our grasp more than that. But it is thought that we can still say that the 'unconditioned' source of finite being must have qualities such as love and goodness in whatever way it is necessary for it to have these qualities in order to produce them in the form in which we find them. This doctrine is particularly difficult to state without seeming to say nothing at all; and therein also lies its weakness. For whatever it yields, and my belief is that it does not in fact yield anything, must be of an extremely tenuous character and provide nothing like the full-blooded claims on which the live practice of religion depends. Its sponsors have been the first to stress this, and have been acutely aware of the caution needed in treading this *via negativa* if we are not to belie the unfathomable mystery of necessary being. They have urged that the conclusions of natural theology, obtained by these cautious deductions from the nature of divine being, need to be supplemented by revealed theology; so that we should still have the problems presented by the latter.

The doctrine of analogy, and the general theological approach it involves, encounters special difficulty also over the existence of evil; for should we not have to say that God must have this quality too in some way needed for Him to be the author of the world that has it? The Thomist theologians to whom we owe the present doctrine tend to equate being in the last analysis with goodness, and this raises many difficulties, not the least of which is to admit the undoubted reality of many forms of evil.

Less plausible, but also in some ways understandable, is the notion of commitment as the answer to problems of religious faith. For religion certainly does require commitment, and it is in giving ourselves to it in a total way and adopting it as 'a way of life' that we have the illumination it offers. The sense in which this obtains will be amplified later. But it must also be stressed that we cannot just invite the unbeliever to change his attitude at will, nor would we do any justice to our own convictions if we represented them as a mere matter of choice. We do not strictly choose to believe at all—in any sphere. On the contrary, as our common expressions put it, we are 'forced to believe', we 'cannot but conclude', and so forth. I do not choose to believe that the grass is green. I can believe nothing else, the evidence of my eyes and all other evidence being what it is. I should be mad if I said that I chose after all that it should be red, and even my form of speech would be incorrect. I do not choose that twice two is four, I can do no other than believe that it is. If I tried to believe as I liked, the hard facts of the world would soon make it awkward for me. And there seems to me to be no exception to this at any point, for how can we in any regard believe except in the sense of taking it that something is in fact the case?

What is of course within our power is to express or refuse to express a belief, directly or indirectly. Under torture I might 'believe' or confess anything, and it is possible that torture and terror could in some way induce beliefs I did not have before. But I do not expressly choose to believe other than I do at any time. A further

concession, and an important one, is that I may cultivate
or induce a belief in myself or others. But a wise person
will only cultivate a belief in the sense of attending as
fairly and sympathetically as he can to the matters most
relevant to the formation of a *true* opinion. This may be
exacting, and may involve living in special ways, but it is
far removed from bemusing ourselves or inducing unreli-
able beliefs, as we might easily do by getting drunk.

These matters seem to me very plain indeed, and they
appear also to be just the sort of things which philosophers should help us to keep to the fore. If philosophers
do not lead in preserving regard for truth, and its objectivity, who will? A philosopher should be the most committed servant of the truth, as Plato never tired of
stressing. But unhappily several recent philosophers have
fallen under the lure of the view that the truth is somehow what we make it. If they hesitate to say this with
respect to science and matters of ordinary fact, they
affirm it boldly in regard to ethical principles. One of
the ethical theories most vigorously expressed at present
is the theory that moral standards are matters of choice
or of policies we adopt. The choice, we are told, is not
arbitrary, we must choose what is consistent with other
choices and the best information about the facts. But in
the last analysis, where the adoption of a policy or 'way
of life' is concerned, when we come to the real choice,
what do we have that is not arbitrary? And why, on this
view, should we even be consistent, might we not adopt
the moral policy of not having much of a policy? In
practice, when we deem something to be good or obligatory, we feel this to be the case in a much more objective
way than by chancing to be part of the way of life we
feel fit to adopt. Faced with an unpleasant duty, we find
this unhappily to be something we must acknowledge—
to ourselves at least—even though we may not in fact
choose to do it or deem it part of our way of life.

The very deep scepticism which the attitude I have

been censuring exposes seems to me to be one of the most distressing features of recent attempts to limit the sphere in which the distinction of true and false applies, or to question its ultimate nature. The quality of mind and character of those who present and subscribe to this sort of relativism prevents their theories, as they affect themselves and their immediate associates or pupils, from having obviously vicious results. But one wonders whether they realize how they build, and what moral and social nihilism may be bred in such distrust of the truth itself. If we merely 'opt' for democracy, or choose to believe that it is the proper form of society, may not others opt in precisely the same way for communism—or worse? Should we not rather say that it is the case or *true* that democracy is better?

I stress this in the present context because I believe that much which is said, with very high intentions, about commitment in religious thought and theology today comes dangerously near to aligning itself with a false and dangerous nihilism with which the upheavals of our days threaten to overwhelm our culture and life. It ought never to be the part of religion to bring regard for truth and its objectivity into contempt, and we ought least of all to sully the qualities of truth where it is most precious—at the heart of religion itself. For this reason, we need the utmost care in speaking of commitment and choice in religion, a warning which needs to be heeded alike in theological work and in practical evangelism. We ought never to let it be understood that we merely 'opt' for our faith, as others may opt for a different one or none. Let us appeal, if we so wish and are Christians, to others to 'commit themselves to Christ', to 'trust Him', to 'choose Him'; for, rightly understood, this is at the very heart of Christianity; but in no such exhortation should we ever suggest that the Gospel we commend is something we blindly and desperately 'choose to believe', we must rather show that it is true, and that our eyes are open. In the long run we shall find that this is not only proper in itself, but the wisest strategy.

It does not follow that there may be no note of urgency in Christian evangelism. There are, moreover, pressures which are legitimate. But we must also remember the patient process of leavening the lump and the much enduring spirit in which it is done. The last thing the Christian should do, at his desk or in his pulpit, is to bully the unbeliever.

For the same reasons, a more directly pragmatic approach is equally unsatisfactory. It will not do at all merely to commend the truth as something it would be good, for practice or in some other way, for men to believe. An illusion might be commended in that way, although it is hard to see how one could put one's heart into commending a 'useful illusion' for long—do cynical leaders in despotic countries do so or do they also delude themselves? If it is good for others to share our religious beliefs, this is because these are also true. To make a case for them in any other way, especially in a free and enlightened community, would be a desperate course indeed. Equally unwise and improper is it to rest our case on success stories, an odd, but not uncommon, form of pragmatism. The triumph of the Christian Church is indeed impressive, and a *part* of the Christian evidence, but a part only. Those who wish to make it more than that, or to treat it as the main foundation of faith, forget how many things have succeeded out of all proportion to their soundness and merit. Islam had an astonishing early success and is extremely vigorous today. But Christians would not, for *that* reason, rate it highly, much less yield it pride of place. Success may even come to thoroughly evil movements, and it is not inconceivable that, with the power available to the tyrant today, that might endure for a long time. But if this should happen, evil would not become good. Despotism would still be an evil thing.

Nor, finally, will it do to appeal to authority. There is a proper place for authority in religion, but it is a qualified one; and an authority must establish its credentials. It should be very plain to us today what evil things come from a blind submission to authority. The appeal to authority may indeed take subtle and elevated forms. But it still remains altogether inadequate. Mr Ian Crombie, for example, brings a most clear and impressive survey of the epistemological problem of religion to a close with the injunction to 'fall back upon the person of Christ, and the concrete realities of the Christian life'.[8] This is no doubt advice in which Christians must concur. But in its context it simply takes us back to the start again. What are these 'realities' and how are they recognized, directly or indirectly? Is any process of reasoning involved? How much historical matter is needed, and in what way? All these questions remain, and we cannot solve them, or dissipate any other aspect of our properly epistemological problem, by pious aspirations, however estimable in themselves.

In any case, all the expedients to which I have briefly referred have to encounter, in addition to the difficulties they involve in general as theories of knowledge, the special difficulty of showing how significant assertions can be made at all about a mystery which is by its very nature, and the mode of our acknowledging it, bound to be incomprehensible. Words and labels will not help us here, and the solution to be commended and discussed in this book will be in terms of experiences which have this peculiarity, that while they remain in themselves finite throughout, that is have a content appropriate only to finite beings like ourselves, yet they can be seen to have also a reference beyond that; and, in their patterns and ramifications in experience as a whole, they afford us the clue we need to the way the unconditioned reality on which we are dependent enters into special

[8] *New Essays in Philosophical Theology*, p. 128.

relations with us and discloses itself, through this communication, as a personal being addressing himself to individuals and present to them. Religious experience, I believe, involves this from the start, and although we can logically separate the apprehension of the mysterious source of our being, already considered, from the articulation of this in further determinate claims, yet in practice this articulation, as we shall see, begins in the moment of apprehending that there is a 'beyond' at all. The reality encountered in religion thus presents itself as at least incipiently personal from the start, although the recognition of this may not always be clear.

It is of extreme importance, for the proper commendation of religion today as well as for the enrichment that comes through right understanding of it, that it be made clear that the 'beyond' which we seek must also be found somehow within. It is this paradox of course that the positivist challenges us to sustain, inviting us either to abandon religion or to conceive of it entirely in humanist terms. But we must hold boldly to the peculiar character of religion that it concerns what is in one sense altogether beyond, and in another sense altogether within. Those who fail to appreciate this are tempted to look altogether beyond themselves and their environment, to peer into the void, and of course they see nothing. They apprehend the ordinary world about them and nothing besides. They declare that religion means nothing to them, and they report their state truly. But what they should be urged to do is to look into themselves and the world for evidence within these of what is also altogether beyond them. And I hope to show in due course that this is not so bewildering as it appears, and that it is the all-important truth about religion.

When it is said thus, in religion, that God is invisible, this has to be understood to be the case in one very complete sense. He is not just invisible in the sense in which a star may be when the astronomer can detect its influence and locate it without being able to see it, as Neptune was calculated into existence before the telescope found it. Nor is He invisible in the sense in which atoms and electrons may be—or a magnetic field. For the evidence for these invisible things, however precisely the scientist understands them, appears as part of the process of rationally interpreting finite existence; it presents us with limited terms in a relation and not with that which passes beyond that and all limited rational systems, namely absolutely necessary and self-subsistent being.

There is then a sense in which God is not known by evidence, and in which the reply to those who ask us 'What would need to be different for your belief not to be true?' must be 'nothing'. But there is a sense also in which we have abundant evidence of what God is like and what He does. My aim will be to show what this means and where the evidence is found in experience.

Some matters concerning the proposed appeal to religious experience must be made quite plain before we address ourselves further to our main task.

The first is that religious experience is not being expressly invoked to prove the *existence* of God. This should be evident by now. But it is worth stressing here, for this is not always how this 'appeal to experience' has been understood and assessed. Normally in philosophy we should consider how certain concepts are derived—perhaps from experience, as we think of winged steeds on the basis of the sort of things we can see; and then consider whether in fact anything exists corresponding to them. And it is tempting to suppose that we may do the same in religion. But if I am right in what I have already maintained, that is just what we must not do. We know that God exists as the inescapable 'ground' of the being of anything, but the way this further defines itself is found in experience.

The only doubt that could I think be raised about this concerns our use of the word 'God'. Is it proper to speak of some unknown 'ultimate reality' as God? I think that it is, when we bear in mind that its ultimacy includes its being complete or perfect in every possible way. But if it is held that it is only when such reality is also apprehended in some personal way that we may appropriately designate it 'God', then I have no serious dispute with this. The question is mainly one of words, and its importance is lessened further when we note, as I have just done, that in practice our apprehension of supreme being is personal from the start.

In the present respect my position must be distinguished sharply from a thesis which in other ways closely resembles it, namely that of Mr Crombie in the essay to which I have just referred, and another which supplements it.[4] Mr Crombie argues that we find the 'reference of theological statements' in reflection upon the contingency of the world, and to my mind he brings out admirably what this sense of contingency, and the 'obstinate conviction' that 'this is a created universe'[5] involves. But what he claims to find here is after all 'a conception of the divine',[6] an 'indicating expression',[7] a 'notion of God'.[8] That gives us 'no right to say even that there exists a being corresponding to such a conception'.[9] 'For the latter one needs to be able to find, within experience, positive indications of the reality of God.'[10] And Christ is thus regarded as 'both the evidence of the reality of God, and also the declaration of Him to us'.[11]

Mr Crombie is only able to sustain this thesis by affirming boldly that Christ is 'of divine origin' and that therefore, in seeing this, we see that the divine must be.

[4] 'The Possibility of Theological Statements', *Faith and Logic*, edited Basil Mitchell.
[5] *Op. cit.*, p. 64.   [6] *Op. cit.*, p. 54.   [7] *Op. cit.*, p. 67.
[8] *Op. cit.*, p. 61.   [9] *Op. cit.*, p. 67.   [10] *Op. cit.*, p. 68.
[11] *Op. cit.*, p. 68.

But this is again that covert appeal to authority to which I referred. What sort of knowledge have we that Christ is divine, and would we have it unless we already knew, as Dr Farrer puts it, 'that God was God before Christ'? I suggest that where Mr Crombie's undoubted insight ought to take us will be plainer if we appreciate better how, in one leap of thought, we ascend to both the meaning and the inevitable being of the 'infinite' or 'underived', and then find, under the guidance of this notion certain finite realities which it claims especially as its own. This, I think, will give us the 'ordinary meaning of words', but with a 'transcendent reference', of which he has written so helpfully himself; and give it in much sounder ways less easily diverted into objectionable courses.

It will, again, be clear already that I do not understand by religious experience the attainment of some literal union with God in which the limitations of our finite nature are completely superseded. God is God and soul is soul in all experiences. Nor am I thinking primarily of preternatural experiences, although I shall attempt to indicate the place these may have in religion. It is wrong also, in my opinion, to suppose that what we have in religious experience is some direct assurance of the truth of some general notions like theological doctrines. Such doctrines do not present themselves 'neat' or in detachment from more initial experience; and there is much in this for existentialist theology and evangelical preaching alike to ponder.

Finally, I do not understand by the appeal to experience some consideration of the general nature of human experience in itself, or what is sometimes called 'the human situation'. Reflection on what human life in itself is like, as a whole or in some part more important than the rest, will not, in my opinion, yield a religious view. We need the importation into such phenomena of some distinctively religious element.

Even when moral or aesthetic factors are put into the reckoning, I do not think that any total view of the situation can properly take a religious form unless there is some explicit way, such as that outlined above, in which we pass beyond any form of finite and secular facts; and I certainly do not think that what has usually presented itself to men as distinctively religious experience takes the form initially of even incipient metaphysical thought about existence as a whole, much though the matter has been represented in that way by religious writers.

Least of all am I attracted to the suggestion that has been much canvassed of late that the difference between having and not having a religious approach to the world is merely a case of some different view we adopt of matters which are quite neutral in themselves. Viewed in one way these are secular, in another religious; it depends how you look at them. This attitude to ultimate questions seems to me generally a very mistaken one. A different 'point of view' involves looking at different things, or features of things. This has been much overlooked in the course of the recent mistrust of metaphysics, it being contended that differences which seemed to be matters of philosophical argument were entirely cases of the slant or point of view we adopted. A celebrated illustration of this is the figure on a page now seen as a staircase, now as a cornice—or Wittgenstein's 'duck rabbit'. But even in these cases I believe we are bringing different things into focus, and I certainly do not know how major philosophical differences are to be settled except in terms of different features of what we find the world or our experience to be; and in the case of religious truth it is, in my view, to certain distinctive religious experiences that we must appeal in the last resort.

On the other hand, in making the appeal to specific occurrences or occasions in human life we must not leave the impression that these can be considered in complete detachment from others or from the general situation in which they occur. Our experiences would never be what they were if they were wholly isolated interludes, nor would the life of one individual resemble at all what it normally is without the close association he has with others and his place in society.

In their concern for these matters, some philosophers and theologians have sometimes written as if the state or society were some kind of entity over and above the lives of their individual members. This happened for instance in the so-called metaphysical theory of the state presented by some idealist thinkers, and in some forms of the traditional doctrine of sin and the Fall. We must not succumb to that temptation, but hold on to the 'distinctness of persons', as the technical phrase has it, and beware of hypostatizing social abstractions. But we must not lapse either, or appear to lapse, into some form of individualism or atomism which overlooks the continuity of human experience and the importance and closeness of social ties.

What counts as 'an experience' is moreover largely arbitrary. The course of what we do and what happens to us presents certain rough demarcations and variations. But which of these we select, and the level at which we consider them, depends on the interest we happen to have. During a morning I may be working in my study and in the afternoon I may go for a walk. But within these divisions there could be countless others. I may interrupt my work for ten minutes to have coffee, and there would be countless subtle changes or interruptions of a different sort, as my interest waxed and waned and shifted from one topic to another; I should be hearing certain sounds outside, some distinctly and some without noticing them much, if at all. I should be aware in some way of all manner of somatic sensations. It may again be possible that I should think harder about philosophy, or to better purpose, during my walk than at my desk, and thus the division into working at a certain problem and going for a walk may seem a rather artificial one. But within the endless variations of what occurs to us and what we do there are some we can single out for a theoretical or practical purpose, and we can do this without implying at all that life is a series of loose or isolated episodes.

Among the ways in which the continuity of experience is maintained, a prominent place must be given to our dispositions. There is much which is true of us which is not strictly part of our history at any particular time. I know (or believe) at the moment countless things of which I am not thinking at all, and I am prone to react in a variety of ways of which there is no indication at the moment; it is daylight, but it might still be proper to say of me that I was afraid of the dark. According to some psychologists we may even have tendencies of that kind without being much, if at all, aware of the fact, and these will sometimes make themselves felt in overt experiences of some kind, usually in too subtle a way for us to detect without expert assistance. Whether psychologists describe this correctly in the theories they propound about 'the unconscious', and whether they exaggerate its importance, as I suspect, is another matter. But it is evident that much of the actual course of our lives depends upon dispositions, some of which we may not clearly recognize, and on changes in our dispositions. We have thus to consider, in this book, not only what particular religious experiences are like, but how these are sustained by our dispositions and how they contribute to the rest of our lives by burying themselves, if the metaphor be allowed, in traits of our nature and in our behaviour and becoming germinative without always advertising the fact.

This is one of the reasons why pragmatic approaches to problems of religious belief have some substance. It is not the case that a belief is true because it encourages conduct of a certain kind. But evidence of the existence of the belief and of its character may be found in ways other than the more overt manifestations of it. And it is at this point also that we find much of the significance of religious practices and of the symbols by which distinctive occurrences perpetuate themselves and become potent in one's own life and that of one's society. These will be matters which will much concern us. At the moment, all that is needed is to remove the spectre of some artificial breaking up of religious life as a whole into isolated episodes, notwithstanding that I shall attach the central importance to distinctive occurrences of a certain kind and their inter-relations.

CHAPTER 3

RELIGION AND
TRANSCENDENCE

I have been urging that it is to religious experience that
we need to attend especially. As preachers and philosophers alike we need to be put in mind of its importance
and to acquire a better understanding of the form of it
which is appropriate today. The core of religion is
religious experience. At the same time we need to appreciate well that it is not possible to give an adequate
account of religious experience solely in terms of the
agent who has it or of his relations to his fellow men.
The object of religious experience is God, and, whatever
else we may find it possible to say about God, it is
certain, as already indicated, that we must think of God
as some reality complete and perfect in a way which is
not possible for any other being or finite creature. He is
the Creator, Himself uncreated, the Lord God before
whom we bow in worship which it would be blasphemous
to render to any other, blasphemous and a violation of
our own nature. The sole object of genuine worship is a
transcendent God.

The word 'transcendent' may not, however, be altogether a happy one here. For it is not always used in
the same way. Some philosophers use it to denote the *a
priori* or to indicate 'non-natural' qualities in ethics. A
recent debate on the limits of empiricism was given shape
by the question 'How may experience be transcended?'
Theologians sometimes concur in this usage to their own

great confusion. For they wish also to mean more than has just been suggested by 'the transcendent'; they sometimes pass surreptitiously from positing one kind of transcendence to acceptance of another, blurring altogether the peculiar character of transcendence in the context of the notions with which this discussion began. The ways of knowing this latter kind of transcendence, and the problems which attend it, are vastly different from the way we know the *a priori* or values, however we understand these and the problems to which they give rise. Philosophical discussions may likewise be confused by the importation into certain logical or epistemological questions of religious associations of the term 'transcendence' which have no relevance to the point at issue. I suggest therefore that we should eschew the word 'transcendence' altogether in any reference other than a religious one and that, in religious discussions, it should be always reserved for the peculiar 'beyondness' or 'otherness' of God implied in the perfection or absolute completeness of His nature to which I have already drawn attention as distinguishing Him altogether from any of His creatures. It is of such a transcendent being that we claim to have experience in religion.

This will seem to many, however, to be much too comprehensive a claim, and before we go further it will be well to consider that objection; it will concern us for the rest of this chapter and the next, but in discussing it I shall have an opportunity of bringing out certain matters, notably those concerned with worship and idolatry, which will have a close bearing on much that I shall say later in dealing more expressly with the particular problem of this book.

Religion, then, so goes the objection, has not always had to do with the transcendent. Men have often worshipped merely natural objects—the sun or the moon, trees, mountains, rivers, animals. They have bowed down in worship before images which they have carved themselves. Then there are the gods of mythology, many and varied, and the semi-divine figures of early legends. Is there not even a notable religion, namely Buddhism, which, in its original and purest form, dispenses with God altogether? Have not men also worshipped the State or great political or national leaders and reformers? Are not communism and fascism often regarded as rival religions to Christianity? Indeed, may we not create a religion for ourselves out of very slight materials? Cricket or fishing seems to be their religion for some people, literature is full of misers who worshipped their gold and of other wretches who worshipped themselves or their power. Does not the lover adore his beloved and the film fan deem his star to be divine? Do we not find almost every lovely thing 'divine' or 'adorable' today?

Now the way we should deal with these examples differs considerably from one case to the other. The film fan, or the lady who 'worships her pet', are normally, though by no means invariably, abusing language or betraying the slovenly linguistic habits and imprecision of their age or set. They are not expressing a seriously religious attitude. But may they not sometimes do so? May there not be a perverted, idolatrous, but properly religious, worship of pets? I think that there may and that crude idolatry is by no means a monopoly of primitive cultures. But we need also to draw careful distinctions, firstly between cases of mere loose use of language and cases of deep and persistent obsessions, and secondly between the latter and genuine idolatry. Not every total commitment is properly religious. A person may give his whole mind and devotion to a cause, possibly a trivial one like ministering to the whims of a pet or perhaps a high one like serving a party or a nation or promoting the advance of science or the cure of disease. But in no case should we straightway describe this as religion, genuine or perverted. It may be a wholly human activity, involving only human or sub-human matters. The resemblance it has to religion must not mislead us or induce us to use the same name for activities or attitudes of mind that are also radically different.

This point should be stressed before we say more about idolatry proper. Religion has suffered much from loose use of language, and in no case is this more evident than in the use of the word 'religion' itself. The adverb 'religiously' has become in common parlance a convenient word to qualify any kind of thorough or whole-hearted undertaking. One may clean one's boots, or tot up one's bills 'religiously'. No great harm comes about by talking in this way, and no one is seriously misled. Only the pedant could object. But once we pass from obviously trivial cases the likelihood of serious confusion is only too plain. Sport, business, politics, art, science and kindred activities become at once religious; and it is not pedantic to object to this practice. For in this very loose use of the term almost anyone will have a religion; most of us have some cause which we are prepared to support or some interest which tends to dominate others; if we extend the term a little further to include whatever happens to be a main interest, any purposive being will be religious by definition. This is, I believe, sometimes used as a way of showing that man is essentially religious, although he does not always have the 'true' religion. But it is an exceptionally Pyrrhic victory that is gained in this way, unless, as often happens, we proceed to load our conclusions with more than the premiss warrants. Questions about the importance of religion or of the relation of religion to other activities are also confused by an undiscriminating use of the term 'religious'. So are questions about the place of authority in religion or the importance of dogma. Dogma in religion is not the same as dogma in politics or science, although there may be features common to dogma in all these cases. If we are to ask helpful questions about religion and deal with them effectively we must be more precise in the use of the term. Some reference to 'the supernatural' is at least required, and I suggest that by far the most satisfactory procedure will be to reserve the term 'religion' for activities or attitudes which involve some awareness of a transcendent being.

This recommendation is not without disadvantages of which I am well aware. For it excludes, not only loose metaphorical uses of the term based on superficial affinities between religious and other activities, but also serious references to 'ethical religions' or religions of humanity or religions with a 'finite God'. Nor can it be claimed that the latter exist only in books and theories. For ceremonies and ritual practices of various kinds have been suggested for them and sometimes adopted. A claim to be describing normal religious practice may also be made by theories, such as some forms of idealism, whose notion of transcendence is at any rate very different from that indicated above. For this reason I would not press my recommendation. But, on the whole, I think more would be gained than lost by its adoption. For I shall maintain that in the practices or attitudes which are described in humanistic terms, such as 'ethical religion', there is in fact often a transcendent object of worship such as we normally find, I submit, in the practice of religion; and, secondly, even if common serious usage extends the term 'religious' to beliefs and practices which do not have a transcendent being as their object as well as to all which do, the difference between the latter and the former is so considerable that philosophical analysis may well be called in here to tidy up our linguistic habits in a way that may be much to the advantage of religion and of our understanding of it. This may become plainer if we look more closely now at allegedly religious practices which do not seem to have a transcendent God as their object.

Consider first the cases that may seem least ambiguous. I said earlier that there might be a genuine worship of pets. But I also suggested that this must mean more than excessive devotion to a pet or obsession with it. The latter may be perverse and unhealthy and present the moralist or the psychologist with a serious problem. It may reflect an unbalanced state of society or bad education, and it may thus call for sharp denunciation or satire. But however distressing such a disorder may be, and however grave the conditions which produce it, it may require nothing for its description beyond the terms normally available in morals or psychology. On the other hand a very similar state or practice may in fact also involve a great deal more. It may be a case of worshipping the pet. How does that happen?

It happens when a creature is invested with a significance that is dependent on some awareness of a transcendent reality and is made the centre of that significance. This is the opposite of religious symbolism. The religious symbol opens out to the transcendent, it refers away from itself. In idolatry the reverse happens, an attempt being made to hold on to a genuine sense of the transcendent but also to diminish it and contain it within the interest which some finite creatures like ourselves, or inferior to ourselves, may have for us. Attitudes and feelings which it is appropriate for us to have only towards God are thus directed to His creatures. This is the most radical of all inconsistencies, the most revolting and the most devastating in its effects on our own natures and on our relations with others. It should not be equated at all with a mere obsession, however complete, or with any kindred psychological disorder. It is an essentially religious phenomenon, possible only where there is at least a spark of genuine religion. The practical importance of recognizing this is considerable. For an attempt to treat a religious disorder, in the clinic or elsewhere, in neglect of the religious factors involved, may be very ill-judged, it may aggravate the ill it sets out to remove or divert it to courses where it is less easily traced.

The best term to describe this peculiarly religious perversion seems to be 'daemonic'. A great deal has been written lately about 'daemonic powers', but not with much understanding or caution. Theologians, anxious to find support for traditional views, have turned to the manifestation of grave disorders in the life of society, especially those which lead to war and accentuate its grimness, for evidence of 'dark satanic forces' let loose in the world. Nervous disorders are also straightway interpreted in this way, the psychoanalyst in particular being often regarded by the theologian, but less often by himself, as a considerable ally of religion for this reason. This is usually bound up with highly questionable notions of sin and human corruption. These latter cannot be considered at the moment. But it is necessary to stress that, however we understand the upheavals and disorders of our time at the moral level or in respect of wickedness and guilt, the facts of social and moral disorder, even grave ones involving much unreason, do not of necessity call for some abnormal explanation in terms of 'satanic forces'. In great measure they can be ascribed to the social and economic complications consequent upon rapid scientific and industrial advances. It would be strange if recent changes in mode of life and culture did not require of us to weather such storms as we have met in our time. The cause of religion is thus weakened rather than strengthened if we quote in support of it matters susceptible of quite adequate explanations at their own level. Much recent theology has been crippled by that particular confession of failure.

At the same time the problems of the individual and of society may be drastically altered and accentuated by the incursion into men's lives of truly daemonic elements, and it would not be surprising to find these coinciding with other ills and disorders. Such elements or forces, if we may retain for a moment these common but somewhat vague terms, consist essentially in the proneness of men to contract their religious awareness in the way described and centre it on lesser objects than God Himself. They involve a genuine awareness of God, but an awareness which is in some fashion also repudiated or misconstrued, the misconstruction being more easy because we can know nothing of the transcendent except as mediated through a symbol. The symbol draws into itself the glory it should only be transmitting. How far the conditions of our time are conducive to idolatry of this kind is not easy to determine. But the following points may be borne in mind. There has been a general diminishing of religious awareness in Western countries as in other countries most open to the influence of the West, and a great secularization of life and culture; presumably this helps the debasing of religion to quasi-secular terms. The repudiation of overt religious beliefs and the criticism of religious dogmas, happening in situations where there lingers also the more radical religious awareness on which the former depend, encourage also the proneness to diminish religious significance and incapsulate it in the finite symbol. The misplacing of religious significance relieves it also of the control and direction to which it is subject in its proper form and allies it with other elements in our nature to which it is not native. The latter become over-charged and inflamed in consequence, a religious disorder which aggravates in turn such other disturbances of human character and society as are accentuated by the conditions of our time.

Detailed discussion of these matters would take us far afield. My concern at the moment is merely to note the way in which an awareness of the transcendent is involved in forms of religion which may at first appear to have some lesser reality as their object. But we shall not stray too far if we note two further points here.

The view is often held that daemonic influences involve the activity of malevolent creatures other than ourselves and not known to us in the normal ways, perhaps not known at all in some cases. The literature of this subject is vast and complicated, including much general literature as well as strictly religious writings; no attempt to sift it would be practicable here. But I should like to stress that little careful consideration has ever been paid to the question of the way in which the existence of such beings could be known. Is the knowledge based on some peculiarity of the events or experiences in which they are supposed to be operative? In that case it needs to be carefully described and its credentials scrutinized. I cannot myself imagine what it could be, but presumably the absence of normal conditions and influences and similar irregularities would come into the picture. So would more positive factors like voices or visions. Whether in themselves these would seriously upset our belief that, with completer knowledge of ourselves, we could ascribe the unusual phenomena in question to obscure conditions or occurrences in our own nature seems to me very doubtful. The evidence would at least need to be exceptionally strong. A more likely possibility seems to be investigations similar to those which are sometimes alleged to establish communications with the dead. If some paranormal evidence of this kind were available, and especially if it could be correlated with cases of moral temptation, or similar situations, which present features suggesting a paranormal explanation, the case might be made. But there would also be need to make large allowance for our proneness to indulge in personification and vivid imaginative presentation of our experiences. It is not enough that temptations, for example, should have an insistence and a repugnance to us or a novelty which seem like the whispering of some other and malignant being in our ear. For 'in a cool moment' the whispering will be found to admit of many other explanations. This will, I believe, apply to a great deal of the more specifically religious reasons and evidence alleged to support the belief in one or more evil spirits. I do not maintain that the existence of evil spirits other than men is inconceivable, although the idea does present difficulties of definition at least which are considerable. Nor is it inconceivable that such beings should influence us. Whether they do so, and can be known to do so, is quite another matter. But what I wish to stress mainly now is the substantial weakening of such arguments by the availability to us of a notion of daemonic powers which, without postulating other finite beings than ourselves, takes due heed of the truly religious character of the facts in question and does not reduce them to secular or humanistic terms. Such a notion seems to me to be provided in the account of the distortions in our own experience of the transcendent already outlined.

Account must be taken here also of what we may describe perhaps as negative religious disturbances. I mean this. If man is made for God, the absence of God in his life leaves a tremendous vacuum. This is apt to be filled by disproportionate developments of other interests, and in a predominantly secular age disorders of this kind also may wreak havoc in the affairs of men and societies. They are quite different from the idolatrous perversions already noted, although they also have a religious origin, and they are less vile in themselves and presumably in their effects; but here again the more positive religious perversion may fuse with other disorders to produce a greater and more insidious total of disruptive power.

In asserting that there are idolatrous attitudes such as those described, and in insisting upon the difference between them and ordinary obsessions, the admission must be made that normal empirical evidence will not suffice here. For, so long as we proceed on the basis of normal observation, the sort of objection adduced earlier against the belief in evil spirits confronts us again. Such peculiarities of some perverted preoccupations as may lend colour to the notion that they are quite different in nature would always be susceptible in principle of an explanation in humanistic terms. The recognition of idolatry for what it is must come in the first instance from within the religious consciousness itself, although that may in due course provide the basis of subsequent discriminations in terms of more incidental considerations.

It is not, however, in perverted or degraded forms of religion alone that we find the worship of natural objects or of other creatures like ourselves. Early religion involves this also, but in a way radically different from that already noted and far less objectionable religiously. The questions that arise here are of course complicated and I know well that speculations about the origins of various forms of culture are notoriously uncertain. I do not wish to involve myself more than I can help in controversies about comparative religion and the history of religions which often require very specialized knowledge. But one can venture, without undue presumption, to make certain observations that bear on our present theme.

One may note, as a matter largely beyond dispute, that in one sense the origin of religion must have been naturalistic; for human life itself evolved out of sub-human existence in which none of the distinctively mental and evaluational qualities of experience associated with religion are found. Ultimately all forms of life appear to have emerged out of inanimate matter, although there are thinkers who question this. But without going lower in the evolutionary scale than the higher forms of animal life we may safely rule out from pre-human existence, as we learn of it, anything which may properly be regarded as religious.

The only challenge to this statement which has a shred of plausibility is that which notes those activities of animals which are not directly utilitarian and which seem to have affinities with the ceremonial performances of human beings. Mating activities, the cries and songs of birds, the seeming abandon of birds swooping on the wing and other forms of animal play, together with certain performances involved in hard discipline, fall into this class. Whether any or all of them could, with requisite knowledge, be accounted for in purely utilitarian terms is a very hard question. It is easy for the ill-informed to ascribe a quasi-aesthetic character to activities like the swoop of a bird when there is in fact a much more mundane explanation in terms of ordinary natural functions such as the search for food. My own view would be, although I would not care to advance it in the presence of naturalists, that there is some kind of inherent enjoyment of animal activities such as I listed and indulgence in them in some detachment from the needs of preservation and reproduction. How precisely this must be conceived is a matter for experts in this field. I do not doubt that they can tell us much which will help us to understand human action also, especially when dealing with animal activities which seem to have been continuous in the evolutionary process with primitive ritual. But when every allowance of this kind has been made, it seems to me obvious that a very sharp line must be drawn between animal activities of any kind and properly religious performances.

A parallel presents itself here with ethics. The beginnings of ethics may well be traceable to animal sympathy and disciplines imposed by the herd. Aesthetic enjoyment may also have its origin in animal enjoyment of the kind already noted. But evolution must not be thought of as if it were like a stream which never rises above its source.

The emergence of new qualities must be allowed, and it seems plain that, however the development of our moral and aesthetic reactions may have been facilitated by animal activities which have affinities with them, the former have a nature not possible of attainment in any measure by creatures who lack the reasoning power of human beings. By what gradations man becomes man or at what stage precisely the animal kingdom was left behind are difficult matters to which fortunately no solution need be attempted here. But radical differences of quality between human and sub-human life must nonetheless be also allowed, and among these, it seems to me, is the total exclusion from the latter of what we understand by morality and religion. A poet may speak of a bird on the wing praising its maker in the elegance of its flight or the tunefulness of its song. But no one takes this as literal fact any more than the 'babbling' of a brook. For we do not suppose that a bird has the reflective power needed to have the dimmest sense of a maker.

This does not mean that events which took place in the world before the appearance of man are of no account for religion, or that we can dismiss as of no importance for religion the processes which take place now in nature independently of human agency and without our knowledge. But they can only have that importance in so far as they enter into the experience or purposes of some beings (possibly God alone) who do not fall below the level of thought and personal relations of some kind. Some philosophers, of course, would argue that material processes do not occur independently of some experient, and I have much sympathy with that view. But we need not go into this question now. For whether we think of the order of nature in the idealist or phenomenalist way suggested, or as having some reality independently of its being experienced, no entity or process in sub-human nature can be of any account for religion except as the scene or medium of activities or experiences of other agents. We may, in the light of our own experience of God and His dealings with us, find in the structure and processes of nature, and the pattern of its changes over vast aeons, an immense enrichment of our understanding of God; and, on this basis, the formulation of religious cosmologies may not be precluded. But we need also to be very cautious, if we are not to lapse into crude cosmological theorizing, such as that which ascribes corruption and sin to processes in nature.[1] A stone has no religion, nor has any other part of sub-human reality, however remarkable its structure. If, with some philosophers, we ascribe minds to material entities, the case is, of course, different, but only if we take our hypothesis seriously. The minds in question must really be *minds*. I myself find the suggestion[2] among the most unplausible of metaphysical speculations—what reasons can we have for ascribing minds to entities which show no trace of intelligent reaction? But my contention at the moment is that only when you have consciousness identical in essentials with our own can you have religion. The universe may, for all we know, contain creatures whose minds work very differently from ours, and whose environments are vastly different. But no being whose consciousness falls below the minimum human mentality

[1] For example, in the very extraordinary thesis of Mr Gerald Heard about 'the Triple Fall' in his *Is God in History?* As part of his account of 'the Physiological Fall of all the animals' Mr Heard refers to the 'Great Refusal' by which barnacles and 'so many other Sea-forms, such as oysters, seem originally to have been free forms, but to have become imprisoned in their shells because the organism failed wholly to dispose of the lime which is secreted', p. 62. Mr Heard thinks such failure shows that 'there is something akin to sloth right through the entire history of life', p. 63. As a scientist's colourful metaphor this might just pass muster, but as substantiation of a religious doctrine of original sin it is preposterous.

[2] The most plausible and cautious form of it known to me is found in G. F. Stout's *Mind and Matter*.

can have a religion. Karl Barth has argued that God, in His omnipotence, could reveal Himself to stones. I find it very hard to know what this extraordinary assertion means, but it is certain that no stone could have a revelation of God without ceasing to be anything remotely resembling a stone in the ordinary sense.

The question of the place of the order of nature in a religious view of the world has, however, many features which do not concern us now. All that we require to insist upon is that we need not look for properly religious life where there is not the sort of intelligence we find in the evolutionary process with the emergence of man. Just how to describe the difference between man and brute is a notoriously tricky question. Some thinkers have denied to brutes any sort of intelligence, interpreting the behaviour of even the 'higher' animals in mechanistic ways or in terms of totally blind response to biological stimuli; others have assumed that the mere interplay of images will account for the seemingly purposive behaviour of brutes. But few who have paid serious heed to the problem today will think that it can be settled as easily as that. An animal looking for a way through a hedge or obeying its master, as when a dog is penning sheep, obviously shows intelligence which is in some way closely akin to our own. Professor Price's discussion of 'primary recognition' opens up one very promising way of accounting for such intelligence, and the vast material afforded by the scientific observation of animals also puts us in a better position to explain their behaviour. But whatever the success we expect in these ways, there also remains a very sharp distinction between the mentality of human beings and animal intelligence of all other kinds, giving to man a power of reflection about his environment that is sufficiently overt and systematic to give him a conception of his environment as a whole. Reasoning processes, when properly developed, always lead on to new questions, and curiosity which involves such questions is one sign of a developing intelligence such as we ascribe only to human beings. Just when, in the history of the race or of an individual human being, the stage is reached when properly human qualities are present, and what sort of tests we should apply, I leave to others to consider. For what is most germane to my present purpose is, not to deny that brutes can be religious (although I do that), but to affirm, more positively, that once the properly human stage in evolution is reached, however precisely we describe it, it is very hard to deny a genuine continuity of essential nature to the rites and performances in which religion had its origin among men and to religion as we know it.

This is for many reasons. Prominent among them is the continuity of essential nature of other major human interests at various stages of development, notably in art and morality. The vogue of primitive art is very high today, mainly because we have reached the stage in our own culture where extensive sophistication calls for the infusion into our present attainments of impressions derived from starker and more immediate contact with things. This may lead to an exaggerated estimation of the significance and worth of various samples of early art. But it seems also impossible to deny that there were produced in times very remote from our own many works of art whose beauty must have been intended and appreciated by those who created it. This does not imply a conscious detachment of artistic worth. The purposes served by primitive art were probably very complicated, including much that is bound to remain obscure to us. But they seem to include a delight in capturing impressions in various patterns and representations for their own sakes which alone accounts for the fascination and expressiveness these productions still retain for us. The beauty of very early art seems thus unmistakably contrived and must be placed above the incipient artistic enjoyment which animals may be presumed to take in play and any other non-utilitarian movements in which they may indulge. To give one example which has been in the news lately, the opinions of those who have paid expert attention to drawings discovered in caves believed to have been inhabited by men of very remote times and primitive habits confirm the expectations of the layman that such drawings had for their makers an artistic quality recognizably akin to that of our own works of art. This in turn is confirmed by the study of art among backward peoples today.

In the case of physical performances, like ritual dances, the line is harder to draw between strictly aesthetic enjoyment and the animal activities with which they have most affinity. But here again the line must be drawn somewhere, giving in the case of properly human activities a contrived delight in significant or expressive pattern which we can separate out in the total complex from sheer physical enjoyment and religious or sexual or utilitarian urges. That most forms of art have a great antiquity seems beyond doubt, and, whatever their permutations and the complications they present to the student, there remains a core which is one with art as we know it.

Ethics has also a very great antiquity *as ethics*. The difference between the morality of primitive people and our own is admittedly vast. Primitive persons do not usually distinguish as sharply as we do between the overt action and the intention and motive. They also hold the community as a whole accountable for the misdeeds of individual members in a way that sometimes leads to savage injustice. The range of their moral sensibility is also seriously circumscribed, the limit being usually set by their own community, although less severely and uniformly than was supposed until recently. Nonetheless moral distinctions are drawn which are substantially the same for them as for us. Devotion to accepted standards is praised and deviations denounced in tones and contexts which show their affinity with blame and remorse as we understand them. The more enlightened views which we claim are a refinement and clarification of notions which are themselves properly moral. The latter may be much overlaid by religious ideas of a very different character, but the presence of a moral factor is also unmistakable. No reader of ancient writings, notably of the Old Testament, can fail to detect in the parts of greatest antiquity a very pronounced moral element which points in turn to the operation of moral principles of some kind in much remoter times and among peoples of much simpler and cruder ways of life than ourselves. Morality did not first appear with civilization, it is not the invention of sophisticated men, but part of the raw material which civilization refines.

This is what we should expect. For art and morality alike have their roots in reason, although by no means in the sense that they can be regarded merely as exercises of reason. How this comes about need not be considered here, for we are not now investigating the relation between art or morality and the sort of rationality which makes us human. But we do need to look more closely at the connection between our exercise of reason and our consciousness of God. As has been noted, reason enables us to organize experience and thus establish relations within it in a more complete and self-conscious way than is possible for brutes, the detection of one sort of relation carrying with it a predisposition to look for other similar ones wherever they may be met. One question thus leads on to other questions, and before we have gone very far in this process we find ourselves asking a very different sort of question, namely why anything should be as it is. This is on a very different level from the question 'why' which I ask normally when I want to know, for example, why there is a patch of ink on the wall or what chemicals induce petrol to explode. But for that very reason it does not presuppose attainment of any particular stage in the normal, the common-sense or scientific, process of explanation. It is a 'limit question' which concerns the process as such, and for that reason can arise at any stage of it. Admittedly, to hold a question of this kind self-consciously and reflectively before our minds requires a high stage of sophistication, and we have seen that it is a peculiarly difficult question to formulate and handle philosophically. But that does not in any way preclude our being acutely conscious of it long before the sort of systematic reflection which leads to philosophy or theology is started. Primitive people may not have theorized much in the abstract, although some kind of rude speculation about the world as a whole may be found in remote times and is reflected in early mythologies. But to become aware of an irreducible mystery at the limit of all explanation and perceive, however dimly, that this calls for some kind of 'power' or perfection or completeness quite different from that which we normally expect objects of rational explanation to have is not only within the reach of simple-minded people, but also more likely to happen in the absence of the kind of sophistication which compels us today to discover those original intuitions at a new level and in a new way which counters the scepticism and confusion engendered by mistaken attempts at abstract formulation. The likelihood that, even in remote times, man had some consciousness of God similar to that which moves us to worship, and that, in spite of superstitions and crudities, this animated the practices which have most kinship and continuity with our religious ways, seems thus very great, although it need not be supposed at all that a genuine awareness of God would be maintained at all points in the religious ceremonials and practices in question or experienced with the same intensity or clarity by all participators.

I shall return to this last point. But a further word may be added here, in the form of recalling what has been already discussed, about the consciousness of God as an original intuition or datum of reason. We have noted the distinction between necessity for thought (or logical necessity) and psychological necessity. No idea is psychologically necessary, there is no absolute guarantee that anyone will, in point of fact, think in certain ways. Certain necessary sequences of thought in mathematics are plainly beyond the reach of most of us, however hard we try. Nor is everyone equally sound or consistent in reasoning about matters which concern us from day to day. The necessity claimed for ethical principles is not jeopardized by the absence of general agreement about them. Similarly, those who claim necessity akin at least to logical necessity for the idea of God are fully aware that there are many, including exceptionally intelligent persons, who do not share their confidence. The latter feel no compulsion at all to believe in God, although in many instances they would like to. The explanation of these differences is important, and it is part of the business of philosophy to provide it, but, whatever form such explanation will take, it must come to terms with the fact, without which life and communication would be impossible for us, that we can normally expect our individual thinking to conform to what is necessary 'for thought' or logic. If, therefore, I am right in the view that the idea of God has this necessity there is the presumption that it will present itself in that way normally to those capable of it although exceptional circumstances, which call for investigation, may hinder this. In consequence the expectation that men have, from earliest times, had a consciousness of God's existence substantially the same as our own is much reinforced, especially since, as we have seen, it does not presuppose any particular stage in the process of understanding the world about us.

In addition, primitive people live more closely to nature than we do and lack the amenities and shelter which keep our minds away from questions that go beyond the limits of normal experience. There are undoubtedly dangers and insecurities enough of a certain kind in the civilized existence of men today. The most obvious perhaps are wars and social upheaval, but, even when these do not menace too obviously, the reflective person will find in the delicate, vast and complicated web of our economic relationships food for sobering thought. Dark shadows are cast in this way on our peace of mind, and the prevalence of nervous disorders shows that at certain levels at least we are more the prey of uneasiness than we care to admit. This in turn may have much to do with the greater proneness of men in western countries to turn enquiring minds anew to religion. Nonetheless these disturbances come in the main from thoughts of a few calamitous inroads that may be made on our way of life. There may of course be other further causes of neurotic worry, the lack of unifying purpose for example. But so far as insecurity goes, it appears at the fringes of normal civilized life, and spasmodically at that. On the other hand, the normal day-to-day life and interests of primitive people are more shot through with insecurity and a struggle to provide for themselves directly by their own immediate efforts in an environment, if not actually hostile, at least not obviously charitable or subdued by cultivation to seem so. They are more at the mercy of forces of nature and seasonal changes. To this extent they would also be more prone to the sense of absolute dependence in which the idea of God, as we also think of Him, has its birth.

This brings us to a closely allied point. I shall be urging later that there are certain experiences in which specific knowledge of God is communicated to us and our relations with Him deepened and secured. These take various forms, and there are certain 'limit situations', to use one of Jaspers' terms, which favour them. Closeness to nature in its starkness and exposure to its various moods would have prominence among these. If the voice of God may be heard in nature, savages are in some ways at least very well placed to hear it. Sudden changes of fortune, for good or ill, would also play their part; the unrelieved grimness and finality of death, from contemplation of which few would be sheltered, the ruder play of elemental human passions and the vagaries of an undiscriminating ethic, would also help to create situations of tension and relief full of a rawness and inevitability to which some counterpart seems to be needed in the situations of more refined sensibility and culture by which we are most moved religiously. If the savage has in a pre-eminent form, but by no means in the form which makes for most richness and refinement of religion, certain seemingly indispensable ingredients of specific experiences of God's presence, then we have here also an increase in the likelihood that he would have some participation in the awareness of God which we have ourselves. Those who live closest to nature today, farmers and sailors for example, are noted for the hold religion has upon them.

But the main test in these matters must not be sought in likelihood and expectations along the lines outlined hitherto but in the impression we ourselves have directly of certain early practices known to us *when these are viewed from within the religious experiences we have ourselves.* This also, more than consideration of what is overtly claimed by the practitioners themselves or explicitly put into religious utterances, is what we should heed, especially in that important part of the study of religion which examines the religious practices of backward people today and compares it with the evidence available about people most similiar to them in modes of life and circumstances in the past. This is a test which only religious persons could apply, but this holds in the final analysis of most matters that have to do with the history and comparative study of religion.

To consider in detail what are those features of early religion which show most sharply an affinity with the kind of religious experience we have ourselves would take us very far afield and keep us from the matters with which I most wish to concern myself in this book. The well-known work of Rudolf Otto is an admirable instance of what I have in mind. The most that I shall do here is to suggest that those who do consider the religious life of people at lower levels of culture than ourselves will find in it items which awake striking echoes in our own experience and convey to us the impression of genuine religious reality such as would be meaningless to us without some apprehension, however dim and confused, of the transcendent being we worship. This test has of course no complete finality, since we can have no direct inspection of the phenomena in question. But this holds even of our present knowledge of one another. This is also mediated and depends on correct interpretation of evidence. In this latter case the evidence is so complete and overwhelming as usually to leave us in no doubt, but its indirect nature must not be overlooked. The fragmentary and sometimes exceedingly perplexing evidence about people in times and conditions very remote from our own calls for exceptional caution from those who consider it, as Sir Henry Maine and other historians have repeatedly stressed. Where points of detail and interpretation of specific phenomena are concerned we may not often get beyond tentative speculations. Whether we do, and how far, is a matter for the experts, but it seems to me that even the very partial acquaintance which the casual student or amateur gains with early religion shows that in its general nature it presents, to those who consider it from within a religious life of their own, elements identical with our own experience of God. But there are now certain more specific features of religion to be noted in support of the main contention.

CHAPTER 4

RELIGION AND IDOLATRY

The first consideration to be adduced in support of the
conclusion at which I have just arrived is that of our
own indebtedness, for the purpose of evocative religious
language and ceremony, to terms and practices which
come into the context of a civilized existence from a
much earlier setting laden with associations and hints of
an irreducible mystery not evoked in the same way by
analogues from modern life. It is of course possible
that borrowings were made from the practices of a period
prior to the emergence of religion in the sense we have
defined it, these having a quality which suited them to be
taken up and transmuted in the genuine religious life
that appeared in due course. But this seems to me not
the most likely explanation. For although factors which
are not themselves expressly religious are constantly being
taken up into distinctively religious experiences and perpetuated as elements of it, I doubt whether any pre-
selection of the factors in question is possible, or any
sharpening of their suitability for the purpose, in the
absence of some genuine religious awareness. The relation between religion and, for example, the majesty of
kingship is two-fold; for the peculiar aura that has
surrounded the royal office and makes it so apt a religious
symbol, owes something to religion from the start. Nor
is it easy to believe that traditional forms and usages
in religion, some dating from very early times, could

have retained their efficacy and persisted through so many changes of culture and religious temper had they not gained initially something of the significance which they had at later times. Certain continuities of form in religion strongly suggest a continuity of substance.

This argument is not, I admit, conclusive. For there could be certain resemblances between, for example, out-and-out paganism and true religion without real identity of aim or motive. But, taken in conjunction with other considerations such as those already adduced, the striking resemblances we find in various religious practices, together with concomitant variations with other factors, make it hard, I suggest, for those who find their own religion pointless without a certain kind of God as the object of worship to doubt that consciousness of the same being has had something to do, if only initially and intermittently, with attitudes and practices that present close affinities to their own.

Moreover, to pass to a further point, it is widely believed by religious people, and especially by Christians, that our knowledge of God comes to us mainly, and on some views exclusively, through the special initiative of God in revealing Himself to us. Some adherents to this view hold that the revelation is confined to a specific tradition, the Judaeo-Christian one; and, according to some theologians of note today, revelation derives exclusively from certain notable central religious events. Those, however, who do not feel impelled to accept restrictions of this kind, but who find themselves persuaded to the view that God does intervene in men's lives and in the course of history to make Himself known to us, will find it hard not to believe also that it is God who is stirring men's hearts and inclining them towards Him in the practices which, in times and places remote from our own, have affinities or continuity with our own religious life.

To this the objection will perhaps be made that we can

hardly associate with the God of Christianity or of other 'higher' religions certain barbaric and savage practices in which men have sometimes indulged under the promptings of their religion. That men's apprehension of God should be very incomplete and limited at certain stages of human development might, it will be argued, be compatible with God's progressive disclosure of Himself in all religions; but, the argument continues, we have to reckon also, not only with much backsliding and unevenness of religious development, but with cruel and repellent practices hard to ascribe to the intervention of the God we worship. This is a most important point, and it is only by dealing with it that some matters of much importance for my present theme can be brought out. But before I take it up there is one other point to be mentioned.

This is the drift of the evidence adduced by anthropologists and students of comparative religion today, and the view they take of it. I must here repeat the warning already given about the limitations of anthropological studies of religion, there being needed for the full understanding of early religious phenomena certain deep-level religious judgments not always available to the preoccupied investigator or heeded by him. The case of art presents again a helpful parallel. As was observed earlier, we deem certain early works of art to be the product of much aesthetic sensibility. This is not mainly due to investigations of matters incidental to the quality of such works of art themselves, such as some purpose they may be presumed to have served or the conditions and conventions of the time, highly relevant though these may be in their place. We rely mainly on our own immediate aesthetic response, in the absence of which we might produce elaborate and plausible but widely erroneous theories. In the same way the study of religion at various stages requires insights derived from present religion.

This may appear not altogether fair. Does it not make the apologist of religion judge in his own case? The answer is that that is perhaps true, but that in this matter it cannot be helped, any more than in the analogous case of art where it is not inconceivable that a similar complaint should be made. This will not satisfy the religious sceptic, and he must continue to provide his own theories, making, one hopes, some allowance for the possibility that there are some matters evident to others which he is not able at present to appreciate. The religious person must in turn be careful not to presume too much on his favoured position, especially as the insights in question are not to be straightway identified with the acceptance of religious doctrines. This is however to anticipate matters which will require close consideration later. I believe that anthropologists, especially in the late nineteenth century, have jumped to hasty conclusions, even when most sympathetic to religion, by not taking religion itself sufficiently as their guide in looking below the superficial meaning of certain phenomena. But the most I wish to do now is to be sure that, in calling the anthropologist to witness, we do not put ourselves too completely in his hands.

What, then, is the usual position of students of early religion today? The view used to be that religion had its origin in some form of purely naturalistic pluralism, a view by no means of necessity opposed to religion, evolution certainly involving the emergence of new qualities at various stages. Herbert Spencer made this view popular,[1] and he was ably supported by anthropologists like James Frazer and E. B. Tyler who maintained that religion began as the worship of ancestors or of personified natural objects. By gradation, it was argued, a craving for unity reduced this colourful multiplicity to more specific localized deities. In due course these were in turn deposed in favour of one

[1] He had of course been brilliantly anticipated by Hume.

supreme being, the Ruler and Controller of all things; this at least happened in some cultures. Doubt was however cast on views of this kind by evidence, such as that adduced by Andrew Lang in his notable book, *The Making of Religion*, which established the existence of 'High Gods' even among very backward races. An example of such a High God is the 'All-Father' of the Australian aborigines who, in the words of Professor E. O. James, 'is thought to have made himself and to have lived on the earth he created before he retired to his heavenly abode'.[2] The High God was too remote from ordinary human concerns to have a permanent hold on men's interest, and in course of time he figures more sporadically in early worship. This suggests to me that there is probably much that we do not understand well about the evidence for the existence of early High Gods, for there are reasons, arising from what we ourselves know of religion, for expecting the religious situation to have been much more complicated than would be the mere reduction of the function of the 'High God'. But the evidence available in these and similar ways strongly suggests that we should be nearer the truth in reversing the earlier theories of the development of religion from some kind of primitive animism to various forms of monotheism in the higher religions. It would, I admit, be hasty indeed to ascribe to primitive or backward people the overt consciousness of one God, and explicit beliefs about Him, which we associate with monotheism in the context of sophisticated cultures—the account sometimes given of High Gods savours too much of that. We do, however, find support for the view that pluralistic forms of religion are corruptions of some more unified religious life and capable of being understood in relation to religious attitudes which have more centralized objects of worship. It seems to have been a case of unity diversifying itself without always doing so

[2] *The Concept of Deity*, p. 26.

in the most estimable forms. The researches of sociologists like Durkheim and Lévy-Bruhl, notwithstanding some tendency to exaggerate the mystical qualities of the primitive mind, also lend much support to this view.

There remains, however, the difficulty already noted, namely the spread and perpetuation of idolatrous polytheism and the barbarous and cruel practices for which it was often responsible. If the original motivation of religion, and its prime inspiration at all times, is some consciousness of a relation to a transcendent being (or, if we wish to be even more non-committal at this stage, reality), how did this come to be so perverted and to expend itself in practices which are so hard to associate in any way with the One God of enlightened religion, much less be ascribed to His initiative or direct intervention? If man was made in the image of God, at least to the extent of having a genuine awareness of Him, how did the image come to be 'marred' or 'lost', to use the stock theological terms?

Traditional theology has a simple answer here, far too simple in my view. It is the doctrine of the Fall and original sin. Man was created innocent, his innocence consisting in right relation to God, albeit, according to some theorists, a somewhat restricted relation and a limited innocence. But something 'happened' to mar this original innocence and make man thereafter a creature alienated by his own sinfulness from his Creator and Lord. The evidence available of early forms of monotheism has not infrequently been eagerly put in the service of this form of traditionalism by its upholders. But this doctrine seems to me open to the most serious objections, especially as normally propounded. It involves conceptions of guilt and sinfulness, as notions including certain ethical elements, which can in no wise be accommodated to the plainest deliverance of the moral consciousness. It also involves an assumption of human solidarity which will bear little scrutiny and which appears to leave totally out of account the independent ways in which human life has developed in various places and at different times. These objections will not be pressed here. But I want to suggest that an alternative explanation of the relevant phenomena, and one more consistent with religious experience as well as with ethical principles, may be found if we recur at this point to the observations already made above about idolatrous worship.

It was noted there that consciousness of the transcendent tends to set up some form of resistance to itself. The consolation afforded by the thought of our union with a supremely perfect reality, although it is the final source of contentment and peace to human beings, is also in one way disturbing and unwelcome. For it makes exacting demands upon us, not only through its effect on our moral and cultural standards, but more expressly and peculiarly by requiring certain mental or spiritual adjustments. It takes us out of the sort of securities on which we normally count and shows us the everyday world in which we are at home merging into a background which cannot be made familiar or mastered like our normal environment. This is all the more disconcerting because of its effect on normal experience, the ordinary certainties are called in question. But the shock is greatest when this ultimate mystery comes into human life with a positive power of its own, as also happens in religion. This not only constitutes a threat to man's own independence but is felt more positively as the impact of an alien power with which he is unable to cope, a power, indeed, by which he is apt to be crushed altogether. That is a well-known moment in religious experience, to which familiar religious utterances and the history of religion bear ample witness. The God of love is also the God of terror and wrath, and He is not the one, in the full religious sense, without the other. There is thus a sense in which men in turn are apt to resist God, to be in conflict with Him or try to escape Him, *just because He is God*. But they will not do this in the first instance by merely forgetting or disregarding God. For they are also drawn to Him and need Him. They will thus try to limit or restrict their own consciousness of God by containing it within the media and symbols which are needed for its articulation. This seems to me the essence and beginning of idolatry.

The process is however complicated by its affinities with other phenomena, cultural and ethical ones in particular. The more conscious a man becomes of God the more does he feel the horror of the guilt which he bears for his wrongful actions. He thus not only feels himself 'as dust', 'as nothing', but woefully unworthy, 'undone' and 'a man of unclean lips'. Nor does religious utterance always distinguish sharply between these moral reactions and the peculiarly religious element in religious experience, the relations between the two being so close; they are usually merged in one general expression of destitution and despairing unworthiness. This is one further reason for the superficial plausibility of tradition-alist theories of sin. The latter seem to chime in well with notable prophetic utterances whose worth and authenticity it would be hard to doubt, and they have been made much of by upholders of traditionalism. But these are matters which we shall need to consider more carefully later. All that we need to note at the moment is that, if man's sense of moral unworthiness is intensified by religion, this affords an additional inducement to limit the power of religion upon him, in other words, to fly from the judgment under which he feels in the presence of God by containing the God to whom he is so irresistibly drawn within forms more amenable to his own imperfections and waywardness.

Such idolatry may take one peculiarly insidious form. It may coalesce with moral evil. The essence of immor-ality is that a man puts his own aims before the greater claims of others, he puts himself 'at the centre'. And in putting himself thus at the centre he is also apt to draw into himself the religious overtones of his experience which he is trying to enclose in a finite symbol. The contraction of his religion is in the expansion of his own importance, and he finds the media of religious perversion in himself and in the excessive assertion of his own aspirations. This intertwining of moral evil with properly religious perversions is a most significant characteristic of religion; it presents us with two strands in the history of religion which we need to distinguish and consider carefully in their relations to one another—in distinction from the common practice of taking the religious utterances which reflect these two strands in the web of the religious life as relating to one indiscriminate whole. By pursuing the course suggested we shall find many matters clarified for us and we shall more easily avoid those strange aberrations of traditional theology which lead to pronouncements completely opposed to our simplest moral convictions.

The history of the higher religions bears out these matters well. For the progress of religion has been far from even, and the backslidings and lapses into idolatry from which certain peoples had been emancipated, the Hebrews in particular, throw a peculiarly interesting light on paganism which helps us to understand it better in all its forms. The idolatry we read of in the Bible is not only, for the most part, condemned expressly as the lapse of people who have known the true God and forsaken Him, but seems to call for peculiarly violent denunciation because it is in this way a perversion seen very clearly as such and abhorred with exceptional intensity by the prophets in the white heat of their own religious experience. No doubt the detestation of corrupt moral practices comes into this also, but who can fail to detect even there the peculiarly religious horror at the investment of these practices with the false values of a perverted relation to the living God. This does not prove that idolatry has always taken the same form, but it creates an additional presumption in favour of that explanation which the detection of parallel cases elsewhere may strengthen.

Significant also is the common reaction of Christian converts to their former religion. In many cases they do not merely deplore it for its limitations or stupidity or for barbarous practices which it may have prompted or sanctioned, but detest it actively as the worship of idols— that is what was wrong most of all with their old religion —the worship of idols. It is doubtful whether such violence could be engendered did not the idolatry in question contain some element in common with the new religion, something which is now seen to be peculiarly abhorrent in its old perverted form, as a discord to the musician who might not be unduly worried by mere noise. Here also then we have a strong suggestion that idolatry and 'true religion' have the affinities suggested.

But we have also to remember how much religion requires certain rites and ceremonial practices of various kinds for its perpetuation. These are apt to acquire a momentum of their own, especially as they are the habits of societies and not, as a rule, of men in more individual capacities, societies in many cases moreover of a very conservative temper. It has often been remarked by historians and anthropologists that the reasons for many practices of primitive people, sometimes practices to which great importance is attached, are beyond recovery except in the form of wild conjecture, and not always of that. One need not therefore be surprised if religious practices were also in many instances continued when the real motivation which made them properly significant had been lost. This would be peculiarly likely to happen where the interest and prestige of a privileged élite was involved. A priesthood has some vested interest in religious rites, and it is apt to become narrowly devoted to the institutions and customs it serves on their own account as part of a way of life and an attitude that have become habitual to its members and are deeply rooted in the traditions of which they are bearers. To suppose that a priestly élite deliberately exploits its position, and even does this when its own belief is weak or lacking, is, in most cases, far too great a simplification, although we are not without evidence of cunning and naked deception of that kind. But there are many other subtler ways in which a body vested with certain responsibilities, such as usually fall to a priesthood, would be inclined to perpetuate religious practices when the true religious life has gone out of them.

I much doubt, however, whether this would in fact be a permanent state of affairs. For not only are there the normal occasions and promptings of religious experience already noted, but it is hard to believe that the life would die out altogether from the ceremonials which have become religiously enervated, or that it would not flicker again and revive from time to time. The rites would themselves have an initial appropriateness to their purpose and their perpetuation would carry with it associations which would live as part of the common culture of the community. The history of religion is not usually the history of an alternation of live and dead religion, but of religion glowing with various degrees of intensity. But the fact that the forms in which religious life is expressed, and by which it is cultivated, can be continued in a nexus of social custom when their true purport has been dimmed or lost, makes it easier to understand how there could be seemingly religious practices in the absence at least of the consciousness of the one transcendent God which, I have suggested, is the origin and motivation of religion and the main source of its life at all times.

A peculiarly sinister consequence of this perpetuation of empty forms is that, as the life of religion rarely dies out altogether but only flickers feebly, these forms readily yield themselves to the more radical, inherently religious, types of corruption I have also noted. As the life of religion returns these become inflamed into dae-monic worship of a ritual, a creed or a book. Of this, most unhappily, we are not without some manifestations today. It is a sobering thought that our own adherence to a doctrine or our regard for the Bible may become themselves a vile form of idolatry. Few things have more horror in them than such distortions of Christianity, most of all when they unmask themselves in violent de-nunciations of morality and avail themselves of enlighten-ment to darken counsel.

Note was taken earlier also of another form of religious perversion, one not so insidious in itself or at the properly religious level, but fraught with grave consequences. When the consciousness of God is dim or absent there is created in human personality a vacuum which is apt to be filled by distortion of other interests developed beyond their proper place in the whole personality. To the extent that this has happened in the past, and especi-ally where there has supervened upon this malformation the properly daemonic perversion of truly religious factors of experience also described, it can well be understood again that there would be initiated and perpetuated many ugly practices which we should never associate directly with religion as we know it, and of which the enlightened religious sense is the first and most fierce censor, but which nonetheless are not unre-lated to religion understood in terms of the consciousness of the one God.

Finally, account must be taken of the context within which religious experience is formed. Religious experience does not happen in a vacuum. For while it is true, as I have stressed especially, that any object may prompt the consciousness of some absolute transcendent source of all things, this knowledge remains formal and bleak unless it is linked, as we shall see that it almost invariably is in actual fact, with some divination of a special relation in which an individual stands at a special juncture in his own life to this supreme reality. The knowledge of the being of God is bound up for us with the transmutation of some particular experience, perhaps that in which the thought of God's existence comes vividly home to us, into a specific embodiment of God's relation to us. If this can be shown to be true of all religious experience, then one can also see how religion is conditioned by the social and cultural media in which it finds this embodiment. If the latter are crude and undeveloped, these crudities cannot but reflect themselves in the completer religious experience which is so organic to them. Crudities in religious life must, therefore, be largely ascribed to undiscriminating ethical or aesthetic reactions, to ignorant and erroneous beliefs about the world around us, and to the imperfections of the first attempts of men to understand their religion and formulate some kind of cosmological system. The problem of the existence of mistaken and inadequate notions of this kind, and of the distressing consequences to which they lead, does not directly concern us now. It is part of the general problem of evil and the gradual evolution of higher forms of life out of lower ones. But it can at least be seen that there is nothing peculiarly discreditable to religion itself in its suffering certain defects and limitations from its involvement in other human defects and limitations, once we find that the latter do not in themselves present insuperable obstacles to religion.

I think we shall find that many of the practices of unenlightened religion which would at first give us pause in maintaining that the God of the higher religions is present in the former too and making Himself known to men in the manner appropriate to their condition, are due to the conditions on which religious life supervenes, and only indirectly to religion itself. But we have also to remember that much which may seem superficial and unintelligible to us with a different knowledge of the world and a different religious background may have much significance in another cultural context which it is not in our power to understand. Those who merely laughed at the 'superstitious' savage for bowing to his carven image or offering it food and sacrifice seem certainly to have failed to appreciate certain reasons which the savage himself had for doing this. It was not *qua* stone, *qua* merely natural object that the image, or whatever it may have been, elicited these attentions; and it is now widely agreed, in consequence especially of the studies of R. R. Marett, that it is not as the habitation of some spirit that inanimate objects are reverenced and worshipped. It seems to me thus very likely that intimations of God's dealings with men came to man in early stages of human development, and still come to backward peoples, in ways whose considerable religious worth can not be gauged at all from superficial inspection of its outward forms and accompaniments. Thus, what we might describe as idolatry is not always false; nor is it inevitably corrupt, it may only be immature and incipient. This is why a Christian, for example, may find sympathetic responses in himself when he enters imaginatively into the atmosphere of certain pagan religions. Is not the reader of Pater's *Marius the Epicurean*, if he reads at all appreciatively, gently stirred into a genuine religious glow as he enters into the descriptions of pagan ceremonies in the opening pages or later when presented with Christian practices which he would not adopt or find meaningful for himself today? This happens independently of one's own particular religious persuasion, because there is something deeper than the overt practices which animates these and has varying measures of affinity with the substance of our own religion.

But while we may regard paganism as, in some degree, an anticipation of the religion we consider to be true or an incipient form of it, we must not ignore its darker side, which is partly due to general limitations affecting the setting in which religion comes to birth and partly due to the various forms of corruption we have noted. The task of maintaining and developing true religion is thus two-fold, on the one hand to maintain the integrity of the specific religious factors in religious experience, and on the other to refine the material which is indispensable for it in such a way as to lead to better cultivation of the whole religious life. The history of religion must be approached on a similar basis. Both these matters will be subject to close consideration later. My purpose at the moment is to remove what may have seemed a grave objection to the suggestion that religion should always be regarded as involving some conscious relation to a transcendent reality.

I have said nothing about high religions which do not come into the class of idolatrous worship with which I have been largely concerned. But I do not think these present a very grave obstacle to what I have been urging.

In the case of Islam we have plainly a religion of the transcendent, and one of the most interesting questions in Islamic studies today is that of the adequacy of the conception of the transcendent in the Koran itself and in subsequent Moslim writings, especially those which most influenced European thought in the Middle Ages. Was the transcendent understood by Mohammed himself in too anthropomorphic a way, and did the contrast between it and created being come to be understood in ways which deprived finite beings of importance and freedom? Are there mistakes in Islamic theology similar to those which some of us find in the work of Karl Barth? Can a better understanding of what Mohammed himself meant by revelation[8] place his claims in a new perspective? These are fascinating questions on which our recent understanding of the way we should think about God throws a flood of light.

But some forms of Buddhism and Hinduism and Confucianism might be thought to be in a different class altogether. Here again, however, the difference appears to be mainly on the surface so far as the present issue is concerned. Is the Buddhism of the Pali Canon agnostic? Superficially, yes. Buddha is represented there as opposed to any form of metaphysical or speculative enquiry, for example about after-life, finite and infinite, and so forth. These are not even possible questions, they cannot be answered one way or the other, and I have been much surprised that our contemporary positivistic agnostics have not made more of this obvious and striking affinity with their own position. But the agnosticism of Buddha is nonetheless agnosticism with a difference; it is certainly not mere preoccupation with ethics, prominent though ethics is within 'the doctrine'; it is part of a way of 'release', and I would argue that, if we take it in its context and consider all that is said about Buddha in these writings, and most of all the account of his 'Enlightenment', we may well find in his agnosticism the caution of those who apprehend well what the transcendent really involves and how misleading the attempt to characterize it may prove. This is the sort of agnosticism which such Buddhism shares with many Christian writings; and if Buddha, as represented in the source in question now, was at fault in supposing that this agnosticism could never be relieved, that is a further matter and leaves us at the point where the special problems of the present study begin. But consideration of what is achieved, and what is lacking, in writings like the Pali

[8] For an extremely suggestive treatment of this subject see Richard Bell's *Introduction to the Koran*.

Canon, is much facilitated by the understanding of the transcendent reference of religion possible for us today, just as such writings in turn can much illumine our present thought about religion.

Similar approaches are possible to other forms of Buddhism, including those on which much information has been made available quite recently. As to the commoner established Buddhist practices, much that I have said about idolatry retains its relevance there. Hinduism likewise, whether in the form of naïve superstition or of exalted belief and practice, is hard to understand without some reference to the Godhead, the One, the Supreme; and this is especially the case if it is true that one cannot be a Hindu without veneration for the Sacred Writings of Hinduism. The Chinese notion of a Heaven and Earth relationship, so important for the ethical and social teaching of Confucianism, is again highly relevant to the point where controversy has taken us today, for it refers to some reality beyond the here and now which is too elusive for us to lay hold on it and describe it expressly, but which we can still recognize as a power working for righteousness in the present world. It does not follow that the differences between these religions are slight—far from it. But I think it can be shown—and I hope elsewhere to do so—that there is more underlying identity in the various religions than is appreciated in studies of religion at present, and that the course of recent philosophy much helps us to understand this, most of all as it concerns the idea of the transcendent.

The same thing cannot be said of humanism as a religion. But, as a *religion*, humanism seems to me to be largely the invention of intellectuals and has rarely thriven as a religion proper. To the extent that it has thriven, as 'ethical religion' for example, it has been largely parasitic on other religions, borrowing from them emotional attitudes and habits which it could not properly generate itself and which soon reveal their hollowness and irrelevance in this artificial setting.

The suggestion has, I know, been made that as the usual forms of religion have (it is supposed) been exploded and abandoned, the traditional dynamics of religion may be transferred to other causes. Professor Flugel, for example, wrote : 'There is at the present time an increasing tendency to look for "religious" emotion elsewhere than in the company of metaphysical belief, in "religions of humanity" or "nature", or even in the high "devotion" of the scientist, artist, or social reformer to their respective tasks.'[4] He continued : 'The religious emotions must be largely or entirely secularized and be put in the service of humanity. The religion of humanity is surely the religion of the nearer future.'[5] I should myself, however, much doubt whether religious emotions could retain for long, after the suggested secularization, the power for good, and sometimes for evil also, which belongs peculiarly to them, and, even if they could, it seems to me that there would still be a strong case for making the dissociation with religion a very complete one and thus avoid the confusion of issues resulting from using, in an entirely new sense today, certain terms which had been given another meaning in the past.

Admittedly, from the point of view of the convinced atheist, there may be something to be said for avoiding too severe a rupture in the process of secularization envisaged, lest emotions or attitudes which need to be maintained, in the interest of the individual or his society, suffer loss of vitality and perhaps undergo complete inanition, in the dissociation with practices and terms, and especially poetic or moving language charged with much power accumulated over long periods, that have gone with them in the past. It is thus tempting

[4] *Man, Morals and Society*, p. 270.   [5] *Op. cit.*, p. 275.

for the sceptic, most of all if he is also a reformer with a shrewd sense of the delicate balance of social forces, to exploit the prestige of religious language and baptize it into new uses. Writers like Eric Fromm[6] appear to be adepts at this task and they also manage to say many illuminating things, in what we may perhaps call the 'religio-secular' context of their work, which have a freshness and penetration which should be well heeded by those who adhere to religion in the traditional sense. But I much suspect that they owe their success largely to the persistence of religion in the forms they wish to repudiate, and I am very certain that, on the whole, their procedure engenders a confusion for which it cannot compensate. Those who do not profess a religion or who question its claims, and whom others may wish to convince, would not normally be thought, least of all by themselves, to be thereby rejecting the moral or social recommendations of writers like Fromm. In short, the claims that are usually made on behalf of religion would need to have been very generally and finally abandoned before we could reasonably divert its language to other purposes, and even then such procedure would be very misleading in allusions to the past.

We have on our hands a problem somewhat different again in respect of the panthea of gods of some of the civilizations of antiquity. But when these ceased to be symbols of a transcendent reality, they lived on for a while, I submit, in men's minds and practices through some social significance which they retained or on account of their place in literature and art. They would only remain features of a living religion because the worship of them in some way referred beyond itself, not perhaps in ways fully appreciated by their votaries, to a more mysterious and absolute reality which found symbolical expression in them.

[6] *Psycho-Analysis and Religion.* See also the note at the end of this chapter.

These are not, however, the topics with which I shall be mainly concerned, and I have ventured in the preceding passages to make some suggestions which will not be followed up in detail later. Even if I were wrong in suggesting that the practices which we generally describe as religious do involve a reference to the same transcendent object of worship as is claimed for 'true religion', and had for this reason to abandon the recommendation to reserve the word 'religion' for worship of that kind, the main problem would remain, namely, granted that, in some religions at least, there is a conscious relation to this transcendent reality, how does this come about and what can we say about the specific experiences in which it happens?

Note

SECULAR RELIGION

There has appeared very recently an unusually attractive statement of the case for a secular religion, or a secular substitute for religion as it normally appears. It is found in the closing chapters of Mr Ronald Hepburn's *Christianity and Paradox*. My own book was in the press when Mr Hepburn's book reached me, and I can thus insert only the briefest reference to it. Mr Hepburn devotes most of his space to criticism of religious belief, and especially belief in the existence of God. With a great deal that he says, in criticism of the traditional arguments or in rejection of desperate expedients adopted by some apologists today, I am in close agreement; I also think that Mr Hepburn's criticisms have no force against the view which looks beyond the arguments to the peculiar insight they reflect in the way outlined above. But my reason for referring to Mr Hepburn's work here is the attractiveness of his case for retaining a 'religious orientation of mind' 'despite the theological breakdown'.

Mr Hepburn has been much influenced by recent linguistic empiricism and is skilled in presenting its case against religion. He is also very clear-sighted and has no illusions about his own position. He knows what he is doing and, unlike many other linguistic philosophers interested in religion, he fully realizes that he cannot hold the views to which his arguments lead him and profess himself an adherent of any usual form of religion. He obviously knows the Christian religion well from within, and one suspects that he much regrets finding himself outside its fold. But he makes no pretence of being within the fold, or of supposing that inability to believe, for example, in the existence of God, is no bar to being a Christian. This is where Mr Hepburn's view seems to me a great improvement on that of Professor Braithwaite whom in some other respects he closely follows and to whom he seems much indebted.

Mr Hepburn's position seems to be that of an erstwhile Christian, or a near Christian, who looks back longingly on the wreck of his beliefs and wonders what can be salvaged out of it. His main suggestion is that the agnostic may find in religious discourse a parable or myth which will determine 'his total imaginative vision of nature and man', drawing for this purpose on imaginative work in general as well as upon sacred scripture and theological writings. The main example offered of this is the notion of life as a pilgrimage or 'journey to the hereafter'. Strip this of reference to the hereafter and the 'pilgrimage-motif' may still have worth as an illuminating way of looking at the moral life, especially when we consider what new decisions are constantly required of us in implementing our moral principles. We may then find in the idea of pilgrimage 'an over-arching controlling symbol within which all other symbols, myths and stories can find their setting'.

Mr Hepburn does not develop this in detail; it is little more than a hint he throws out. But it seems to me that his suggestion is more attractive as a general project one may entertain than it would be if worked out in detail. No one can object to the atheist's trying to salvage as much as he can out of discarded religions or drawing upon the imaginative life of religion whenever this is possible without misleading himself and his fellows. He can enjoy the Bible, for example, as great literature. But whether one could do more in this fashion than nourish one's life in a very general way on great symbols and imaginative writings, seems to me doubtful. I am not at all confident that a certain distinct 'over-arching controlling symbol' or symbols will appear in this way or that they will have anything of the tightness of structure or unity of a religious faith. The attempt to elevate symbols deliberately to this position might in fact prove very artificial and frustrating, and could easily become rather ludicrous.

The atheist, adopting Mr Hepburn's procedure, might not of course be required to be as consistent or systematic as the religious believer, nor need he have the same concern to commend his symbols to others. There may be alternative ways of going to work here. But once we make allowances of this sort, it is hard to see what could be left us beyond a special enlivening and while that would be a very good thing it would have little in common even formally with religion.

Mr Hepburn has, moreover, chosen a rather easy example. The idea of a pilgrimage can no doubt be adopted in many contexts. How would one deal with the ideas of the world as a created world, of a cycle of rebirth, of the Fatherhood of God, of the Messianic work of Jesus or His divinity, of redemption and reconciliation, or of being 'washed in the blood of the Lamb'? What could we do with detailed Biblical images like the shield of faith and the helmet of salvation? We might no doubt find literary uses for the latter, but to accord them a specific function in some imaginative scheme for directing our life as a whole would be rather strained; and it would seem to me exceptionally hard to adapt the other examples mentioned, without absurdity, to any purpose other than the one they originally served.

But even if Mr Hepburn's recommendation could be implemented effectively and in a fairly comprehensive way, the religious believer would still insist that this is a poor substitute for what he claims to find in religion, and that the special richness and significance of great religious symbols is largely lost in the projected metamorphosis. Mr Hepburn would probably not dispute this, but I wonder whether he has considered sufficiently how much the vigour of religious imagery is bound up with the context in which it appears and the associations set up in situations where belief was central.

I leave the last observation as it stands for the present. But I shall later be discussing the 'life of images' and the relation of art and religion. In the meantime there is one further submission made by Mr Hepburn in the present context which I wish to note. It is that certain 'basic experiences' of the Christian are also available to the sceptic. The example offered us is the sense of the 'numinous' or the holy. It will be evident how basic I myself consider this experience to be, and I have no quarrel with Mr Hepburn's choice of an example. But he seems to me quite wrong in what he says about it. He appears to think that the experience itself is neutral, that it may be interpreted in a normal religious way or theistically. This is only plausible if we exclude what is vital in this experience. It is not *any* impression of awe or 'quite inexpressible strangeness' which constitutes the sense of the holy. The strangeness, in this case, is the peculiarly religious one of finding God in some way present in the world, and whatever further interpretation may be in order here it is certainly not one which leaves it open whether God exists or not.

Mr Hepburn is, indeed, entitled to say that the sense of the numinous is 'ultimately non-intellectual', but this is only because it is a sense of something beyond the world as we are able to understand it. That the experience should be peculiar and elusive in this sense does not preclude its being in its own way cognitive. Admittedly it does not tell us what God is like in the way 'a visit to the Zoo can tell us what a tiger or racoon is like'. But has anyone thought that it would? Mr Hepburn seems to me to fall well below his standard in making such a comparison (on page 206), and one suspects here the influence of the cruder forms of positivist scepticism.

It would, I think, be more consistent for Mr Hepburn to deny that there ever is numinous experience in the sense I have described, and to ask then what may be done with impressions of awe and strangeness we derive from nature, as in much poetry. But it confuses the issue for him to use the word 'numinous' to cover the latter; for although some writers, not excluding Otto himself, in unguarded moments, have been careless in their use of the word, it is normally understood to refer to some religious experience in which there is some awareness of an infinite or transcendent reality. We do not reason from the awe and strangeness to something which warrants them, but find the strangeness preeminently in that of which we become aware. For the same reason we should avoid suggesting, as some do, that there might be numinous objects, or a quality of numinousness, independently of the way certain objects function in our awareness of the transcendent.

My quarrel with Mr Hepburn here is not merely one about words. I suspect that in laying claim to the numinous as something of which religious persons have no monopoly, he is trying to salvage for atheism more than the case allows. The mistake is the more easily made because art and religion have a great deal in common, and because poetic and kindred impressions of nature and of the affairs of men have so large and appropriate a place in religious experience. This is also why some persons who have genuine religious experiences may suspect them of being merely poetic ones, and perhaps many today are helped into Mr Hepburn's position in this way. On this head I shall have more to say later. In the meantime I suggest that there is less available in common to the atheist and the religious person than Mr Hepburn seems inclined to think.

CHAPTER 5

RELIGIOUS EXPERIENCE

Religion begins in wonder—this has often been said, and I think it is profoundly true, but we have also to consider carefully how such a statement must be understood and what sort of wonder is involved. For we could very properly use the word 'wonder' today in many ways that have no specially religious import. We may, to begin with a fairly trivial example, make good use of 'wonder' to make a polite request or to convey various degrees of doubt, the tone of voice helping to accentuate our meaning and give it precision; thus we might say, 'I wonder whether you could help me', or 'I wonder what sort of day it will be'. How these turns of phrase are connected with the more basic meaning of the term need not be investigated now, but it is evident that we have a more basic or substantial meaning of the word 'wonder' when it is used in connection with some unlikely or unexpected facts or events when these prove also to be very impressive or agreeable—a 'wonderful achievement' a 'wonderful device', a 'wonderful cure', and so forth. The term in such cases sometimes qualifies the facts in question themselves, sometimes the attitudes they evoke; and quite often we have an undiscriminated reference to facts and attitude together. Such nuances of meaning may be very interesting to investigate and rewarding for certain philosophical purposes. But they fall entirely outside my purpose, as they tell us nothing which calls for any specially religious interpretation. The humanist is as entitled as anyone to the word in such cases as those already noted.

A more serious claimant to religious import is the use of 'wonder' in designation of elaborate or complicated general features of our environment, especially when these again are agreeable or in some way comforting to us. The structure of our bodies, the eye, ear, the general nervous system, is wonderful in this sense and shares that quality with other 'wonders of science', the microscopic and macroscopic patterns of the natural world and the unity these exhibit. But neither in these nor in the intellectual feat which discovers them have we any properly religious phenomena. They may provide highly suitable material for the religious imagination to transmute into religious insight, and they may evoke attitudes which predispose us to have religious awareness. But in themselves they can be shared and well understood by the secularist. The unbeliever may quite legitimately, and without any mitigation of his unbelief, marvel at 'the starry heavens' or the 'dance' of molecules, as he may also be amazed or profoundly stirred by contemplation of 'the moral law within'. For none of this wonder is inevitably religious. It may concern only the nature of finite facts and of our finite reactions to them, there being surely nothing in the nature of religion to preclude features of human life and of our natural environment from having qualities which astonish or impress or evoke admiration.

Indeed, the more we take a religious view of the world the more we should expect it to present features which impress or astonish on their own account, the main reason why this has been doubted being, in my opinion, the very discreditable one that many people assume that the main interests of religion are imperilled unless everything can be expressly accorded a religious hue. Our minds may be led by the thought of anything to contemplation of God, but this involves taking a step additional to any understanding we may have of finite facts as such or any reaction they may evoke in themselves. To query this betokens that excess of zeal which usually ends in the attenuation of religious claims which is most unfavourable to due appreciation of them.

Poetic or artistic wonder comes nearer to religion, and it is no disrespect to science to emphasize this. The part which science has to play in the total life of religion, when science has been duly consecrated in the service of religion, may be as important as that of art. But in itself art is much more closely related to religion, a truth which should not be obscured by any view we hold of the relative importance of art and science in themselves or as human enterprises. The main reason for this is that art has to do with reality in its more elusive individual form and exhibits to us those features of existence which touch off most readily the sense of the irreducible mystery in which all things, even by the mere fact of their existence, are set. This is not all that art does. It makes the world, in its distinctiveness, yet more peculiarly and positively articulate, presenting us with significant mysteries which border on being religious and may merge almost imperceptibly into properly religious experiences. The artist may not always appreciate this and he may display overtly the greatest antipathy to religion. This is due in part to misunderstanding of what religion is; but that is accentuated by genuine tensions which do subsist between some of the requirements of religion, especially in its full form in the life of a community, and the pursuit of some forms of art. This applies especially to conditions incidental to the proper functioning of art and religion, but it may present itself also nearer the core. Art may combine with the requirement of fine sensitivity a certain ruthlessness and imperviousness to some conditions of our conduct of more mundane affairs to which religion brings enhanced importance. The artist is bound, to some extent, to inhabit a world of his own and so to give himself in his work as not to be as free as he should in wider fields where religious loyalties are elicited. But it is not to the purpose here to pursue this further or to consider the varied and perplexing questions of the devices and shifts of mental attitudes by which tensions and conflicts of loyalties are to be met at this level. Nor need we go here into the perversions and abuses of art and religion which have sometimes brought them into violent conflict. For what concerns us now are the very deep affinities between these two, often reflected in the very tensions they may also manifest. This affinity appears especially in the fascination exerted upon the artist and the religious person alike by some reality which they feel to be peculiarly beyond the world in which they are normally at home, alien and even hostile. This is not offered as an exhaustive definition, and it would be going too far to say that all art is essentially a form of religion, except in the loose uses of the term 'religious' which I have already censured. There has to be some extension of the strictly artistic attitude to make it religious, and that I believe takes the form of bringing artistic perceptiveness into more explicit awareness of what it really is in itself than the practice and appreciation of art itself require. Art is incipient religion, and the conversion of it into the limpid recognition of itself which makes it properly religious may never happen, and where religion takes certain inhibiting forms is not likely to happen. We have therefore to admit that there may be poetic and artistic wonder, the sense of the exciting, living strangeness of the world about us, which is not religious or associated with religion. There are certainly atheistic artists and artists who have not even a religion disguised from themselves. In consistency with what has been earlier maintained we must admit this, but I think such artists must be in a curiously half-lit world where the lights and shades are never quite what they should be, and this may have much to do with the present state of art and religion alike. It is certainly possible to be in that condition, and we must thus admit the possibility of art which never even in substance, much less in the overt attitudes and declarations of the artist, does more than border on religion. But this will perhaps be plainer if we try to deal more expressly with the nature of religious illumination and the peculiar wonder in which, I have alleged, religion begins.

The wonder which is basic to religion, and in which it begins, comes with the realization, usually sharp and disrupting, that all existence as we know it stands in a relation of dependence to some absolute or unconditioned being of which we can know nothing directly beyond this intuition of its unconditioned nature as the source of all other reality. This may seem a highly sophisticated statement to associate with the primitive and rude origin of religion, and it would certainly be out of place if it implied the slightest ability on the part of primitive man to formulate his new-found conviction in such terms as I have just used. Philosophy comes late with a high and sophisticated state of culture. But certainties which we may recognize best perhaps today in their philosophical garb, or which need some infusion of philosophy into ordinary thought for us to acquire and recognize them, may nonetheless be obtainable more simply, if also in some respects more dimly, at much more naïve and less reflective levels of experience. Support for this has already been sought in allusions to early art and morality, and I think we may add to what was said above that the notion of a Creator, Himself uncreated, has such a directness and simplicity and a reference to experience of any kind whatsoever as to be as much within the reach of the untutored mind as of any other. Peculiarly difficult to treat philosophically and elusive in the sense that it is exceptionally, perhaps uniquely, hard to designate or to present in formal terms, the idea of God may nonetheless come more naturally to us than many others which mark some great advance in human culture. It is the philosopher's grasp that it especially eludes, and it is in the hands of the philosopher that it is perhaps most apt to be given forms that belie its real nature and make it hard to recognize and accept. But however elusive in the sense of lacking a precise specifiable content and passing beyond the world which is properly comprehensible to us, this idea may not be elusive in the sense of being confined to a few times or places or of occurring to individuals only in very rare moments of special illumination. I believe that, in fact, it lies in the background of most of our thinking, although more dimly in lives that have a secure routine of pleasing preoccupation with features of present existence, as happens often in civilized communities. The savage as much as the man of enlightenment, and in some ways more easily and inevitably, finds himself startled into sobering and perhaps terrifying realization of the limitations of his own existence and activity and their involving a source beyond themselves which seems to him free and powerful, and thus overwhelmingly mysterious, as nothing can be which is normally comprehensible to him, in short what the philosopher later describes as unlimited or absolute being. This realization will be embedded in many others and come in the context of such anthropomorphic lore as may be developing independently under other stimulus and to meet other needs. But however hard to disentangle from the folds of the anthropomorphic garb in which it appears, it is only with some dawning in the minds of men of this realization of all existence being rooted in unconditioned being and a sense, humbling and elated at the same time and in many ways akin to aesthetic joy, of the complete but unexpected appropriateness by which the world comes, with a peculiar inevitability of its own, to have a sustaining wholeness, that religion proper begins—this is the wonder that gives it birth, having as its core some awareness of the beyondness we name the transcendent.

How far this comes about in solitude and how far it is social is by no means easy to assess. The swing of the pendulum in anthropological studies today has brought considerable stress on the social and collectivist aspects of primitive life; and as a corrective to naïve and unhistorical individualism, such as found its heyday in the seventeenth century but persisted very markedly until late in the nineteenth century and which sometimes recurs today, this is very welcome. We must be careful not to approach the phenomena of early life with presuppositions derived from our own self-consciousness and sense of individual distinctness and responsibility. On the other hand we must not overlook the fact that, however far back we go in history or prehistory, we shall never find any community which is not made up of individuals, and it is not out of accord with evidence or normal expectation to allow for the play of wayward individual impulses in the moves which see the beginning of creative and cultural activities. Even in animal life the influence of the herd varies, and even where it is close and powerful there seem to be cases of misfits and rebelliousness, and this is all the more significant in view of the harshness with which they are treated. In human society the likelihood of similar variation is greater, and where the activities concerned are the prototypes of precisely those interests of our own in which the play of individual initiative is greatest and most indispensable, we should not be surprised to find some anticipation of such initiative from the start.

Some features of the early history of religion certainly confirm this expectation. Initiation ceremonies, for example, among some of the most primitive peoples we can find, often require a period of seclusion from the tribe in which there occur to the initiate experiences very much coloured by his individual history and relationships. The emotive excitations of the communal ceremonies are only indirectly effective here. When we turn to the earliest records we have of remote and formative periods in the history of more fully developed religions, and to the scriptures of the Hebrew-Christian tradition which we understand best in the West, the importance of notable religious experiences of outstanding individuals is very evident. Questions of strict historicity are not to the point here, the identity of the Old Testament patriarchs may be as clouded in ambiguous evidence as we please; for what the legends certainly reflect, directly or indirectly, are highly personal and distinctive experiences. Even if, as some have alleged, the patriarchal stories only represent mythically the personified history of a community, they would still at some removes point to intense stimulation of individual minds, and this is not less but more the case if the records as we have them suggest the merging of several historical or legendary figures and the stories about them. The original impetus in the formation of most of the great religions has come from inspired individuals, the founders or their forerunners, and these appear in turn to reflect a general tradition in which the recurring inspirational excitation of peculiar persons seems to have had no mean part to play. But if the stirrings which first gave shape to the main religious cultures of history afford some clue, as we should expect, to the yet more elemental stirring of religion in the background from which these emerged, we have reason again to suspect that much was due to exceptional individuals and rare moments of illumination.

In this the general course of religion appears to mirror the religious development of the individual. For in the latter case also there is an 'awakening', not of necessity sharp and disrupting, in which religion first becomes properly significant, followed at later stages by periods of renewal and enlivening of religion. But whether the initial prompting of properly religious awareness comes mainly, as I have suggested, through the occasional illumination of rare individual minds and persons peculiarly circumstanced, or whether it owes more to the simultaneous and collateral heightening of perceptiveness for members of a community generally in the performance of communal practices and mutual exchanges, there must at some point be a realization on the part of individuals in some way that 'behind' or 'beyond' all occurrences and facts of present existence there lies, not merely other facts or occurrences of like nature, but a totally mysterious reality on which all else depends. Except where this happens, religion properly does not supervene upon the practices and attitudes which predispose men to it and prepare its way. Its proper awakening, even if it comes by more imperceptible gradations than I care to think, must be in the wonder to which I have already alluded. This must not be obscured by the difficulty of tracing origins and identifying periods of advance and awakening, any more than the sharp distinction of 'ought' and 'is' should be jeopardized by difficulties we may have in noting when and how it first comes to be observed. Such transitions there certainly must be if progress is to be intelligible.

It would be wrong, however, to assume that the consciousness of an absolute or unlimited reality, which lies 'beyond' the world as we normally apprehend it, comes in the first place, or indeed at any time, in clear detachment from other experiences and the attitudes they engender. That would be peculiarly unlikely to happen to naïve or untutored minds not habituated to abstract thought; but an additional reason, and one more important for us, for expecting the apprehension of a supreme reality beyond finite life to have special association with other kinds of experiences is that the former is almost certain to be prompted by situations which make a deep impression in other ways. Some crisis will precipitate the leap which takes the mind beyond finite things, and the nature of this will have much to do with the shaping of the total religious experience and its subsequent development.

Crises of the sort mentioned will be of various kinds. Some will turn on conditions more external to the agent himself than others, extraordinary or alarming natural occurrences for example—tremors of the earth, eclipses, thunder and lightning, whirlwinds, sandstorms, volcanic eruptions, drought, plagues, floods. Disturbances due to human agencies, such as migrations or battles or extensive social change, will have a similar role. In other instances the crisis will be more personal, exile, solitude, failure or frustration, loss of prestige or possessions, defeat, punishment and shame, triumph or great good fortune. The distinction between these two sorts of conditions of disturbance must not be exaggerated. It is in virtue of their influence upon our own destinies, as well as by the immediate impact they make upon us, that natural disturbances excite and impress. Lightning is not merely an impressive and extraordinary spectacle, it is alarming and destructive. Turns of personal fortune will also have their significance deepened and emotionally toned by physical surroundings, most of all for imaginative minds likely to make a new mental advance. A case where the conditions seem to be nicely balanced as between what is more internal and the course of external events is the changing of periods and seasons in nature. For here we have events likely on their own account to arouse deep reactions but which have also much to do with survival and prosperity. The physical entities which figure most prominently in these, the resplendent sun and the pale, waxing or waning, moon, impress in the same double way. We thus find features of nature or of personal history through which individuals are apt, by close interaction of what lies more without the individual and distinctive events in his own life, to be sharply confronted with their own limitations and the power and impressiveness of what lies beyond themselves in their environment; and these will be also the factors most likely to prompt reflection about what lies altogether beyond themselves and their environment, the infinite or unconditioned.

The situations to which I have alluded will not always take the form of disturbance and upheaval. The reverse of these may be equally potent. Calm after storm, the gentleness of the onset of a new season, the stillness of remote and secluded places, ease of fortune after turmoil and trouble, accommodation with one's enemies and the serenity of age after the wildness of youth, may also set the mind in the mood where it is induced to pass beyond its present transitory setting and awaken to the new notion of what lies altogether beyond all its limitations. God may be found by 'the gentle waters' and in 'green pastures' as well as in the flood and the storms of the desert, and He may be heard in 'the still small voice'. Quite likely, the interaction of peace and storm, of upheaval and normality, and of the emotional and other reactions these induce, has an outstanding role in the development of religion at all stages, and there is certainly much in the history of peoples especially prominent in religious history, such as the Hebrews, to suggest this. The eruptions at Sinai, and events connected with it, which undoubtedly affected them deeply, are offset by the influence of periods of settlement after nomadic roamings.

The importance of these considerations lies for us at

the moment of their bearing on the question of the filling or the content of religious awareness. For it seems to me that this begins to be formed from the first onset of any properly religious life through the way the first apprehension of finite being as having a supreme and infinite source, and the emotional and other accompaniments of this awareness which we have also in mind in designating it 'wonder', impress themselves into the situation which prompts them by lending to that situation something of their own quality and aura of mystery. Certain features of initial religious situations acquire a particular prominence or sharpness of outline in this process through which secular parts of a total experience are toned by their association with religious insight, and those come to constitute for us in this way the first formulations of the 'Word of God'.

This works in two directions, first inwardly into 'the more personal experience and history of the agent himself; and, secondly, outwardly into the external situation in which he finds himself. The nerve of the first movement is found in the reactions directly elicited by initiation into the mystery of dependent being and its absolute source. There is no reason to suppose, as some views of early religion might suggest, that these reactions are bound to be violent, at least in their outward manifestations. On the contrary they may be very sober, and that, it seems to me, is certainly what we should expect them to be at first. To find that the edges of things are not where we take them to be, that they merge, not only into one another in the unities we can understand, but into an entirely different background, rich and inexhaustible and giving them a character totally different from what we normally find in them, to be strained to the limit of understanding and confronted with absolute novelty at the same time as the basic uncertainties are eased and the sense of faltering in an insecure, impermanent, world yields to the com-

pletest of all assurances and the guarantee of reason
by what goes beyond and completes it—all this is more
likely to induce a bating of breath and stilling of the
mind into quiet wonder than immediate demonstration
of excitement. Is not this the attitude of the scientist
when problems that have long baffled him yield to an
obvious solution by a new way of looking at things,
perhaps overwhelmingly simple, or of the artist when
all falls easily and obviously into place, is there not
here a suspension of all activity that might compete
with the process that is so strangely fulfilling itself of
its own accord, and is it not in a similar integrating of
all activity into a meditative mood of suspended animation that a man becomes inwardly silent before the
greatest mystery of all? As the tension is eventually
relieved, the pent up energies summoned up and
arrested in the first moment of wondering awareness
will find release in various ways according to temperament and circumstance, and in the course of this much
in the original experience may lose its purity. But it
seems to me that the note of stillness rather than violence
is that most likely to govern the first dawning of true
religion and its main moments at all times.

This stillness of mind is not, however, numbness or
quietism, but on the contrary an alerting and concentration of all the powers of the mind, the more especially
as 'the beyond' is apprehended, not in detachment but
as involved in facts of the world which are most sharply
presented 'here and now'. There will thus be a heightening of perceptiveness and sensitivity, but qualified
by the selectiveness by which attention is directed
mainly to matters most consonant with the new experience through which we are passing and the new
perspective into which all things are cast when viewed
in the light of our altered notions of their boundaries.
We may thus in one sense be taken 'out of ourselves'
or lifted to 'a seventh heaven' and feel that we have

left behind the more mundane and drabber affairs of our normal existence; but we never quite do this, any more than the poet does so in moments of intense creativity. The world as we normally think of it may be forgotten and our impressions of it effaced, but it will be nonetheless very much with us in another guise. We may be impervious to much that goes on around us, and certain events may fail to make any impression that we notice on our senses. But we may be all the more sharply aware of our environment in other regards, as the poet, to continue what seems the aptest analogy here, may have much in his poem conditioned, directly or indirectly, by things he notices, the colour and shape of a leaf or the gleam of light on a wall or the tinted clouds in a sky, out of the corner of his mind, as it were, not reflectively and self-consciously, but yet acutely and vividly and taken up subtly in some fashion into what he writes or says. The world as remembered will be present in the same way. A poet or a mystic may thus seem quite unaware of some features of present environment, both may fail to observe what happens about them or to be conscious of physical sensations which are normally most obtrusive. But they have at the same time a heightened consciousness of their environment in other ways, and while they may well declare themselves, in some extreme cases, to have been 'out of the body', they are not so in fact, but, on the contrary, more than ever within the body and within the ordinary world differently perceived. In the moment of live religious experience we shall thus be more than usually perceptive of certain things in our present environment and responsive to them, although not perhaps the things we should notice most obviously at other times; and this holds as much for what is occurring within ourselves as for features of the external situation.

Alertness of this kind will be heightened and directed

also by a profounder consciousness of unity in things communicated to us by our apprehension of its transcendent source and guarantee. This reduces the proclivity we have to heed events more as they enter into the orbit of our particular interests and spheres of activity, or to take a romantic view of the world and whatever it holds for us of good or ill. Events which are remote from spheres in which their significance is most evident are thus accorded their due importance and seen to have essential affinity with the matters which impinge more insistently and inescapably upon us. Our judgments are thus corrected and made objective and we incur a discipline which should deepen in every regard our devotion to the truth. How consistent this is with what we know of religion in its living and undefiled forms is easily perceived and it may readily be confirmed by inspection of the progress of religion from its humblest to its most exalted modes. The language and symbols of religion are rich with encomiums of truth, whether it concern God or man, this world or another. Its censure of deceit and hypocrisy is heavy and some of its sublimest and most impressive praise is reserved for those who have no deception in them, either for themselves or for others. Debased religion has often obstructed the search for truth and won for religion the enmity and suspicion of enquiring minds, but it is not hard to see that where religion thrives on dogmatism and intolerance the energies which it has released are being exploited in ways not consistent with the insight which generated them. The long chapter of religious persecution and narrowness needs more explaining than can be accorded it here, although views already advanced about corrupt forms of religion suggest the course which such explanation should take. But I think few who study the main sources of religious inspiration and the utterances which typify best its course in the past will question the extent to which undefiled religion puts a premium on integrity and love of truth. This, I submit, is most consistent with what we must think of religious awareness as involving a reinforcement of our sense of objectivity and bringing comprehensiveness into our apprehension of our environment, and that is a characteristic of religious insight which it exhibits from the start and retains at its core so long as it is able to be true to itself.

Nowhere is this more evident than in our grasp of ethical truth. Values and obligations are markedly external to ourselves, they are not our own creations and do not depend directly on what we feel and think ourselves. We acknowledge and recognize what we deem of worth and own it to comply with our duties whether that pleases us or not. But in having our thought directed to what is so completely 'beyond' or 'other than' ourselves as the absolute source of being which wholly eludes comprehension, we find ourselves also better disposed to appreciate fairly the standards of worth and the obligations which confront us directly, not, it may be, in some abstract form, but as qualifying some situation in which we are placed.

The relation of ethics and religion at this point is in fact two-fold, for just as the apprehension of a transcendent reality bordering all that we otherwise know induces a sharper and truer appreciation of ethical distinctions, so our sensitivity to those distinctions predisposes us in turn to have our minds guided beyond the sphere in which they naturally function to what is more completely external or 'beyond'. There is for this reason a close and persistent interaction of ethics and religion which we may also readily trace in the history of their progress and which has often been made the subject of comment and speculation by the students of both.

To the extent that our apprehension of the ultimate mystery which surrounds our own existence (and all other finite being) has the effect of heightening and correcting our perceptiveness of the world about us and ourselves, and to the extent that it makes us more appreciative of ethical distinctions and their objective or external quality, it will much affect our understanding of ourselves and of our present environment in the situation in which that apprehension is vividly awakened in us. This is one distinctive characteristic of the general enlightenment which religion brings and which gives to religion a content peculiarly its own and yet made up of features of finite experience.

As such it has not the fullness of revealed truth, but, before I indicate what I consider the latter to be, further stress must be placed on the total effect of the state of wonder and suspended activity, by which religion comes to birth and is renewed, on our own state and the conditions which prompt it when it occurs. I have already referred to reactions directly elicited on such occasions, and have contended that they are likely to include a stillness of mind combined with unstrained alertness. We should thus expect emotional factors at first to be subdued, and this I think also conforms with the testimony of notable religious experience. But as the original tension is eased emotional elements have greater play. The excitement initially induced by our new experience and our new view of the world gathers momentum as we realize more fully all that this involves and seek some diversion from the overwhelming nature of its impact upon us. The shock and the strain of adjusting our mental attitude finds relief in deeper emotions and diversion in subsidiary activities. There runs in this way from the live and sure centre of the religious experience an emotional charge and drive which energizes various other propensities of our nature and sets in train various activities. These will concern especially interests that have most affinity with religion proper, the broad imaginative interests that sweep us into a greater wholeness of experience than our fragmentary bits of ordinary living—profound affection, art, the passion for truth and justice; but other deep emotions and overriding aims may be freshly activized by religious excitation and given new forms. Not all these will be laudable, nor will they always have the balance which we would expect the unifying character of the religious awareness to lend them. Much will depend on what they are initially, and here is a point where religious discipline and the guidance of the refinement of religious experience in the past and reflection upon it are needed. The emotional aftersurge of religious insight has had much to do with the stranger forms of activity associated with it and it has to be considered in connection with other ways in which the life of religion may become distorted. Variations of temperament will be very important here also. But we need not go closely into these matters now. Suffice it to note that the religious insight and wonder which has been described may be accompanied by emotional disturbances which may affect various individuals in very different ways. These are of secondary importance and must be considered in relation to the initial cognitive experience, and not vice versa. But they become more integral to the religious experience as a whole as lending to the occasion of religious apprehension a distinctive character and helping to signalize it in a manner that has much to do with the fuller development of religion.

At more sophisticated levels of religious experience emotional factors appear in yet other forms. Our memories of religious occasions in the past will have many emotional tones, and bordering associations will also be charged with feeling. The circumstances in which religion has been presented to us, involving often tender associations with persons very dear to us, will carry their own emotional strain into the later enlivening of our religion, and this is itself a factor of no mean importance in the maintenance of religion. If, in addition, it can be shown that religious events or processes, and the interplay of these with other factors of experience, have some patterns which encourage the belief that they represent the dealings with us in the matters of most concern to us of another personal Being, there is scope again for the excitation of the profoundest emotions according to the turn the relationship takes at particular times; and if, on the basis of the way this religious strand of men's experience as a whole has been woven, there are produced certain general notions about its significance which contain further possibilities of acute dramatic tension, these notions, both when they are warranted and when they are not, will bring additional emotional charges into outstanding religious occurrences. To complicate things further, the process of enlivening a religion when it is dormant or inducing it when absent will involve exhortation and other devices in which the more immediate aim will often be the direct excitation of the emotions which occur in these various ways in religion, a way being sought, sometimes more sometimes less legitimately, along the emotions themselves, or along emotions resembling the properly religious emotions or connected with them, to whatever is thought to be the core of the proper religious response. We need not trace the course of these processes and their variations now. All I wish to do is to make proper allowance for the part which various forms of religious emotion and the activities stimulated thereby may play in characterizing particular religious situations and lending them distinctiveness.

By means of the emotional accompaniments or effects of our initial discernment of all finite reality, but more expressly of what is present here and now, as having a transcendent source of whose particular nature we can have no direct comprehension, and even more, and more importantly, by the sharpening of moral sensitivity and the alerting of the faculties by which we take note of our environment, certain features of the situation in which this discernment or apprehension occurs acquire a distinctiveness and prominence which they would not normally exhibit. Independently of this, such situations are likely to be exceptional and to represent some climax or crisis in our own personal history or in the course of the events which make the biggest impact upon us. In this way the significance we attach to certain secular or finite features of some situations in which we find ourselves, a significance which is itself furthermore finite or secular throughout, has a special connection with our apprehension of the transcendent. The course of such experiences in one's own life and the life of one's society will yield results of distinctive importance for our understanding of our environment and the reactions to it which are fitting for us. If furthermore the features of those distinctive and critical situations which are thus specially highlighted for us have, as religious people claim, a compelling and insistent character which rivets attention upon them, then we are disposed to conclude, and justified in doing so it seems to me, that we are here being afforded a clue to the importance the transcendent has specifically for us in our present existence and to the expectations we may form on the basis of our dependence upon it; and this, moreover, over the continuous history of ourselves and our society will present itself increasingly as a 'dealing' with us of that which is beyond the sphere of finite existence altogether which, along with various reactions or responses of our own, builds itself up into a relationship of intimate and fairly sustained communion which is already presupposed in all but the most initial and incipient awakening of religious apprehension and causes us to think immediately in personal terms of the situations in which this particular process of illumination occurs.

CHAPTER 6

PATTERNS OF EXPERIENCE

The situations which are central for religious apprehension in the way described and the particular features
of them on which our sharpened consciousness of the
transcendent causes us to rivet attention, including of
course the requirement that we respond in a certain
way, have to be regarded as the initial ingredients of
our awareness of God and His dealings with us. They
may be described as the basic or first-order symbols
or media by which divine disclosure is made. They are
symbols only, for they do not enable us to fathom or
reduce the mystery of the transcendent, they merely
make the transcendent significant for us in terms of
the finite realities which do come within our orbit. We
cannot know God as He is in Himself, but we can know
Him expressly and intimately in terms of the sort of
experiences of which we are capable, and the experiences
in which this does in fact happen are symbols in the
sense that by them alone do we know the Supreme
Reality which goes altogether beyond them.

These are our first-order symbols, but they are not
isolated from one another or obtruded into our lives in
a random way. They enrich one another and each comes
loaded with associations from the past. What is new
is not easily detached from renewal of what has appeared already, not only to oneself but to others in
the long history of religion. They clothe one another with

meaning, merge and coalesce, to form an extended pattern of religious illumination in which isolated pieces are not always distinguishable, any more than we can closely delimit the way our affections grow. There are, for most religious persons, occasions which are more momentous than others and in which their own religious experience reaches its peak or a turning-point. But this occurs in a setting to which previous religious events in our own lives and those of others contribute, even when we are least conscious ourselves of this determination of the present by the past; and this enrichment of one experience by another, especially when it takes the form of a significant pattern of distinctive intervention in our lives, may almost be regarded as a further order of religious symbolism, so much does it contribute to making religious occurrences a mode of distinctive communication to us. But the difference is ultimately one of degree, as the essentials of the process remain the same.

There is a further way in which religious experiences proper, in the sense in which we have been concerned to examine them hitherto, may be conditioned by other experiences and extended into them. This is in line with the way most of the occurrences in our lives, even the most distinctive and formative ones, combine with others into what our lives as a whole become. I may acquire a friend who has no interest in what I do professionally, but it is very unlikely that this will have no effect of any kind upon my work or that my professional interests will not influence my friendship in some way. The influence our aims and interests have on one another is sometimes too subtle to be detected, and it may need the insight of a novelist or the training of a psychologist to unfold it, but it can rarely be negligible. Normally we do not keep our interests in separate compartments, and even if we try, as in the case of those who lead a double life, the experiment is rarely, if ever, quite successful.

In the case of a major interest or concern, almost everything we do, or which happens to us, will be touched by that concern. I am not always thinking about my friends or my relatives, but their influence upon me pervades what I do when they are not physically present or present to my thought. In a similar way, a religious occurrence will have, in the first place, a fairly immediate impact on others and merge almost imperceptibly into them. It will owe much to what precedes it and give its colour to what follows; and that in turn will permeate other activities and interests.

The merging of our main aims and activities into one another, such that it can only be in a rough and rather artificial way that we can demarcate them, is made possible by dispositions and character, and I have already remarked upon the subtle interweaving of events and dispositions in our life as a whole. Much may be retained dispositionally and have much influence upon us without our being directly aware of it. In other cases we see the results without heeding much the progress which brings them about. This also will give an extended significance to a religious occurrence and guarantee the continuity of the part it may play in one's life as a whole and which may be overlooked if we think mainly of its episodic character. There accrue in that way to a religious occurrence proper extensions of meaning and importance as it lives on in the remainder of experience, and this, although not directly prompted by the special wonder and awareness which is pre-eminently characteristic of religious experience, can be properly regarded as part of what we come to apprehend in the totality of the religious intervention in finite occurrences.

The extent to which religious occurrences proper are episodic and can be fairly clearly recognized in detachment from other parts of our history is by no means easy to ascertain. This is due partly to the fact that religion itself has so many by-products and accompaniments, some of which have a great deal to do with the renewal and maintenance of it, that it is not always easy to know when we are dealing with the substance, and when with the shadow. I believe that most who profess a religion and observe its practices, in the sense of saying prayers or attending services or reading scriptures, are bound to attain in some fashion to a personal religious awareness. But how far this happens and how far the religious round may be followed, perhaps with great earnestness, without ever mounting into genuine religion, is an exceptionally difficult question which could only be settled, if at all, by exhaustive consideration of a great many matters that have to do with religion, including the moral practices which it inculcates. It is also a moot question what value allegedly religious practices could have if sincerely pursued in the way suggested at some removes from genuine religion as involving some personal apprehension of the transcendent. I have stressed already the perils of pseudo-religion of this kind and the ease with which it may lapse into idolatry of a positive and vicious sort. It may also lose its sincerity and the earnestness of the allegiance to esteemed practices or persons and become crude hypocrisy; and, for these reasons as well as for the supreme worth of religion proper, it should be an especial charge—as I shall show in more detail later—on those who minister to others religiously, as well as upon each person individually, to see that genuine religious awareness is not overlaid by its forms but stirred into life.

But, quite apart from the function of subsidiary activities in religion, the question of the episodic character of genuine religious experience is difficult. Many of its features are copied in others, including those, such as art, with which it most easily coalesces, and in addition the onset of properly religious experience may be gentle and not startling or disruptive. This does not imperil its distinctiveness; for, much as the quiet enjoyment of a natural scene may imperceptibly become the inspired experience of a poet or painter, so religious awareness may supervene unobtrusively on the conditions most prone to induce it. To those who are accustomed to the practice of piety and have aids to appropriate reflection on divine things in the devotions which they observe, this will be the way of things normally, most of all in mature established religions. But even outside our particular devotional practices, and the ideas which guide them, or where these are not much heeded or cultivated, the transitions by which a secular occurrence transforms itself into a religious one may be easy and barely noticeable without the latter's lacking anything of its novel and distinctive character.

In the same way a religious experience may subside, or merge itself into the activities it especially prompts, by gradations which leave it uncertain where its margin is set. It will prompt moods and activities akin to itself, and it will continue to have influence in other ways. In addition, the explicit consciousness of the transcendent which I have maintained to be indispensable for live religious experience need not by any means be formally expressed or reflected upon; it will not in fact be normal for it to turn in on itself in this way. For these reasons it is not at all easy in practice to say when a religious experience is merging into its appropriate sequels, and there will in any case be much variation from one instance to another according to circumstances and temperament. The more habituated we are to live religiously the more unobtrusively will the glow of explicit religious awareness light up the normal round, but if genuine religion comes as a novelty, then it may be expected to have, in its occasion and accompaniments as well as in itself, the startling and disruptive quality usually associated with sudden conversion. Moreover, religious experience happens, not in a vacuum, but to a certain type of person peculiarly circumstanced, and will vary with these conditions. In some cases it will be more explosive and more expressive and violent in its manifestations, and in some it will glow with a quieter inner light. If a religious experience makes possible, as may well happen, insights very markedly different from those we normally enjoy or brings with it powers which neither the agent himself nor others commonly exercise, then it will distinguish itself more sharply from other experiences and be more easily delimited. But in no case, except perhaps some quite peculiar preternatural experiences, will there be an obvious discontinuity, but rather a merging into appropriate sequels and the general change in the tenor of living.

This is exactly what we should expect, if the analysis offered of religious experience is correct. For we found that this involved a peculiar alertness and heightening of attention, together with a special directing of attention and release of activity, consequent upon our awareness of the mystery of unconditioned and perfect being; and it would not be likely that we should normally be conscious of the change in our experience when the direct stimulation brought about in these ways yields to the perpetuation of the various activities in question more by their natural momentum. It must not therefore be supposed that, in attributing very peculiar qualities to religious experience and distinguishing sharply between it and other experience, I wish to circumscribe religious experience closely. On the contrary, just as I have urged that the transcendent becomes immanent when the consciousness of it is led to associate itself with certain features of finite existence and put on these the imprint of what is altogether beyond them, so the live religious experience in which this consists extends itself into yet other experiences by lending them something of its own quality.

Dispositions will plainly have much to do with this, for they will make possible a more permanent influence than the immediate repercussions of one experience on others. The content of the initial experience will be retained and leaven others in ways which we shall not always be able to notice, partly by recurring to us in other contexts, and partly by subtle ways in which our dispositions affect one another. Religious experiences, like other experiences which have a very distinctive character, are woven into the web of our life as a whole and count for us quite as much in this way very often as they do in themselves. They are not isolated or extended in meaning and significance merely in relation to one another, but become a part of living; and much of the wisdom to be shown in the healthy conduct of religion consists in the due cultivation of explicit religious awareness together with the right relating of this to the minding of other affairs that concern us as finite beings, and this will vary again from one person to another, according, for example, to whether we are more prone to contemplation or to practice, or according to whether our particular history has brought us the intenser and more disruptive forms of religious experience. The alternation of the live religious experience with periods in which this perpetuates itself in other aspects of living may be unobtrusive and unnoticed, and where there is settled religious living that may be the normal and the more estimable state, although it carries with it the dangers I have been at pains to stress, those of corruption and the atrophy of genuine spiritual power.

There have been religious persons who have made a special study of the changes of mood and course in the spiritual life and have elaborated various techniques for recognizing the appropriate stages and passing through them. For persons suitably placed and gifted this may have considerable worth, both for themselves and those they may benefit. But it will seem too artificial and studied for adoption by others. There is no one right way in religion any more than in art, where the variety of style and technique contributes much to eventual enrichment. On the whole the maintenance of living religion should be not so preciously contrived as in art, for religion is a vital concern for all and not for persons superabundantly gifted or peculiarly placed, and while one has always to beware of easy acquiescence or the sluggish performance of habitual practice, religion must be lived for most of us as the animation of the normal routine of our station.

The point to be stressed is that, while the distinctiveness of the 'live' religious experience, as I have called it, must not be overlooked or underestimated, we must not regard it as the intrusion of a wholly unusual factor into the normal occasions of life, or something peculiar which happens to us oddly now and again, but, normally at least, as the renewal of a formative influence by which the remainder is deeply affected and which, in consequence, the latter is more and more predisposed to receive. And the more we are enabled to regard the renewal of insight and power in this way in vital relation to the fullness of a religious life which it animates and out of which it arises, the more we shall appreciate how there will be extensions of meaning or significance in religion, not only as distinctive religious experiences are viewed in relation to one another, but also in respect of the whole of what comes about in consequence of them, in the way of further insights or changes of attitude, for us and for other members of society; and this may also be regarded as part of the story of the way the transcendent enters into vital and intimate relation to us within our own lives.

Much in the course of this story will remain imprecise; the spread of the difference which it makes to us can not be carefully mapped, but will rather have very uncertain and fluid edges. Much will pass into total oblivion, just as a friendship may be sustained and extended in innumerable ways of which it would be quite impossible to give a detailed account. It is the general impression which stays as a rule. But while it will not be possible to note and record precisely the part which distinctive religious experiences play in our lives, or to determine exactly when they arise and fade again into others, we are able to recognize in a general way, not only the more direct impact of one religious occurrence on others and the pattern of the course such occurrences take, but also the manifold accretions of meaning and importance as this process immerses itself in our life as a whole; and this gives a further reach and dimension as it were to the distinctive media or symbols from which we detect, in the indirect way which alone is possible to us, what are the particular ways in which the transcendent may come to count for us and be, in this manner, disclosed.

Of this process there will be two forms we need to distinguish. There will be in the first place, as again in the case of friendship or love, a general or over-all impression of the way the relationship builds itself up. We may find, for example, that the moments of religious insight are sharper and more pointed in their significance on occasions of grave and outstanding need, in grief, perplexity or doubt for example, and there may thus be produced the general impression of an ever-present help in trouble. We may find comfort when comfort is especially needed by the new breadth that is given to our mental or spiritual outlook, and we may find sources of strength when despair would otherwise overwhelm us by finding ourselves feeling and thinking in ways that are superior to our normal lot, and there may be marked accretions of strength to our personalities in these ways. Occurrences of this sort may of course be easily travestied as we think of them in retrospect or generalize about them, and we may come to think of them in more mechanical ways as a more explicit intervention in the outward course of the difficulties which beset us; and when men are at a primitive stage of development and apt to rationalize their experience in the ways that are more amenable to their understanding and call for the least effortful response, unusual turns of events, an unexpected deliverance for example, may be seized upon to confirm or exemplify superstitious beliefs in magic or totem for which the facts provide no justification. But this is another issue, and I postpone for the moment any observations to be made on the question of a possible divine intervention in external events as it appears in the light of the views advanced in this book. The point is that we may have distinctively religious occasions in the course of which we may have the impression of being helped or solaced or strengthened.

In a similar way we may find that the more distinctively religious moments are also apt to occur on occasions of deviation on our part from the course we believe we ought to be following; they stand as it were athwart our path and may arrest our course in a way which we can regard as a peculiarly spiritual deliverance in which our own personalities, and not merely our particular circumstances, have been preserved from disaster and degradation. Alternatively, we may find, in yielding to a temptation, that we have an accuser other than our own conscience, an accuser which speaks with yet greater gravity from within the heightening of our own sense of worth and dignity in the clearer illumination which religious experience brings and the association of moral values with the general intervention of the transcendent in our lives. We shall then be disposed to conclude that in religion we are confronted with a specially righteous power and that the intervention from outside our finite experience, which is also within it, has to do especially with the moral quality of our lives. God will be a God of righteousness and justice and He will search out our hearts.

This again admits of travesty and misrepresentation according to the stage of moral enlightenment we may have reached and the play of our imagination. But that need not trouble us here. And just as we may find in the livelier moments of religious experience a terrible accuser deepening the accents of our own conscience and making us sensitive to moral distinctions we might have overlooked or considered trivial, so we may also find an eventual healer, a healer whose ministrations may be costing and humbling and whose cures may not always be immediate, but who provides in the last resort the only balm that will work by presenting in the world at large a sustaining of moral and kindred values which gives us confidence in taking them into our hearts again and renewing their hold by identifying them more closely with the religious interventions by which they are extended and deepened. In the same context we may find also that the blunting of our religious awareness, and the relapse into less elevated attitudes towards the world, is countered by unexpected renewal of moods of religious sensitivity, that God, in the simpler language of live religion, does not 'abandon us wholly' or 'leave Himself without witness', and we may come to know of ways in which we may facilitate this process and make ourselves more open to its influence. And here we may see the germ of our thought of God as the restorer of right relations with Himself, as renewer of life and healer, as redeemer and God of grace.

There may be much more than this to a mature conception of grace, and Christianity has, in my opinion, a proper claim to a particular ministry of grace and redemption. But I think we must start from the sort of experience I have just described and which is far from being a monopoly of any religion. And if we find, in the manner of which I have only given an indication in outline here, that there are certain general impressions, such as those instanced, to be obtained of ways in which the alleged divine intervention in human experience occurs, then we have certain general pointers or counters by which to sum up and sustain the faith we acquire, and for which we come to have a special regard.

This will hold also for very different kinds of total impression which we may acquire of the process of divine disclosure. For we may find, not only that there are recurring patterns or modes which the process usually exhibits, but also that it has taken a particular course in a particular history, our own or that of our community. This will be linked up of course with the shape our own destiny has taken at the secular level, but if we find that, at distinctive and outstandingly significant interludes in our own story, the course of our lives has been modified in some fashion such as to give us an altered conception of its nature as a whole, and that this modification takes the religious form we have been discussing, or even if we merely find that the primary religious occurrences in our lives, considered in relative detachment from the remainder, build up into a special shape or story of their own, then we are presented with a very special way in which religious experience is the medium of divine disclosure, a particular revelation in history. And while this again is not the exclusive monopoly of any community or period or religion, it may well be more evident in some situations and periods than others, and there may well be a distinctive form of it which may yield the tenets of a particular faith and substantiate the claim to uniqueness to be made on its behalf.

But of processes of this sort again certain general impressions may be obtained, blending with the more basic and universal over-all impressions of the process of revelation already noted. The God who succours and preserves, and who restores the erring to right relations to Himself, may be found to have done this in outstanding ways which have given shape to our affairs over a particular period, and especially perhaps some period of importance in the story of a people or community; and this will present itself to us, in our total impression of the process, in close and specific identification of God's activity with the particular occurrences in which it has thus been made especially evident to us. God will be the God of Abraham, Isaac and Jacob, the God who led His people out of captivity, who revealed Himself especially to their leader in ways which left their pronounced and indelible mark on the whole of their subsequent story at all its levels, and who created within them the expectation, often marred by crudities and distortions of interpretation, of some triumphant culmination of this process of His dealing with them. And for such a people God will be the living God who discloses Himself to them in this distinctive shaping of their history.

Those who are most sensitive to this process, and they will normally include those who have participated most prominently in it, will moreover have represented the process, both in its general scope and in the particular way in which it impinges most closely upon them and on any part they may be playing in the affairs of their community at the time, in significant and expressive terms peculiar to their age and circumstances; and the more their imaginative and artistic propensities are inflamed, as it is very natural for them to be, by the tensions of the events in which they take part, the more will colourful metaphors and parables appear giving further particularity and concretion to the process of revelation. God will be the great king, the patient long-suffering tender of the vineyard, the husband who never forsakes his beloved however she offends but draws her with 'bonds' of love, and in due course, as profound insight supervenes about superstition and distortion, the blameless victim by the shedding of whose blood the guilty are redeemed and the demands of righteousness and sanctity met.

In this process also God Himself will be given more specific representation in easily recognizable forms, the 'arm of the Lord' will be found encompassing men, His throne will be in the skies and His voice will be heard. In moments of religious exaltation and excitement men will be prone moreover to have colourful visions and abnormal experiences of other sorts which will lend their own imagery to the more permanent representations of God. There will be perpetuated certain established ways of designating Him and these will be such familiar and common accompaniments of religious living and aids to its maintenance that the distinction will be largely blurred in many minds between what is real and what is figurative in such representations. Religion will live in its inspired images, and at less sophisticated stages, where the sense of the religious moulding of life is also marked and vivid, the domination of experience by its more creative and life-giving images will be considerable. It is to this feature of religion that we must now turn.

CHAPTER 7

EXPERIENCE AND IMAGES

Before considering further the part which images play in religious experience, it is most important for our purpose to insist that the religious imagery to which I have just referred, however vivid and indispensable it may be at certain stages, does not represent the truth about God and His activity directly, but only at a certain remove; for the warrant for the images comes from certain experiences and the total significance of these in our experience as a whole. What the images gather together and represent are the patterns and recurrences of certain distinctive events which, in their significant patterns or sequences especially, are themselves the ultimate and irreducible ingredients of our knowledge of God. The latter I have called the 'first-order symbols' and I have allowed this designation to extend beyond individual religious experiences into the course of such experiences as a whole and even their accretions of importance through the part they play in other experience. But the imaginative representations of this, however indispensable and however rarely dissociated in practice from the experience to which they relate, are of a different order and must not be thought to mirror the nature of divine activity directly.

The necessity for stressing this especially arises from the proneness of many influential theologians and religious thinkers of today to regard certain images as basic and final in the process of revelation or divine disclosure. This comes about in large measure, I suspect, from the rather bewildered realization of the urgency, for religious apologetics and the propagation of faith, of the need to provide some ultimate warrant for the claims made on behalf of revealed religion. It has already been stressed, at more than one point in this book, that the crucial problem for religious thought today and that which has the closest bearing on the commendation and practice of religion, is the problem how the limitations of our finite natures may be overcome in our apprehension of a reality which goes altogether beyond them and is not comprehensible in finite terms. I am attempting my own answer to this question, and I have given indications earlier of approaches to it which are current today. Among these are various forms of the appeal to authority, and one such appeal has considerable interest for us at this point.

This is not, directly at any rate, an appeal to the authority of any particular body or church, although that may well be in the background. Nor is it the authority of a set of doctrines that is involved, nor directly the authority of the Scriptures. There is something more fundamental which licenses the use we make of those sources of faith and regulates it. The crudities of blind submission to a church or of a fundamentalist approach to the Bible are thus avoided, and this is a considerable gain. But we do not move altogether away from the notion of authority in the ultimate assessments of truth in religion. For we are told that there are authorized parables and images. God cannot be known directly, we can only think of Him in parable or image whose terms are taken from our finite experience but which has a reference beyond that experience, and as we cannot check the parable or image in this case by any kind of comparison between it and the reality it is supposed to reflect, we must, in the last resort, so it is maintained, fall back on the authority which invests some parables or images.

Among the most influential and distinguished advocates of this view is Dr Austin Farrer, and he states the theory in question very explicitly in several parts of his well-known work, *The Glass of Vision*. No one who has an understanding of the importance of images in religious belief and in the extension and deepening of faith can fail to feel extremely indebted to the suggestive and illuminating observations made upon this subject by Dr Farrer in this book and elsewhere. His account of the way a religious image may have accretions of meaning in new contexts, and almost have a life of its own, is subtle and extremely apposite to the present state of the discussion of the problem of revelation. But when it comes to the crucial question of the adoption of certain images and the rejection of others, or of the selection of certain images as being regulative and more fundamental than others, the most that he can tell us in the last analysis is that there is 'a process of images which live as it were by their own life and impose themselves with authority. They demand to be thought in this way or that, and not otherwise.'[1] There are only two qualifications of substance to be made of this. The first, namely that 'the principal images provide a canon to the lesser images',[2] while of considerable worth in some contexts, does not help us at the present juncture, for it leaves open at least the question of the principal images. The second qualification is that the analogies afforded by natural theology provide us with 'a canon to interpret revelation',[3] a 'way to criticize the images',[4] 'a rule by which to regulate our intuition of what they mean'.[5] But Dr Farrer must be aware, if only on the basis of the importance he ascribes to revelation, that this is not enough.

[1] *The Glass of Vision*, p. 113.   [2] *Op. cit.*, p. 111.
[3] *Op. cit.*, p. 110.   [4] *Op. cit.*, p. 110.   [5] *Op. cit.*, p. 110.

Admittedly, the 'regulative' function of the fundamental notion of natural theology, namely, in Dr Farrer's own words, that of 'a supreme being' or 'an infinite creator', is of vital importance in the process of revelation itself. For it not only provides the reference of the content of revelation, but, if the suggestions put forward earlier are sound, must be actively renewed in the process of revelation and associate itself in particular ways with the substance of further experiences. Dr Farrer speaks wisely when he says: 'The apostles were not, indeed, philosophers: but the philosophy of natural knowledge presupposes the knowledge it analyses and refines, and that natural knowledge, in abundant measure, the apostles had. What God bestowed on them through Christ was revelation of God's particular action. They had not known before that God would send His Son for us men and our salvation, but they had known that God was God; and what they now learnt was not that some superhuman Father had sent his Son, but that God had done so.'[6] This is impressive enough—as far as it goes. The apostles, like all others, must know that God is God, if they are to witness and understand His action. But we have still the difficult question of assessing what the course is which God's particular action takes. Does He do this, or that? And the answer to this question cannot be wholly educed out of the idea of God or the knowledge of His being—or if it could we should hardly need revelation. There is a gap which Dr Farrer does not bridge after asking 'Can we in any way criticize the images?'[7] For we need more than 'a rule of a highly general kind, in the conception of God supplied to us by natural theology'.[8] We need some criterion or principle of selection for what is specifically claimed about God, and it will not suffice, in the absence of this, to insist that 'natural theology, then, provides a

[6] Op. cit., p. 111.   [7] Op. cit., p. 110.   [8] Op. cit., p. 110.

canon of interpretation which stands outside the particular matter of revealed truth'.[9]

One reason for Dr Farrer's failure to see that his account has the lacuna just noted is his proneness to be content with an account of religion as the 'supernaturalizing of events in the existing world'.[10] This is ambiguous as it stands. It might well refer to the sort of process I have attempted to describe myself. I agree with Dr Farrer very readily when he insists that 'What the finite mind perceives in detail and fullness is always finite existence'.[11] But for this reason I feel all the more the need to consider what peculiarities of some finite existences license the claim to refer beyond them. To describe these peculiarities, as I understand them, as the supernaturalizing of some events would not be misleading, provided it were understood that the process does make a real difference to these events and the course they take. It is not a special way of looking at them or some religious licensing of them which leaves them substantially what they were independently. The supernaturalizing must make a real difference, and not a 'difference without a difference' similar to the account which some philosophers offer today of metaphysical differences in terms of different ways of looking at the world. Perhaps Dr Farrer would agree, but in that case he should give a fuller account of what is involved in supernaturalizing a natural occurrence. On the whole he seems to want things both ways, to suppose that an event could be supernaturalized and at the same time retain the fullness of its independent natural character. And this, incidentally, brings him into very dire straits, as I shall note again below, when he attempts to solve the 'riddle of grace and free will' in terms of 'a double personal agency in our one activity'.[12]

It is this tendency to think of the supernaturalizing

[9] Op. cit., p. 111.   [10] Op. cit., p. 12.
[11] Op. cit., p. 29.   [12] Op. cit., p. 33.

process as one which we seem bound to regard as making only a difference without a difference that seems to drive Dr Farrer back on the alleged authority of the divine images themselves, and to make him regard the life of these 'God-given images' as itself the very core of revelation. He declares: 'We have to listen to the Spirit speaking divine things: and the way to appreciate his speech is to quicken our minds with the life of the inspired images.' He continues: 'I have heard it wisely said that in Scripture there is not a line of theology, and of philosophy not so much as an echo. Theology is the analysis and criticism of the revealed images: but before you can turn critic or analyst, you need a matter of images to practise upon. Theology tests and determines the sense of the image, it does not create it. The images, of themselves, signify and reveal.'[13] 'The images', we also read, 'are the stuff of revelation' and 'they must be interpreted according to their own laws'. 'The Bible-reader will immerse himself in the single image on the page before him, and find life-giving power in it, taken as it stands.'[14] 'In the case of supernatural divine revelation, nothing but the image is given us to act as an indication of the reality.'[15] Revelation presents 'the extreme example of irreducible imagery'. 'Unless finite things put themselves upon us as symbols of deity we can have no natural knowledge of God. Revealed images do not do this: they are authoritatively communicated.'[16] 'The ineffable thing happens. . . . Man cannot conceive it except in images: and these images must be divinely given to him, if he is to know a supernatural divine act.'[17]

The primacy here seems plainly to lie with the images, and with the authority with which they are invested. I do not know how far this is, at basis, a subtly disguised form of the appeal to the authority of the Bible

---

[13] *Op. cit.*, p. 44.   [14] *Op. cit.*, p. 51.   [15] *Op. cit.*, p. 58.
[16] *Op. cit.*, p. 94.   [17] *Op. cit.*, p. 108.

as ultimate in itself. The view is sometimes put that, while no case can be made for the literal inerrancy of the Bible, we take the substance of the Bible's message, *ab initio* as it were, as ultimate and beyond question. The only problem is, just what does the Bible as a whole say? This is a very important advance on fundamentalism. But it leaves us, nonetheless, on rather shaky ground, and if the Muslim says that for him the equivalent role is played by the Koran, we should surely in practice seek to go beyond the dogmatic affirmation of the authority of one Scripture and have recourse to argument of some sort or another, notwithstanding that there is some point, in religion as in morals, where argument must stop. But to the extent that the view in question does commend itself and is persisted in without much heed of its difficulties, it can well be understood how the supremacy of certain dominant images in the Bible could come to be regarded as the clue to its message as a whole, the appeal to any extrinsic criteria being precluded.

Whether something of this sort is at work in Dr Farrer's own case is not easy to decide. But it does seem certain that his final appeal is to some kind of authority, and that he wants to ascribe this to dominant Biblical images, or at least to the images that have the main place in a certain religious tradition. Perhaps he would allow some degree of this authority to the similar images of other religions. But, whether he would or not, he seems to me quite mistaken in ascribing this finality to the images as such, even when considered closely in relation to each other and their contexts. We certainly 'cannot point away from the image to that which the image signifies', if this means going beyond them directly to the ultimate reality they mirror. But there is an intervening stage, however hard in practice to dissociate from the life of the images, namely the course of the experience which the images help to sustain and guide.

The importance of recognizing this is enhanced when we note the matters which Dr Farrer himself has helped us to appreciate, namely the play of religious images and the fact that they seem to have a life of their own. One image sets off another, and an image like that of a divine king gathers significance as it moves from one context to another or is renewed in exceptional situations. If, as is invariable and wellnigh inevitable, the king is the centre of a story, the story being probably dramatized and re-enacted in various ways, the story will gain new forms in the impact of different people and cultures on one another and, subject also to the moderating influence of conservative established usages, present new features in repetitions of it, particularly where the social or political setting changes. Cultural developments will affect it, and there will be refinements of it as one imaginative representation sets off others, and the story may have an internal momentum, especially if it is forward-looking, which actually calls for elaboration in changing situations. There will also be the interplay of vivid images within an elaborate mythology, the whole will have a life in the sense in which creative literature has life and principles which extend and elaborate it. Indeed, there is more than an analogy here, for primitive mythology and literature will largely be one, at least if we extend the term 'literature' to cover not merely what is recorded in writing but what is preserved orally and by dramatic and ritual enactment. It is only at sophisticated levels that literature is set apart to be cherished and revered on its own account. And thus the ways in which literature generally develops will be at work in combination with other forms of imaginative activity, none of which will be sharply set aside, as we nowadays distinguish lay and secular matters, from other features of the varied but largely undifferentiated life of a society. Religion in primitive communities has the advantage of having to do unmistakably with the whole of life, and one of the problems of riper periods of civilization is to restore or retain this unity in the richer forms made possible by more differentiation and the concentration of energy on more delimited interests.

But the more we appreciate the integration of functions in early societies, the more apparent will it be that, while religion contributes stimulus and depth to artistic activities of various kinds, the more inherent determination of such activities, or the course they are prone to take on their own account, will exert its pull on that functioning of imagination in religion which is religiously the most appropriate. That matters not directly or obviously relevant to it should enter into the imaginative life of religion may be most valuable, and lead in due course to new insights and a wider range of application. New images, or the extension of old ones, evolved in the first place in the more spontaneous operation of imagination as such, or at least in detachment from express religious stimulation, may come to do excellent service for religion as the prompters and vehicles of insights which might not be otherwise forthcoming. But they may also be distracting and direct attention to extraneous matters, and they may even corrupt the religious imagination by diverting its energy to concerns not consistent with religious ends.

This warning has had to be repeated at various times in the past when the enlivening of religion has influenced men's imaginations in ways not wholly subdued to the interests of religion itself. The creative power which religion releases ought indeed to be welcomed as a source of general inspiration, and the view I have taken of its working clearly accentuates this, but the perils of this release of energy, especially in the explicit service of religion itself, have also to be heeded, and disregard of them has often brought the 'enthusiasm' of which religion stands in continuous need into ill repute. In short, religious imagination needs to be controlled, and this holds not only of early stages where art and religion are peculiarly integrated, but also at other times when enlivened imagination is apt to centre attention on whatever matters happen to be most suitable to its own operation, matters perhaps of subsidiary or incidental importance for religion, or, it may be, inferior or even degrading in themselves. We cannot put ourselves wholly at the mercy of the life of images—that way madness lies.

Dr Farrer can no doubt reply that it is not *any* 'life of images' that he has in mind, but rather a particular life of images which is subject to very special control, a divine one. But where I seriously fail to follow him is just in this supposition that the divine control is exercised primarily and directly on the religious images. His theory seems to be a far cry, for example, from the centrality we generally accord to ethics in religion, even if the images should turn out to have, in point of fact, a pre-eminently moral character. It seems highly artificial to suppose that God works primarily in the world through His 'given images' and not more directly in the very substance of living. The emphasis seems wrongly placed, however much the images arise out of real situations or refer to them.

This reflection is prompted also by consideration of the way imagination works. We must not lapse into the error of what is sometimes known as 'faculty psychology'. The imagination is not a thing apart, but a feature of a total experience, and it has its material on which to work. It is not some odd separate gift of imagination that Shakespeare had, but imaginative insight into what life is like, and the more there is insight of this kind in the exercise of imagination, in distinction from the sheer precipitation of one image by another, the finer it is. Possibly it is by this test that many modern artists and poets—Dylan Thomas perhaps?—are found lacking. But however that may be, imagination never works quite in a vacuum, and the rightful stress today on the importance of 'image thinking' will become one-sided unless we bear in mind also the need for imagination to be duly integrated with living.

The moral of this for our theme is that the images which figure in religious belief have their proper significance in relation to the experiences which they sum up and reflect and whose life they help to sustain. Images must thus be anchored in experience and never allowed to take wing very far on their own. But subject to this qualification, and bearing in mind that the qualification must not be understood too mechanically or allowed to become a curb on enterprising exercises of the religious imagination, we must award a very prominent place to the work of imagination in giving sharp and impressive delineation of the course which religious experiences take, both in themselves and as a leaven of life as a whole, for the individual and his society. Nor must we crudely and slickly attempt to unpack this imaginative presentation of the truth into its ultimate elements in experience. For the particular merit of images lies in the fact that they enable us to gain a total or over-all impression of certain presentations and occurrences in such a way that the contribution of each to the total impression is not explicitly noticed, and in this way we can also retain an over-all impression of the character of certain occurrences when the memory of them individually has passed into oblivion. This does not preclude the control of images and the vetting of them on the basis of experience. But it does mean that such work requires to be skilfully and patiently carried out by remaining sensitive to the inherent dynamic of the image and sufficiently conversant in a general way with the facts out of which it arises to be informed by the images and not misled. Sanity and wisdom in living turns much on the skill we exercise here and the ease with which it comes to us by custom. We need to be imaginatively at home in the real world.

This has outstanding importance where images refer to stretches of experience that extend beyond the life of the individual. 'The life of the individual' is of course a rather loose expression, unless it is understood in a strictly temporal sense. No one lives entirely in a world of his own, and the impact our immediate environment makes upon us is coloured by the context in which we meet it and the impression conveyed to us by others in thought or deed. In the case of friends and nearest acquaintances our environment and the lives we live in it are very closely shared, and it may not be easy to distinguish the contribution of one from those of others in the imaginative representation of the environment we share and help to constitute. But we can draw a sharper, if still imprecise distinction between the impression the world makes upon me more directly, or through those involved in my life, and the impressions that owe more to my participation in the general life of society. And while within the latter there are again some boundaries which may be roughly drawn, these are fluid and in turn they merge into stretches of history that reach beyond the span of my own life.

The religious images which draw their power from wide ranges of human experience, and whose vigour is due to the life they have had in being carried from one social situation to another, resemble in some ways the archetypal images of which much has been written of late, especially by Jung and some of his followers. We certainly owe much to Jung for the prominence given in our studies today to the role of dominant images in the experience and history of men. But the 'archetypes' of

Jung do not in themselves straightway fit the part I have been ascribing to images in religion. The origin of our archetypal images, according to Jung, is to be found in the alleged 'collective unconscious', although they are 'activized' when an object is presented to the conscious minds of particular persons. There is thus a co-operation or 'complementarity' of conscious and unconscious. But how then has the 'unconscious' to be understood in this theory? The personal unconscious is said to have as its content elements forgotten or repressed by the individual—they have *become* unconscious. But the 'collective unconscious' is a more basic constitutional capacity or proneness to produce certain kinds of images which is native to us as human beings and thus common to the whole of mankind.

Little is explicitly said about this alleged source of images or capacity for forming them. Jung is very properly cautious here and is anxious to regard himself as engaged in strictly scientific work without venturing beyond the limits of what he thinks can be established empirically. From the study of dreams and other investigations conducted by him as a psychoanalyst he believes it is shown that certain types of images are precipitated by us in all kinds of situations, and that the constancy of these warrants our ascribing them to some innate disposition to form just these images in specific situations. Comparison of various cultures and communities, including those which seem least likely to have influenced one another, and of the dominant features of their mythologies, is taken to reinforce the main contention. But further speculations about these alleged findings of a scientific investigation are treated, when they are advanced at all, with great reserve.

At one stage Jung seems to have inclined to the view that recurrence of very similar experiences among primitive peoples everywhere and in very early periods of human history had a great deal to do with the formation of our capacity for archetypal images. He also considers a more physiological explanation in terms of certain creases or tracks in the brain. He furthermore seems to think in general of the capacities we actualize in images and in other ways as themselves the determinants of a certain dynamic power or psychic energy. But whether we are individually endowed with a certain amount of this energy, or whether it is to be thought of more obscurely or imprecisely as some general force like the *élan vital*, is not very plain. Nor is it clear how far explanations of the scientific findings are thought to encourage the notion of some kind of universal mind or a strictly corporate existence or solidarity of human beings. Jung has, I believe, been interpreted, especially by traditional theologians, in the latter sense. But how far he really wishes to encourage that view of his work is not very clear. He is certainly much more conscious than Freud ever was of the dangers of hypostatizing abstractions, and while seeming anxious, as Freud was, to do nothing that would jeopardize the alleged 'reality' of some kind of collective unconscious or minimize its importance, he also calls himself back from speculation to his proper concern as a scientist with the exhibition of certain structures of an otherwise unspecified nature which govern some psychic energy not wholly controlled by consciousness in its own way.

On the value of the scientific evidence adduced by Jung I shall make no pronouncement here. For the points that need to be made for my purpose are these. In the first place, if it can be established that we have in some ways an innate tendency to form certain kinds of image in certain situations and to ascribe to those a distinctive role in the imaginative manipulation of elements of our experience, then this will have obvious importance for our study of the way images are formed in religion and contribute to its development. But if I am right in the view I am taking of religious experience

and the part which images play in it, any innate disposition we may have to form images in certain ways
will only have relevance in so far as it enters into and
helps to give shape to the process whereby the perpetuation and development of a certain kind of experience is
made possible by the images which that experience itself
precipitates and which owe their essential character
to the particular nature of the experience. It is as part
of the mechanism of image-forming, and as some explanation of the appearance of certain kinds of image,
rather than as indication of what is distinctive and essential in the images religiously, that Jung's views, if sub-
stantiated, will be illuminating to the student of religious experience.

I must also confess that I find it initially unplausible
that images should have any kind of determinant other
than experience and that, for me, the evidence would
need to be very overwhelming before I accepted an
alleged general proneness to fashion certain images as an
ultimate datum of human nature not derivable even
from a common lot we share.

But the point I most wish to stress is that dominant
images, whether they arise from the course our experience takes or from some native propensity to form them,
do not, by the mere fact of being dominant or being
made inevitable for us in some fundamental way,
acquire a religious character. They can only be religious
when they reflect some religious insight or experience. As
far as the archetypes of Jung are concerned, the most
obvious candidate for the role of a religious determinant
of them is the initial intuition of the being of God,
since this is not connected as directly with particular
features of nature and human experience as our specific
beliefs about God. But there is nothing in the fact of
being innate or very pervasive to establish a proper linkage of any of our images with this religious insight. The
evidence for such a linkage would need to be provided

empirically or by some analysis of features of the images in question which justify an association of them with belief in God. So far as I can see, Jung himself provides nothing of this sort. The nearest he comes to it, in his later writings and the ones, as it happens, most sympathetic to religion, is the ascription to archetypal images of a character of mystery which is repellent and attractive at the same time in ways suggestive of the numinous as religiously conceived. But this, while very significant if it does arise out of the evidence, does not give us what we need. There needs to be firmer indication that the mystery is properly religious and not merely akin in *some* ways to the mystery in our awareness of God. And this applies generally. For whether we think of the archetypes as belonging to some alleged structure of human nature or as reflecting the course which men's experience has taken and the embodiment of it in imaginative forms, the dominant character of the images, or their seeming to be imposed upon us from an alien source or arising from levels of human experience which are not normally manifest in ordinary consciousness, does not immediately amount to a religious phenomenon. The findings of Jung could be described in purely humanist terms; the depths which the images uncover or the alien source from which they emanate, together with other quasi-religious characteristics they exhibit, may not go beyond the peculiarities of human nature or accumulations of human experience preserved in extraordinary ways.

In the main it appears that it is this humanist version of his views that Jung himself intends, although he borrows the language of religion and seems often to fall under the spell of it. In the earlier stages of his work his religious scepticism was less disguised and his programme, in respect to religion, not substantially different from that of Freud in regarding religion as an illusion which needs nonetheless to be handled very gently. In his more recent work the position is less clear, there is more venturing into what seems to be properly religious territory. But this takes a form which is worth noting.

It is this. As a psychologist Jung seems very anxious not to commit himself to anything other than the exhibition of certain facts about human beings, this being the limit beyond which he must not venture as a scientist. *Qua* scientist he must be neutral on metaphysical or philosophical issues. But he allows of the possibility that, when metaphysical questions are raised, the answers may be religious, and there are hints that, while he does not wish to be distracted or diverted from his own scientific work by consideration of metaphysical questions, he favours a religious view. The issue is not unlike the one concerning the origin of our perceptions —have they some origin beyond themselves, and is that a material reality or, as Berkeley held, God? One thinks also here of the controversy about 'things in themselves'. But so conceived Jung's approach to a possible religious significance for his findings seems to me very mistaken.

For in essentials it is not radically different from the argument from design or from the objectivity of moral standards and other variations on the attempt to proceed from certain general features of human life and the world as we find it to conclusions about God; and I have argued that, while we have an intuition of the being of God as the unconditioned source of all other being, no specific features of the world, or any combination of them, can provide, without the alleged intuition, adequate grounds for believing in God. Indeed, any attempt to build up a so-called 'ontology' by propounding metaphysical accounts of finite facts in terms of entities which fall altogether outside any kind of experience we have, except for the very special requirement that all things derive in some unknown way from some supreme unconditioned source, appears to be just the wrong kind of speculation of which our empiricist critics have helped to disabuse us. I suspect that Jungians have not quite learnt this lesson yet, and that for this reason some are more sceptical than they need be through failure to seek indications of religion in the right way, while others flirt with religion in ways that are bound to be self-defeating.

The lesson to be reiterated here is that, although God is transcendent and thus beyond our experience, He is also within it in the sense that all that we know about Him comes from within our finite experience and in particular from the occurrences which we have reason to consider to be distinctively religious. Our problem is not how to get outside experience but how to discriminate within it, and I believe that if this were understood aright the likelihood of psychoanalysis of the Jungian and kindred types uncovering matters of great importance for religion from the study of images and dreams would be very much enhanced. What we have to suggest to the Jungian is that he should consider how certain images may be connected with a particular type of experience, in this case a religious one, and invite him to look out in his investigations for evidence of dominant or recurrent images which bear traces of such a source.

This will mean that the psychologist must free himself of any obsession he has about being merely a fact-finder or a severely empiricist investigator. The mistake has marred the work of the psychologist in many ways. It has been argued for example that considerations of value are irrelevant to psychology, which is not a normative study. But questions of value cannot in fact be kept out, and a sound notion of their nature is of the greatest importance to the psychological investigator when he encounters valuational factors in the beliefs and experiences he examines. Likewise the consideration of religion as having relevance to the work of the psychologist is not to be postponed until the findings are obtained, as if it were solely a question of a gloss to be put on the findings or a further way of viewing them: it is rather itself part of the investigation of the appropriate material.

This brings me back to my main contention here, namely that images have significance for religion, not by being outstanding or relating to large tracts of human experience or to subtle ways in which past experience is accumulated and made potent in the present, but solely in the measure that they reflect, directly or at some removes, a distinctively religious strand in experience; and this, I have suggested, they do mainly by enabling us to acquire firmer and more germinative over-all impressions of the patterns of the occurrences in which the character of God is disclosed. All that we can independently learn about the way images are formed and develop and their course in contexts not expressly religious will have the highest worth for our understanding of their religious function, but only provided the latter is rightly apprehended on its own account. Nothing in the nature of images as such or the mode of their appearance is specifically religious.

CHAPTER 8

HISTORY AND DOGMA

There can be little doubt of the important place which images have in religion, but it would be wrong to conclude that it is by images alone that religious experience sustains itself. The consciousness of the pattern which the distinctively religious factor in experience takes may yield certain overt or deliberate reflections about its outstanding features, and in this way there will appear more formal affirmations of what is made most significant for us by religion and what affords thus our clue to the character of the transcendent reality exhibited within it. This requires some maturity and sophistication. But in saying so we have need also to be cautious. For the line between overt reflection on the course the peculiarly religious illumination of experience takes on the one hand, and its imaginative representation on the other, is not one we can always draw very sharply. Initially there would be a very close blend of the two, but in course of time the more sustained attempt to sum up the meaning of the sequence of religious events in formal terms will assert itself as a separate religious activity not wholly determined by the 'life of images'.

I say 'not wholly determined', for it would be very difficult, if not altogether impossible, to capture what is most distinctive in a large tract of experience independently of figurative ways in which it finds its most spontaneous expression. Much of the work of making religion articulate and critical of itself depends on a proper fusion of the direct inspection of the religious facts with the due and sensitive discernment of the significance these have as preserved in imaginative forms. This not only makes possible a sounder understanding of the significance which the facts themselves have, but also provides a way of filling the lacunae left by the facts no longer available to us. Religious sense consists in some measure in skill in allowing the imaginative presentation of religion in the past to carry us over the gaps in our knowledge of the religious course of things which they mirror. We have to learn when to trust religious imagination, and when to suspect it, in regard to matters where detailed vetting is out of the question; and this is accomplished mainly by the habit of living at the same time in the more rarefied sphere of imaginative religion and in the world of live religious occurrences, including the renewal of genuine religion in our own experience. There are no foolproof checks or absolute guarantees here, but only the sort of confidence which comes from habituating ourselves to the appropriate disciplines and being at home in the relevant milieu, in this case the interplay of imagination and fact as presented especially in our personal experience. The situation is not unlike the one by which practical wisdom is acquired in ethics.

With the ripening of religion the attempt to extract and express the matters of greatest moment in its course in the past, and thus provide it with more explicit claims to make, dissociates itself sufficiently from the general maintenance of religion and its part in the life of a community to become a distinctive religious discipline. Leaders of religion and those most concerned in the practices by which it is perpetuated and renewed, its priests and officers, will normally have charge of this, and it will probably begin with pronouncements and codifications of practical requirements to which religion has lent its sanction most notably. At what stage this takes the form which we should describe as theology is a moot question, and it is largely a matter of terminology. Is there theology, is there a recognizable 'creed' or 'doctrine' in the Old Testament, as there are certainly beliefs about God and His law and His dealings with men, or does theology proper appear in the Hebrew-Christian tradition only in the first centuries of Christianity? Are the Epistles theology or prophecy, or both? Something may be gained perhaps by so fixing our terminology that fairly precise answers to these questions will be possible. But in actual fact the line to be drawn between the immediate utterances of religion, as arising from our sense of the course it is taking, and the extension of this into more deliberate reflection and formal expression is not to be clearly drawn. Suffice it to observe that a certain stage is reached where religion yields certain formal pronouncements about itself in which are made explicit the course it has taken and the meaning to be given to that.

It is here, as already suggested, that religion presents one of its main danger-points. For in throwing its claims into this particular prominence and making them explicit and formal, much intellectual activity may be involved which takes a course of its own not subjected adequately to the processes it seeks to interpret and extend. The lure of the often deceptive neatness of intellectual systems is hard to resist, most of all when its rigidity conduces much to the upholding of authority and the imposition of discipline; short cuts are taken at points where the logic of live religion would require greater subtlety and circumspection. The errors and confusions which strew the paths of theology are often to be traced to this source, and in quite recent times we have witnessed a spate of lively and often prophetic theological thinking which has been very distressingly marred, as I have endeavoured to show elsewhere, by proliferation of theological pronouncements taken in detachment from the initial living course of religion in which the expressions which give plausibility to those pronouncements had their birth.

The proper task for theology is an extremely difficult one, and it requires today a great deal of technical expertise in combination with imaginative understanding and devout religious insight. It is not merely a criticism of images, as some would have it, least of all criticism based solely on the alleged general notions of natural theology. It involves scholarly investigation designed to yield an appreciation of religious matters not possible for those not steeped themselves in the true life of religion, and with this must go a consecration of imagination which will provide for a balanced heeding of the figurative forms in which religion found expression in the past, on the one hand, and, on the other, of the course of the initial live religious occurrences, themselves extended and sustained in imaginative ways, as these occurrences permeated secular experience in its fullness, including the devious turns which the histories of societies have taken. And along with this must go acuteness and integrity in the more severely intellectual task of deploying the concepts found most useful in the process of interpreting formal expressions of religious truth in the past and providing the appropriate equivalent for today.

The work to be done in imaginatively interpreting the imaginative expressions of religion, I have elsewhere[1] compared to the work of an art-critic; and that work, I have suggested, consists at the core, that is where we get beyond the provision of relevant information, of super-imposing one art on another. The critic is like the reciter or singer who 'renders' a composition already complete of its kind. Theologians may in a similar way

[1] 'What is theology?' *Philosophy,* October 1952.

'render' the great figurative utterances of religion by creating them afresh in the context of the later life of religion and their own experience. But it needs to be also stressed that in providing this service of inestimable worth to religion more is needed than skill in manipulation and creation of imaginative forms. Imagination must here most of all be closely related to fact, and in this case, moreover, the basic facts are the subtle and elusive ones of the religious illumination of secular things already described.

It is this character of religious facts in particular that accounts for some of the very close interpenetration of religious facts and images; for the state of wonder and rapture in which the world is made anew for us in religion is also the one most likely to precipitate moving and impressive images for the expression of itself or of the overall sense of the process of which it forms a part and which continues within it as a major determinant. There is thus hardly any point at which the assessment of religious fact can be dissociated from the imaginative re-creation and interpretation of religious imagery. No doubt we may describe certain historical occurrences as such as religious facts, the Israelite crossing of the Red Sea, the rule of David, the committing of Jeremiah to the dungeon, the trial and execution of Jesus, the journey of St Paul to Damascus and his other travels. But as ordinary facts these are not religious. They become religious as part of something more than the 'brute' facts as a secular historian might describe them, and this something more, I have maintained, is to be recognized in terms of a peculiar religious feature of the total experience of some of the persons who had part in those events. It is a religious fact in this sense, as involving normal historical fact *and more*, that I hold to be peculiarly closely connected with figurative forms which express them.

This does not mean that I underestimate the place

of imagination normally in history, or that I am unaware of the need there too for the creative reconstruction of ordinary facts of which the record is sometimes
available only in metaphorical terms which the gifted
secular historian also has to interpret and assess. There
is more than one way in which history without imagination would be mere chronicle, although that by no
means implies that history is not objective. But there
is a special work of imaginative interpretation, and
one which lies even more at the core of our task, in
the process of establishing 'religious facts', whether we
think of this in the form it presents in the normal or
initial process of religious understanding, which must
be present to some extent in all religions, or in the
more sustained and self-conscious form into which this
understanding develops at the level at which we call
it theology.

A very difficult problem which arises here is whether
the religious understanding of historical facts can be
relevant itself to the determination of them as historical
events. There are plainly some matters within the occurrences deemed most important for religion which are
settled as conclusively as we could wish in purely secular
ways, dates, names, journeys, battles, reforms and social
changes, the composition of important works, and so on.
For the most part the religious scholar will proceed
in precisely the same way here as his secular colleagues,
and a great deal of the work to which we normally
apply the word 'theology' consists in precisely the same
kind of investigation as the historian or philologist and
kindred scholars undertake. The less we deviate, if we
are to deviate at all, from these where the paths of the
theologian and the secular scholar converge the better.
But a question does arise whether there are some points
where the assessment of fact in the sense of the secular
historian could be affected by understanding of 'religious fact' in such sense as I have given it. One would

certainly be reluctant to appeal to evidence of the latter kind in matters where independent evidence was strong or seemingly conclusive. The theologian would need to be very bold to risk discrediting himself by disputing 'plain facts' of history on any religious grounds. But not all of history is plain fact, not merely in the sense that we distinguish between history and chronicle, but in the sense that the narrative to be presented has many gaps and many conjectural and debatable elements, most of all where it involves imaginative reconstructions and is wide in its range. And we have thus to ask here whether a religious insight may not only help to bring out the significance, for the proper religious narrative, of facts independently known (making use of course in a secular way of 'sacred' sources), but may also help to find solutions to historical problems as such, and whether this goes beyond providing suggestive hints to be subsequently confirmed solely in a secular way.

The answer, if what I have already maintained is sound, must be plainly 'Yes'. For if there are insights of a distinctively religious kind which men obtain, and especially if these involve finer understanding of secular facts, and if this is in turn a leaven in the whole of life, then plainly a narrative may not be complete or even sound in what it actually says, if it leaves out the possible relevance of the insights in question and their effects. I shall not look closely here at the methods and aims of the historian or pause to ask in what way precisely an historian is concerned, for example, with the motives of actors on the stage of history. For it seems to me evident, without any close consideration of such questions, that if there are occurrences of a distinctively religious kind, and if these are capable of far-reaching influence, the historian overlooks them at his peril and is handicapped if he is not in a position to appreciate them fairly, much as an historian who has no understanding of art or who is insensitive to certain moral feelings is seriously limited, although it does not follow that he is precluded at all points from doing sound historical work.

An historian is entitled of course to deny that religious experience has the status ascribed to it by religious people and in other ways to question claims made by religious believers. He cannot, for this reason, straightway disregard religion. For even if the claims which religious people make are without substance, certain beliefs have in fact been held, and no one could deny that the course of history has in fact been very extensively affected by certain phenomena which the word 'religion' may designate in a general way. No historian would wish to query this. Even the out-and-out materialist has something, often a great deal, to say about religion. But if religious occurrences are held to be susceptible of an exhaustively secular account, it is for the historian to provide this if he wishes and he must in any case proceed in accordance with his convictions. My concern at the moment is not to refute the secularist, but only to observe that the account to be taken by him of religion as it enters into the study of history will be different in certain ways, and liable to error, if the claim I myself make about the occurrence of distinctively religious events is sound.

I admit that it is possible, to an astonishing degree, to handle material historically without probing to the very core of it or assessing its inherent worth. A writer who is at home in a general way with the forms which religious beliefs, and the attitudes they engender, assume may be able up to a point to give an admirable account and analysis of events in which the former have prominence, even though he has no interest in these beliefs himself and deems them to be sheer nonsense. For he knows what it is like in general to have convictions, how people are affected by very profound beliefs, what it means to draw nice distinctions and how the relevant distinctions are recognized or labelled in the case of the controversies with which he may be concerned. If he understands human nature sufficiently well and is normally an historian of sense and discernment, he may get on well and without blunder even when dealing with matters to which he ascribes none of the importance attached to them by the principal participants in the scenes he describes. An atheist is not precluded from studying the Reformation and describing it, or making discoveries about it, in ways which would earn the respect of the Christian scholar; he might likewise write a valuable and understanding study of, let us say, St Thomas More. For he has not to cash all the counters he handles, and he can extend the rules of intelligent discourse formally, so to speak, to fields where he does not consider they apply materially. Whether he could also bring the proper enthusiasm to his task is another matter, but there is nothing to preclude a non-Christian from having very great esteem for the character of a notable Christian.

At some point, however, the non-believer, and even the believer who has not the right insights, may be led astray by inability to pay due heed to occurrences, and the dispositions and habits that go with them, which have a uniquely religious character to which the effect they have had on the course of things is mainly due.

It is to the course of peculiarly religious events, and the ramifications of these in matters not expressly religious, that I think we should be referring most of all in dealing with such topics as 'religion and history' and in making the claim that there is revelation in history. These topics have been very widely discussed of late and there has been considerable renewal of emphasis on the importance of revelation in history and the 'mighty acts' which God has wrought in the world. But it is also very surprising how few of those who are most clamant in calling us back to these themes have the courage of their convictions. What they mean by 'history' is often completely divorced from the course of any particular occurrences, and very little heed is paid to the question how the word 'history' should be understood and how some things may be said to have more importance than others for the historian. A very common attitude is to suppose that the religious factor in the notion of divine action in history is simply a religious gloss to be placed on the story as told by the secular historian or a special over-all interpretation of the normal course of events. Some speak, very obscurely, of natural events being also supernaturally determined, or of the process of history as a whole being seen to carry a hidden 'transcendent' significance disclosed to the eye of faith irrespective of any deviation from the normal course of events due to religion. Others find illustration and confirmation of dogmas, such as 'original sin', in the ordinary course of history. It is rarely noted how little, in substance, such theories deviate from the despised deism to which they are supposed to provide an arresting alternative.

By contrast with the theories instanced, which I do not propose to examine on their own account here, I should ascribe the distinctive features of divine intervention in history to the fact that there have been distinctively religious occurrences which have taken a course of outstanding importance for our relationship with God and the apprehension of His purpose in the world. This does not preclude our regarding all events as sustained by God or the scene of His activity, although I should myself, as I shall stress later, exempt responsible choices from this. Indeed, such belief is indispensable from my point of view. For I have accorded a very fundamental place in my general account of religion to the intuition by which God is seen to be involved in the being or occurrence of anything at all. But while this does give us an overwhelmingly profound and sustaining sense of the nearness of God, it cannot give us what is normally suggested by the notion of revelation in history. I believe, however, that God has in fact been peculiarly active in history, and not exclusively in Hebrew-Christian history, through the special disclosure of His own character to men in certain experiences and in the effect of the insight so obtained, and the lives men lead in the knowledge of God thus given them, on other events. It is in the pattern of this illumination, and its by-products, that we find God peculiarly at work in the world.

The pattern of the religious experiences of men, and of the place of these in life as a whole, is the one a theological thinker has to unfold; and in the Christian religion he will be especially concerned with an alleged culmination or fulfilment of this on which the distinctive claims of his religion are based. In tracing the pattern and considering the conclusions it yields about the dealing of God with man the theologian will only be making more articulate and self-conscious the activity which is at work at all times in religion and by which man's consciousness of God becomes increasingly personal. And it is in this work, moreover, that we need, over and above the use of imagination normally required in history, the exercise of imagination to recapture the meaning of figurative forms in which religious awareness has bodied itself forth in the past and the interplay of these with the live events they sustain and extend.

The reflection on religion in which imagination has this part to play is much helped to assume its more articulate and explicit form where there appears independently a distinctive interest in reflection on experience in general and appropriate apparatus for it. Philosophy is a good generator of theological thinking, and theology as we know it has been much encouraged and expedited by the meeting of marked philosophical thought with a sharp consciousness of a particular course which religion was taking, pre-eminently in the union of Greek philosophy and Hebrew-Christian experience. This union is in part a confluence of two religious cultures, but it involves even more a germinative obtrusion of a religious process into a secular setting exceptionally well suited to extend it; in both regards we have an important part of what Christians should mean by 'the fullness of time'.

It must however be added, in consistency with the warning already given, that the limitations and errors of philosophy may also mar the process by which religion reflects upon itself and becomes more aware of the import of the course it is taking as it unfolds itself in the whole of life. There are two ways in particular in which this may happen, firstly when speculations about God, or other philosophical notions which come close to religion, venture beyond the very strict limits appropriate to them and thus encumber theology with a framework which does not fit it, and secondly when thoughts about God, or those that come closest to this, bring a certain remoteness or static quality of their own to their union with a process which is essentially dynamic. An evisceration of live religion is apt to result in these ways, as is very evident in some forms of Indian religion, but by no means absent from Christianity. To this the correction very largely will be appropriate heed to the imaginative presentation of the life of religion and the close integration of this with more direct inspection of what may have happened religiously.

The importance to be ascribed to general formulations of belief, and to the explicit profession of these, will vary a great deal from one religion to another, and even within a particular religion very different attitudes may be taken towards creeds, doctrines or dogma. There are many reasons for this variation. One of these is the extent to which, in some cases, doctrinal differences are due mainly to philosophical differences. This is the situation where normally differences of opinion are viewed with considerable toleration, the obvious example being that of Hindu religion within which many shades of doctrinal belief, ranging from the absence of anything we should call properly a creed to elaborate doctrinal systems, are included together and manage to co-exist in the main without undue discomfort. A complicating factor here, however, is the institutionalizing of religion and the acquisition by a priesthood or other persons of an interest (not necessarily selfish) in the perpetuation of certain rites and practices, with associated beliefs, and the hardening in kindred ways of religious habits. Individual factors come in also, for example the teaching of a particular person and the loyalty or veneration rendered to him or to his memory. But in general the differences of belief which spring mainly from philosophical sources are vaguer and held with more toleration than those which reflect more expressly a difference of religious experience.

The latter variations of belief are normally more specific, as we should expect, and held with a greater tenacity. They will be more closely involved in local customs and traditional symbolism and carry with them the weight of much social and political prestige and social habits of belief and practice apt to be very inflexible. But there are also reasons more inherent to the structure of the beliefs in question now which account for the status accorded to them and the way they are viewed. These concern especially the way those beliefs are rooted in particular experiences which become formative influences in the life of a people. For there is something here at stake to be preserved in a very special way. It is not a case of reflecting on some common lot of mankind or of eliciting some reaction or understanding of which individuals normally placed are capable. The truth is bound up with a pattern of events to be apprehended in a particular manner, and the danger of missing what is significant is much increased in the absence of permanent pointers to it.

The supreme example here is the Christian religion, and Christians have very naturally and properly ascribed importance to dogma. In making their faith explicit they have understood it better, and the soundness ensured for their sense of relevance by theological reflection has brought into greater splendour the initial terms of their faith. Instruction has been helped, and worship and meditation have been provided with clearer directives. Perils have been averted, especially those which beset the religion of the individual or a group when religious life is slack; for there has been maintained a continuity of the tradition and practices by which initial insights are preserved for the later proper apprehension of outstanding events of the past. The confusion and uncertainty engendered by the merging of Christian bodies into an alien or indifferent environment has been much lessened, and the dispositional factor in religion has been helped to germinate in a more healthy way in the whole of life. In these ways the uniqueness of the Christian claim has been preserved, both at the level of imaginative presentation and in the linkage of the latter with appropriate fact.

CHAPTER 9

ABUSES OF DOGMA

We have seen in what ways dogma may be important or indispensable for a religion, but I have now to add that there are few things more fraught with danger for a religion than dogma. It is not very clear to me what merit, if any, should be accorded to a religion which is centred mainly or exclusively on creeds and dogmas without penetrating deeper with the aid of these. There seem to be persons who have accepted their religious beliefs merely as part of the ethos or custom of their set or community, an attitude which owes a great deal to the institutionalizing of religion. Such beliefs need not be insincere, nor need it be thought that they are accepted altogether blindly. They are taken, without much reflection perhaps, to be initially plausible and might have been seriously queried if they did violence to other accepted notions, such as our ideas of good and bad. There may also be some critical thinking within the accepted framework of religious belief. But there is no personal experience which would make possible due appreciation, and absorption into one's own experience, of the religious events by which the dogmas are warranted. Religion is here lived entirely at second hand, and the loyalties and enthusiasm which it may arouse are pseudo ones in the sense of being concerned with matters incidental to genuine religion. We move, as it were, along the proper course, but not through the power of the live current. Has this any worth?

Part of the answer to this question may be that complete examples of mere adherence to dogma may be very rare. Sooner or later contact with the proper current will be made and there will be a spark of genuine religious life. At the same time it may well be the case, most of all at times when religion is at a low ebb, that a great many people adhere to religion largely as a habit and subscribe to certain beliefs as part of the routine of their station or set. This is not downright hypocrisy. It may involve very genuine zeal of a certain kind, but it is a case of holding, as a rule one suspects in a lukewarm way, to the shadow rather than the substance of religion. And it is by no means an easy matter to determine whether this superficial, tenuous religion, religion so much removed from the warm heart of it, a religion of the husk without the grain, has any value at all.

One's first reaction perhaps is to deny any worth to a religion of this kind or even to denounce it outright as an evil thing, a hollow imposture or caricature of the truth like sentimental poetry or bogus art; and when it offers in an effortless form the sort of consolations and rest which are only to be gained properly in the costing disturbing experience of meeting the Living God, then one is apt most of all to resent its smugness and falsity. Jung, among others, has represented dogma as an escape device or bulwark against the mysterious and tremendous realities of religion, and while we may not agree with Jung as to what constitutes these realities, we may nonetheless find in his reports evidence of a very discreditable reluctance to be realistic in religion. In so far as it offers cover to an evasionist attitude of this sort, the blind adherence to dogma may be positively evil or at any rate a hindrance to be put solely to the debit side.

It is thus not for nothing that so many prophetic voices have recently been raised in a paradoxical denunciation of religion itself, and, while this represents in some measure the mere flamboyance and extravagance of existentialists pioneering for a new cause or of authoritarian theologians resentful of the slightest departure from orthodoxy, it does reflect at the same time and even more the resentment of religiously inspired people at the mockery of true religion which merely formal profession of belief involves. Religion, we have been repeatedly told, is encounter, and while this, as I shall note again, is often presented in exceedingly questionable forms, it is significant how important a word 'encounter' has become at those points in our culture, and most of all in religion, where there seems to be a quickening into new life. We certainly need to stress, as a vital theme of religious and theological thinking today, the centrality of living encounter and personal experience. Religion counts little in the end without the sense of the presence of God, and there is no theme to which I wish to give more prominence in this book.

At the same time I cannot altogether avoid what I may almost describe as a sneaking regard for the formalities of a profession of faith as such and the expectation that, if the warmth of our concern for vital inspired religion, which alone has saving power, be tempered by an even judgment, we may wish to qualify our condemnations and be able to do so without moderating our enthusiasm for the life and fire of genuine religion. What should we say of the mere acceptance of doctrines, and the practices which they require, if the doctrines happen to be true? Is it better to entertain them or not, if worship is honest but never gets beyond the delusion that it is the reality it never attains? If the appropriate shell is genuinely taken to be the substance, is this wholly without worth? One cannot but think of many whose religion appears to be very uninspired and formal but which somehow elicits reluctant regard from us all the same. This may be partly due to the fact that seemingly lifeless religion may often have a genuine vigour within it not evident to casual inspection. But I suspect that there may be more to be said than we are disposed at first to allow for the acceptance, fortuitous in the final religious analysis, of familiar religious beliefs. In itself, one should expect such belief to have good consequences, in the sphere of moral and personal relations for example. And even if the believer is merely entertaining himself with shadows in the cave, may there not be shadows worth holding to?

I think at any rate that this possibility needs consideration and have gone a little out of my way to present it, and even to write somewhat against the grain, lest we should overlook here a part of the truth and disregard concessions that need to be made. But in all other respects my allegiance lies with those who stress the dynamic character of religion, not, as I hope will be plain, in the sense of violent manifestations, but in the sense of alert and wondering awareness which becomes an illumination of the mind in its wholeness and the source of deep and vitalizing personal insights into the truth about God in the highest form attainable by us. Some recent pointers towards this dynamic kind of religion, carrying in itself a sense of momentous possibilities in the relationship of men to one another and to God and of new and venturesome courses to be taken in new cultural and social settings, seem to me extremely timely and most welcome features of contemporary culture. And this presents a constant challenge to the religion which is mainly centred on dogma on its own account to transform itself into the living wholeness of religion in which dogma has its important, if not indispensable, but quite subordinate part to play.

The trouble about the 'religion of dogma', if I may so style it for convenience, is however, most of all, not that it presents an inferior form of religion or even, if that should be the truth of it, that it should be positively bad in itself, but that it is so fertile a breeding ground of the vilest forms of religious corruption. From genuine delusion to naked hypocrisy the distance may sometimes be disconcertingly short; from sincerely loving the shadow which we take to be the substance we may come to love the shadow for itself, we may acquire a taste for the spurious goods in which we have trafficked and cultivate them even when the deception is exposed. It is not surprising that Plato, who could show such sincere respect in the opening passages of the *Republic* for the mainly conventional piety and high principle of Cephalus, should also straightway proceed to devote the substance of the remainder of the dialogue to a most deadly exposure of the perils to the soul of living in the shadowy world of merely conventional belief. Here and in the *Theaetetus* we have pleas, than which few, if any, outside sacred scriptures have been more discerning and eloquent, for the full and individual acquisition of truth, however 'steep and rugged' the ascent.

For Plato, however, the evil was the 'lie in the soul' as such, and mere opinion was censured because it was apt to offer itself as a substitute for truth and knowledge. This 'lie' had also power to corrupt the whole person and subject the 'man' in us to the beast. Life as a whole would be out of harmony. But Plato knew little of those peculiarly religious corruptions which present themselves so grimly to us in the pages of the more prophetic literature of more profoundly religious peoples. And the main evil of dogma, divorced from the genuine life of religion, is that it becomes so easily the medium of idolatrous perverted worship. On this I have already dwelt above, and I have referred to the ambivalent character of religion whereby the object of worship is at the same time overwhelmingly attractive and also, in respect of its power and strangeness and mystery, as these are included in 'the holy', a source of awe and disruption which induces us to set up barriers against it;

and while this is to some extent an indication of the genuine character of our insight and the reverence it should induce, there is also involved immediately a tendency to ease the strain of this profound and disturbing experience by containing it within the media by which our contact with the divine is established. Dogmas lend themselves easily to this abuse; for while, on the one hand, they do help to deepen and extend our understanding and also make it easier for us to carry our knowledge of God into the normal transactions of life steadily and without undue distortion, they are also the means, to some extent necessary, by which the tension and concentration of live experiences is slackened and religious energy diverted to its proper secular ends; and in this latter capacity dogmas, in becoming a more attenuated form of religion, lend themselves easily to distortion and corruption.

A form of this distortion which is not expressly idolatrous in itself is found when the attempt to co-ordinate and systematize our religious experience and reflect upon it, provides also an opportunity to detach ourselves sufficiently from the searching experience of encounter with God to moderate the demands which this experience makes upon us, most of all in the moral sphere, and suit them to our own convenience or present them in less exacting forms. In much of its history doctrine appears in this guise of providing some cover for departures from the harder exactions of religion other than naked betrayal, and a great deal of the odium which often attaches to dogma and the criticisms levelled against it by opponents of religion, or of the more credal forms of religion, have been due to this particular abuse. Examples of doctrines which exhibit this evasiveness in a marked degree may be found in much recent theology, but Christians, having peculiarly exacting requirements to meet and not aided by being encouraged in their Scriptures to meet them by

wholly forswearing the world, having to be in the world
but not of it, have always been exceptionally open to
the temptations of seeking sanctions for unwarranted
modifications of their ideals by adapting their doctrines,
or even fabricating special ones, to suit the purpose.
Some forms at least of the doctrine of the Fall illustrate
this well.

The procedure or reaction deprecated here finds much
encouragement when the prestige of religion is high and
its secular success extensive. A means is provided of
ensuring the incidental advantage of religion, and to
some extent also its spiritual consolations, without the
price to be paid in the way of conformity to testing
moral and spiritual requirements. But while this may
have yielded forms of religion devoid of genuine piety
and in some cases the adaptation of religion to political
and secular ends, it seems unlikely that this would have
occurred in the form of sheer hypocrisy on an extensive
scale. Some genuine self-delusion or acquiescence by habit
rather than by contrivance for an ulterior end can at
least be presupposed in the case of the majority of participants in this debasement of religion. And I think it is
extremely likely that within these false adaptations and
distortions of religion there will constantly be induced
in its adherents renewals of its genuine life.

This is where it is most apt to breed idolatry. For the
proliferation of doctrines and preoccupation with their
refinement as a sheer intellectual exercise or profession
afford means of blunting the impact of genuine religion
or of drawing away its force when that is not sufficient
to keep it firmly to its own course. The energy which
religion releases is thus drained away into subsidiary
forms of religion, or its by-products, not all of them
healthy. And, in particular, the impact of the divine is
reduced and diverted by drawing the transcendent significance it has for us, and the sense of wonder and ela-
tion and newness it induces, into the credal forms made

only too easily available by excessive preoccupation with them. The credit is given to formal notions for what only properly belongs to them in the service of something else, namely live experience of God. In this way the dogmas become themselves the ultimate terms of religion and are allowed to attract to themselves the glory and splendour they should be transmitting. Being first degraded to barriers and absorbers of energy they become counterfeits, false gods or idols reverenced, with all their appurtenances, in a properly religious way on their own account.

The most tragic feature of this is the snare it presents to the prophetic mind which rises above the shams and delusions of a religion living mainly by the momentum or incidental prestige of its outward forms. For the loneliness of such a figure, living in a rarefied atmosphere which others do not share, makes it harder for him to sustain in its purity the glow and radiance of a new and disturbing awareness of God. The saints have often confessed themselves the 'prince' of sinners, and while there are many facets to this sense of unworthiness and, occasionally, historical factors to account for some of its forms, one recurring feature of it, I think, must be the lively consciousness of the temptation, and not infrequent yielding to it, to reduce the strain of an ecstatic experience and the reaction to it, immediate and consequential, for which the appropriate communal support is not forthcoming, by diverting its power to more familiar and manageable courses in the form of an inflamed preoccupation with refinements of formal profession of faith—to the extent of perverting the religious life. This temptation is peculiarly vicious where a great need of reform in doctrine or forms of worship has become evident, and it is thus a very understandable and illuminating paradox of religion that those best suited by their gifts and insights to liberate a religion excessively restricted by its forms have often been the ones to rivet its inhibiting restrictions more firmly upon it.

Is not this the sad story of many an inspired reformer, and is it not significant also how common a theme in such cases is the sinister preoccupation with the bondage against which the spirit has to contend and by which it is almost inevitably restricted? Can it be an accident that it is from such quarters in particular that there have emanated the rigidities of doctrine by which the bondage, sometimes complete and sometimes provisional and partial, of the spirit to the law is most insistently proclaimed? May not part at least of the explanation of the propagation of gloomy and inhibiting doctrines, such as well-known doctrines of inevitable sin and predestination, on the part of undoubtedly inspired and godly persons, be found along the lines suggested in the psychology of the religious experience of such persons? This is no doubt only a partial explanation. Many other matters, some noted already, and including much intellectual confusion, have to be heeded before we understand fully how notions so contrary to the true spirit of religion have so strong an appeal to persons of deep spirituality. But I do not think we should neglect the repercussions on the general outlook of some prophetic characters of their own yielding in the very moment of achievement, and because of its strains, to a perverted idolatrous centring of their religion on doctrinal forms.

It is of aristocracy, as a form of government, that Rousseau says in one place that it is the best type of government and also the worst type of government—it depends which kind you have. Adapted to the subject, this may well sum up the truth about dogma. Religion is a live and tender concern, like all personal relationships, and it involves a subtle interweaving of all experience with the peculiarly elusive experience of the religious illumination of the present. To retain and foster this, and to make it yield a continuous and over-all impression of a personal dealing with us from within our own experience of the world, we need the assistance of set and formal notions, at the very least as pointers and reminders. This becomes exceptionally necessary when the personal encounter, in which religion consists at its core, is seen to depend also on participation in a community by whom the experience is shared. For the maintenance of the sort of attentiveness by which effective meeting points of a shared experience are ensured calls for regulation and discipline through agreed formulations around which communal practices and meditations are organized, it being made more certain thus that there are genuine rapports of kindred spirits and not seeming and misleading ones. The vagaries of the co-operative maintenance of religious insight, and of the attitudes and conduct appropriate to it, are kept within restraint, and the waywardness of much religious excitation corrected, by the steady focusing of attention on the points which the formulae indicate as the basic ones in the impression of God conveyed in the varieties of our experience of Him. But the more indispensable dogmas become in these and other ways mentioned, the greater is the need to preserve them from the distortion and corruption to which they are exceptionally liable; and when that is done the religion which distils itself into appropriate, and appropriately regulated, credal forms may have a freshness and health which put it in the sharpest contrast to the religion which has become fossilized and perverted by misuse of dogma. The vital point, here as elsewhere, is that dogma, like every other feature of religion, should have its appropriate place in the fullness of a religious life which has at the heart of it the constant renewal of personal experience of God and the sense of His presence.

CHAPTER 10

MATERIAL FACTORS IN RELIGION

I have now noted a number of different senses in which we may speak of religious symbols. The first is what I have described as the live experience in which we become personally conscious of God, the initial ingredients of religious awareness. Secondly, we have the significant patterns which these form, in themselves and in their permeation of life as a whole, and thirdly the presentation of both these features of religion in imaginative forms. Fourthly we have the doctrinal formulations of belief which are themselves in turn organic to experiential facts and figurative forms, as these are organic to each other. I have now to examine a further form of religious symbol.

This consists of ritual acts and the material entities which figure in them, the instruments or ornaments of religion as they are called, a little strangely perhaps, in some religious traditions. On the performative side we have obvious examples in ritual dances, religious processions, the adoption of bodily postures such as bowing the head or clasping the hands in prayer, and the various activities deemed appropriate for special occasions such as initiation, marriage or burial. On the side of the material entities we should first note sacred natural objects, mountains, trees, rivers, holy places, sun and stars and so forth. Secondly, and often attached to the former, we have human artefacts such as religious buildings, of which temples and chapels are the most obvious instances, altars, fonts, crosses, prayer wheels and rosaries, vestments, incense and oils, religious paintings and sculptures and sepulchres, together with a wide variety of objects used in particular ceremonies like the Christian sacraments of marriage and the eucharist. The diversity of symbols of the present sort is very great, and I have only noted a few of the best known examples.

In some forms of religion the ritual element, and with it the type of symbol just instanced, has more prominence than in others. But it is rarely, if ever, that the ritual factor is absent. It may be subdued and not clearly defined in some cases, but religion can hardly subsist without some kind of ritual. Even when a point is made of dispensing with ritual, as in cases of strong or violent reaction against excessive or perverted ritualism, the reaction is itself apt to assume a ritualistic form appropriate to itself. Excellent instances of this may be found in the history of puritanism where simplicity of dress and deportment, for example, has sometimes acquired a rigidity and conspicuousness of its own not wholly in accord with the religious intention. The Quakers come to mind especially. They aspire to reduce the formal features of corporate worship to a minimum, and in all other regards to make their practices as simple as may be. But not only are they forced, by the requirements of any public transaction, to have some formal procedure and indicate thus in some manner how matters should go, but also their union in outwardly simple or silent worship, the common quiet meditation in particular perhaps, can hardly fail to have a subtle ritual character of its own which is deeply affecting and to have symbolic overtones of a profound and revealing nature.

This is only one of many cases where ritual and outward symbol may have much importance although not formally prescribed and directed. Demeanour and tone of voice will likewise count a great deal, and these may owe much to associations and expectations set up in the course of time and for which there is no explicit rule. They function in their own way within the prescribed order of service, but they may well make the main formal contribution to the efficacy of public worship. An instructive example, as it seems to lie half-way between the more and the less formal type of ritual, is the custom of reading the text on which a sermon is preached. The preacher usually makes a point of reading his text—he has no need to. The text may consist of very few words which could be, and usually have been, committed to memory; they may be very well known, and they may be frequently repeated in the course of the sermon. All the same the preacher will read his text, he will open the Bible in the right place and literally read, not pretend to; his eyes follow the words on the printed page. (Some have even confessed to panic because they could not find the place in time although they knew the text well.) The reasons for this are many, among them rhetorical ones. Reading the text may help in the first awkward moments of establishing a more personal contact with one's congregation. But it is also much more than a device, more or less conscious, of this sort. It stands for the sense the preacher has of giving a message which is not his own, of speaking the word of God as he finds it in the Bible and of rooting his discourse in the Scriptures, variable though the accounts may be of the human factor in the delivery of the message, within the Scriptures and in the contribution of the preacher. Other subtler associations and undercurrents of meaning may centre on the reading of the text. The reading is thus usually a symbolic act, and not a mere rhetorical device, and as a rhetorical device it owes a great deal no doubt to its symbolical meaning. The way this delicate little ritual is performed will vary much from one person to another, and this further illustrates the subtle interplay of form and spontaneity on which much of the efficacy of ritual turns.

Other examples of the more subdued or less explicit kinds of ritual and ritualistic symbols are the sombre bindings and the format of sacred books, clerical tones of voice and demeanour, the music found appropriate for the voluntary before the commencement of a service and at its close, repeating the hymn, muting the voice or raising it in exhortation in tones to which specific religious significance is accorded, intoning as in the Welsh 'hwyl' for which there is no prescribed form or occasion, reverent movements and the making of gestures to which association brings religious meaning; and we may even include, I suppose, the religious cough with which some preachers have been known to punctuate their sermons and prayers. There are also the nervous and physical movements more or less violent which accompany some kinds of religious excitation and help to produce them. Not far removed from symbols of this sort are images and decorations of sacred places to which a more specific meaning is attached but which do not come directly into the form of service, consecrated banners, the eagle on the lectern, carving and sculpture and religious art in general. By gradations we pass from these to stricter and more specific forms of ritual where a precise performance is required and given a definite meaning at every stage. Strictness of adherence to the ritual is accorded great importance and centrality in some traditions.

The varieties of outward religious symbols, the ways they are viewed and the varying importance accorded to them in different religions and denominations, are a most important and fascinating subject of study. But this is not expressly our concern now. What I shall venture to add will not be without bearing on specific points at issue among religious persons regarding ritual and liturgy. But the question it behoves us to consider expressly here is the general one of the place of outward forms or manifestations of religion in the life of religion as a whole.

One answer which might be proffered to this question is that, in some cases, material factors function in religion in a purely causal way. This would be the case, for example, if the taking of drugs could induce a spiritual state in the properly religious sense. The question whether this does in fact happen is very debatable and has been the subject of much recent controversy. Some take the line boldly that it is out of the question for drugs to produce such a religious state, and they seem to do this on the general or *a priori* ground that strictly material causes cannot produce spiritual results. The worth or dignity of the spiritual state is thought to be impugned by the dependence on physical factors. This seems to me unreasonable, for every mental state, under the conditions we know, has variable physical conditions. We are usually brighter, for example, after relaxation or sleep or if we have fresh air. A tonic or stimulant may, for a period at least, quicken our mental faculties, and an injury from a blow to the head deaden them completely. Nor is this merely a matter of enlivening or deadening our mental activity in general. There seems to be nothing in principle against there being specific physical conditions of elevated mental states, as there are certainly parts of the body connected with the various sense-experiences we have. Much further study of the brain and of physiological conditions in general seems to be needed before very reliable conclusions can be reached on such questions.

At the same time we need to recall the highly complicated character of the higher and more distinctively human mental operations. The interplay of many conditions is needed for these, including very subtle and complicated modes of the fusion of past experience with the present. This should make us suspicious of the notion that restricted physical conditions, such as taking a drug or applying some similar physical stimulus, could have more than a very minor part in enlivening a particular propensity, such as that for poetry or philosophy, in distinction from producing a state of general heightened activity which could affect each person variously according to his gifts and interests. A major physiological change would of course be another matter. We have learnt much of late about operations which diminish the sense of moral responsibility, and it is not inconceivable that the reverse should happen, by restoring for example the original condition, although in both these cases the specific physiological change would be operative in combination with a number of other factors.

Where, as in the case of music, the high attainment is closely connected with a specific sense-experience, the likelihood of its having a close dependence on specific physiological conditions is greater, although here in course of time the dependence may be weakened, as would presumably be the case with deaf musicians who can still read the score or hear the music in their heads. Possibly this holds of poetry and the plastic arts also, and the question of the dependence of religious experience on specific and variable physical causes will thus turn in part on the affinities or connection it may be found to have with attainments like art or music.

The relation of sex to religion calls for some note here also. For it has often been observed that the heightening of certain forms of religious experience is accompanied by some kind of sexual excitation, it being likely that there is involved a causal relation which works both ways. But here again we have to recall that both sex and religion are very complicated things. How far the strictly physical aspect of sex affects religious states directly and how far it influences religion through the attitudes of mind and sympathies generally involved in sexual relations or stimulated by them are questions which can certainly not be settled easily. The great likelihood, it seems to me, is that the strictly physical or sensual aspects of sex do not much affect religion directly, although there are important affinities at other levels which it is not appropriate to investigate here. But of course we cannot *a priori* rule out the possibility of closer relations between sex in its strictly physical features and certain religious states, least of all can we do this on the ground that the former is *physical*. For in some way physical conditions do affect religion like everything else in human life.

The considerations to which we ought to hold, in examining questions of the present sort, seem to me to be these. Firstly, that not every state of excitation is a worth-while one, and that it is not by its emotional intensity mainly that we estimate the worth of an experience. Secondly, the unusual or abnormal character of an experience is not a very reliable clue to its value—otherwise one might rate a state of delirium highly. Thirdly, a state of mind may be unusual or exceptionally lively and also of considerable worth without being expressly religious. This has very close relevance, I think, to the question of inducing religious states by drugs. It is one thing to establish that supernormal and elevated conditions of mind may be induced by a drug or by sexual excitement, another to exhibit the properly religious character of these conditions. I have myself little doubt, having regard to the evidence available now, that there are interesting and revealing resemblances between some of the extraordinary states induced by drugs and religious states, and the investigation of these matters may thus prove very suggestive and illuminating for the student of religion. The account of the general heightening of experience under the influence of mescaline and the peculiarly sharp perceptiveness of the world around us so induced will obviously have interest for anyone who shares the view outlined above about religious experience, and it may help us to understand why conditions of this sort should be taken to be religious, if it is the case that they are not in fact properly so. Likewise we may appreciate better how such conditions may become religious, by what transitions this comes about and what part, if any, this should play in the normal inducement of religious awareness. But in all questions of this sort we should have particular regard to the following further considerations.

At the centre of all properly religious experience lies the awareness of God, as unconditioned being, involved in the being of all other things. This is awareness of a widely general kind, in the sense that it is not bound up with discernment of some particular feature of the world. It has the affinities already noted with moral experience and the disinterested pursuit of truth. But these in turn cover the widest areas of human experience. One should thus not expect religious awareness to be connected in any particularly intimate way with our enjoyment of some very peculiar kind of experience. We do not need to confine ourselves to very specialized tracts of human experience to encounter God, and to that extent we should not expect the stimulation of extraordinary mental states, subject moreover to the limitations and detachment from normal experience consequent upon the exceptional and predominantly physical mode of their stimulation, to have any peculiarly religious feature.

On the other hand, we have also seen that disturbance of the normal tenour of existence, setting the mind on courses which confront it with the inherently limited character of all finite existence, initiates us into the awareness of God and has much to do with maintaining and enlivening that awareness. The propulsion of a personality into some highly abnormal state, especially a state of much excitation and disruption, may thus have the further consequence of predisposing us to have religious awareness also. If, in addition, the states in

question are states of heightened alertness and intensified impressions of our environment, real or imagined,
and of the inter-relations of its contents, we have
further conditions of close affinity with those by which
our awareness of God is shaped and directed. We need
not then be surprised or religiously upset if we discover
that mental states induced in the first place by highly
artificial physical means are found to have a religious
quality.

At the same time we need to be sharply aware of the
dangers of religious states which involve extraordinary
conditions of mind, whether deliberately induced or
not. For not only have we to reckon with the ill effects
over a long period on mind and body alike of powerful
and peculiar stimulants, but there is also the danger
of dissociation of at least a part of our religious life (and
that the one that may have most appeal for us) from
the practice of religion in general and normal experience.
This is of course an ever-present danger of all religion,
and the corrective to it is certainly not the avoidance
of all heightened and intense religious awareness. The
emphasis of the present study has been throughout
on the need to enliven religion and preserve it from
stagnation and staleness. But we need also a rounded
religion and the controlling of moments of intense
awareness by integration with the wholeness of life
religiously lived. In states which are artificially induced
and which involve much detachment from normal experience, the exercise of such control is not easy. Nor
is it a simple matter, when moments of ecstasy are
ended, to know how much substance and how much
delusion there was in them, as notable mystics have
themselves stressed.

We shall return to the last observation. But, subject
to caveats and qualifications such as those noted, I
think we may take it as possible, and even likely, that
distinctive physical conditions, such as the taking of

drugs, may operate fairly closely and directly in a causal way in inducing a religious state of mind. The place accorded in the practice and mythology of early religions to sacred foods and drinks, usually of a very potent kind, supports our conclusion, as it may also in turn be susceptible of a better understanding, and one more consistent with our respect for some of those religions, in terms of the observations just made. We may also find in these ways that, in restrained forms, certain physical stimuli may still legitimately function causally in the inducement of religious states. Aromatic flowers would be innocent candidates for that position.

Abstemiousness and various physical impositions of the same sort may also have effects, similar to those we may ascribe to positive physical stimuli, in inducing or perpetuating spiritual states. How far this comes about psychologically, that is by suppressing desires and interests that may compete with more elevated interests, is not easy to settle. Plato and others have thought that sensual enjoyment and much physical ease would hinder intellectual pursuits, and no doubt there is truth in their view, whether or not we endorse the severe asceticisms which Plato counsels. But whether we have to do here with more than the removal of hindrances is another matter. Does physical privation conduce positively to mental alertness? It seems to me conceivable that it does and that the mortification of the flesh in ascetic practice has partly that explanation. It is a further question whether privations or pain could have a special causal connection, not only with mental alertness in general, but specifically with religious states. Here again, it seems to me, we should retain an open mind. The subject has been much obscured no doubt by confused ideas of sin and the corruption of the body. Nor would it be very easy to sift the evidence which points to a helpful removal of distractions from that which suggests a more direct connection of physical states with spiritual ones. But I am inclined to the view that the history of asceticism, especially in the lives of very noble characters, indicates that there are physical privations of some kind, fasting perhaps in particular, which are directly conducive to spiritual attainment.

It is a yet further question whether this has to do only with peculiar or very exalted spiritual states obtainable by exceptional persons or in extraordinary conditions, or whether it can play a part in the normal religious life. The question is complicated by the fact that there are other aspects of asceticism, not all of them by any means due to discreditable theories. But I should think that we ought not at any rate to be unmindful of the possibility that certain restraints and disciplines should be found a part in normal religious practice, or be given some special form, expressly on account of their direct connection with spiritual attainment. That there should be safeguards against abuses and superstitious misrepresentations is also evident. But what we have to note mainly now is that there is at least some likelihood that physical privation may function in some way causally in connection with both normal and extraordinary spiritual states.

From physical impositions we pass fairly easily to other bodily states which have a place in religion, such as the adoption of certain postures of the body and breathing exercises like those which have prominence in yoga practices. The comments already made on food and drugs as inducers of spiritual states apply here also. We have to ask, for example, what does the Yogi attain? That the physical practices in which he indulges, often together with extreme abstemiousness, do produce extraordinary states of some sort seems beyond dispute, notwithstanding that there be many fraudulent practitioners. But is there more than this? Is there some genuine awareness of God, whether or not described in language which discloses easily the identity with more obviously theistic experiences? I think there is and that fresh investigation of these extraordinary practices and states, as known from the past or the present, in the light of a better understanding of our knowledge of God, will be a very rewarding task. And here again I think it very likely that the physical practices themselves will be found to be those which long experience has shown to have some direct causal connection with spiritual states. They will not of course function exclusively in that way —nor, I should imagine, mainly. They are, one presumes, more important, not only in a symbolic way to be noted in a moment, but also as powerful aids to concentration and to the exclusion of thoughts and preoccupations not consistent with the required contemplation. But we should not rule out their operating more directly by initiating further physical conditions which release extraordinary powers of the mind.

CHAPTER II

INSTRUMENTS OF WORSHIP

The reference I have just been making to exceptional physical disciplines brings us an important stage further in our discussion. For it seems highly likely that these have importance in a way we have not yet considered, but one much more central to our theme, namely as symbolical representations of the truth. The physical movements and postures will have acquired certain meanings, if only through associations with past experiences of like nature, which help to induce the appropriate state of mind. In all likelihood they will have some inherent appropriateness for the purpose, as the seated position of the Buddhist in contemplation appears naturally to suggest to the agent or the beholder a condition of great inner calm. It seems likely therefore that bodily postures or exercises, such as those the Yogi commend, may be effective in a two-fold way, the exercises which are causally efficacious on their own account acquiring associations, some more and some less subtle, of a spiritual kind and being taken up into other physical states or attitudes which have symbolic religious significance. It seems to me very likely also that fasts and kindred religious disciplines operate in the same subtly dual way.

A proper appreciation of this dual operation may have much importance for our understanding of some religious practices and the way they may need to be altered or developed. But this in turn will be furthered if we are clear how material entities and practices feature in religion in a properly symbolic way.

To this end we must first distinguish two ways in which material factors may affect worship. They may in the first place help to provide a favourable atmosphere and thus predispose a person to be exceptionally aware of God. This in turn comes about in two ways. We may, firstly, find in our environment features which have some general kinship with our attitude of mind when we are especially aware of God and heeding Him. The quiet of the sanctuary, the lofty receding heights of the cathedral, the solemn peals of the organ, the bareness of a wayside bethel, the magnificence or the simplicity of a landscape, may all in some fashion reflect some general quality of the religious state, its peace or grandeur or strangeness, and thereby help to evoke it. But within this general helpfulness of our environment there may be found also the representation in material tokens of the beliefs which sustain our spiritual life, the interplay being again close and subtle between the general conduciveness of our environment to a religious frame of mind and the more explicit representation within the former of the content of the latter.

But, secondly, in worship we are not merely aware of God, and of His dealings with us; we react to this awareness and adopt certain attitudes towards God, reverence, love, submission, penitence and so forth. And it is a further function of the material elements in worship to elicit and express those worshipful attitudes. This occurs also in a dual way. For there is again some general suitability of our environment, through resemblance or harmony, to the attitudes they are to express, together with the explicit representation of those attitudes in certain features of the environment. The lofty vaults of the cathedral or the 'dim religious light' that filters through to some quiet sanctuary may not only elicit or express our sense of the majesty and holiness of God; they may also elicit, by an affinity of what they present in themselves and our moods, the awe and humility which it is fitting for us to feel in the presence of God, and in eliciting this reaction they will at the same time provide reflections or echoes of it in which the reaction can begin to find proper expression. In course of time an association will be set up between these outward forms and our states of mind, such that the appropriate mood is induced or expressed more spontaneously and certainly by its material counterpart, and the way will be paved in this fashion also for the further more specific and deliberate adoption of material tokens by which appropriate spiritual reactions may be outwardly expressed.

The expression of our reactions will indeed be peculiarly important in religion, for the right personal relation is always best maintained by expressing it fittingly. The lover is expected to 'tell' his love and provide tokens of it, not mainly to assuage doubts but because the telling of love affords an enrichment of it, it is an extension of the lover's willingness to give himself to his beloved, a favour which has no purpose beyond the completion of the lover's surrender and which may thus have tokens which are of minimal worth in themselves. But in religion we have the paramount personal relation, our relation to God, and although God searches out our hearts and knows them to the full, it is preeminently true of the personal relation we have to God that it requires communication from us as well as from God, and this not merely as a discipline by which we maintain in ourselves the due love of God, but because in finding ways to express our love we extend it and make our surrender to God complete. When the union of man with God is seen to involve his union in the bond of this same love with his fellow men, we are, in expressing our love to God, expressing it to one another;

and this further deepens the need to express our love or adoration in praise.

Much of the detailed development of material religious symbolism may be traced to this source. Sacrifice, and the ritual by which it is performed, is perhaps the most significant example. For at the heart of this lies the notion of giving for giving's sake, of making a gift consumed in the giving as the seal of love. This has no doubt been combined from the earliest times with superstitious fears and the propitiation of powers not solely jealous for righteousness. But the correction and sublimation of the cruder features of sacrifice have been much aided by the fact that it is a natural and proper religious reaction to make a gift to God in which the essence of the gift is the giving. The relevance of this to specifically Christian thought and practice need hardly be underlined. Elaborate ornamentation and forms of worship, while they reflect reprehensible ostentation and sometimes the baser forms of rivalry, have also been due in part to the enthusiasm with which it has been sought to complete the giving of oneself to God in the splendour of one's praise and its tokens.

The visible tokens of reverence and other spiritual attitudes will however be largely identical with those by which an enlivened awareness of God is induced and maintained. The person who bows his head or kneels and clasps his hands in prayer is doing many things. He is shutting out the world and helping himself to concentrate. His pose is one we should naturally associate with deep concentration, but it is also one which seems to harmonize with the inner religious frame of mind, to draw into itself as it were the sustaining wholeness and calm of religion; and in these and kindred ways the worshipper will be aiding himself, by the posture of his body, to induce the appropriate reflections. In this he will be further helped by the traditional associations of the prayerful attitude. But the worshipper, in prayer, will also be conveying to God what he himself feels, reverence and gratitude, penitence and the humility with which petitions are made, and so forth; and this will also have its part in the kneeling posture, the clasped hands and the tone of voice. The same physical attitudes and gestures will thus carry a double load of religious significance.

Nor will the worshipper himself be very much aware, as a rule, of any sharp dichotomy within his experience and performances. The more formal sort of prayer may proceed from reverent salutation and descriptions of the greatness and goodness of God to more explicit expressions of praise or humility. But the distinction is largely artificial and procedural. Praise will be present throughout, and no one could easily call to mind the goodness or greatness of God, or put himself in any other way effectively in mind of God, without this involving immediately certain reactions of his own, including those which it is most appropriate to express in worship. There is likewise a peculiarly intimate fusion of many facets of worship in the outward embodiments of it. Variations of gesture or of felt bodily tensions there may be, according to shifts of emphasis. But what is more striking is the way the very same attitude or gesture wraps up in itself the many sides of our worshipping state.

Within this blend of the significations which material religious symbols may carry, there will also function whatever directly causal power the physical entities involved, and our own bodily states and movements, may contain. In more mature forms of religion the directly causal efficacy of material elements will presumably be very slight in normal religious activities and overlaid by long accumulations of symbolic meaning. But they may be present in ways too subdued to be normally noted, and we must at least allow of that possibility in a full account of the material factor in worship.

In any advanced religion, and probably at all times, it is mainly by their symbolic meaning that material entities come expressly into worship. We may of course use the word 'worship' so widely that it covers most, if not the whole, of religion, and in this sense the use we make of material things for practical ends, as required or sanctioned by religion, is a part of our worship. We may also find, by using things in this way, that they are invested for us with a symbolical religious meaning, and this may happen extensively for some devout persons; these will be able to make everything a sacrament of some kind. But these extensions of the sacramental character which things may have are best understood in the light of the distinctive adoption of certain material things as symbolic elements in specific rites or religious practices.

To understand this we must first recall the peculiarly close integration of religion with the rest of life. Religion does not take its course in a void or a world of its own. On the contrary, I have especially stressed that religion is in a sense parasitic on other activities and comes to life as a formative influence within other experiences. This is what gives it body and content. But in that case much in its course will be determined by interests and conditions which are not in themselves expressly religious. At early stages the contrast between sacred and secular will be faint and not sharply drawn, as students of religion have much emphasized of late, and this reflects both the permeation of the whole of life by religion and the contribution to religion of factors which have not in themselves an initially religious character.

There will thus be much in the development of religious ritual and symbolism which is due to a natural tendency to provide figurative representation, in outward forms, for various experiences and interests, especially impressive ones, and to give some of these representations permanence and prominence by repeated or regular recourse to them. No one who has watched a young child at play can fail to appreciate how natural and deep-rooted is this proclivity to dramatization of experience. Indeed, it is incipiently present in the play of animals, just as it is instructively evident, most of all in the case of infants, how fortuitous the connection may sometimes be between the symbol and its object. There are, no doubt, certain conditions which generally affect our adoption of symbols, for example certain similarities of form and content between various items of experience. But personal idiosyncrasies and turns of fortune will also have much to do with it, in the lives both of individuals and of societies. A close investigation of the outward forms of religion will thus extend into many aspects of experience and follow paths too devious and long to be entered upon here.

One comment which may be elicited here perhaps is this, that ritual is always religious ritual, as the associations of the name suggest, and that it has always been under the propulsion of religion that ritual practices have developed. This is however rather misleading, or only partly true. It overlooks the point already stressed about the integration of religion with the rest of life. For while everything may become religious, and ideally should do so as was largely the case in the early stages of religion and history, nothing completely empties itself of its own characteristics in becoming religious; and there are thus many features of symbol-making habits and the development of ritual ceremonies which derive from other sources than explicitly or properly religious ones.

The latter do not however concern us especially now. The point we need to emphasize is that the strictly religious contribution to the rites and symbols which we find in religion is determined throughout by religious experience, it is part of the general representation in imagination of religious experience. Of this there are several forms, two of which in particular call for notice.

In the first an experience may be said to be represented by a part of itself. This is of interest to us primarily here when some feature of our natural environment has a place of some prominence in one's religious experience at a particular time. It has already been noted how a vivid awareness of God extends itself into our immediate environment and invests it with a significance it would not otherwise have, our sense of God associating itself with those aspects of our situation which it most illumines or throws into prominence. The latter may in turn enrich and enliven the total experience by providing a focus for it, drawing into themselves the wealth and radiance of the whole and reflecting it back in a more concentrated form into the total experience again. By their sharpness and distinctness of form physical entities immediately present lend themselves well to this service.

The same result may moreover be achieved when some feature of our physical environment is merely prominent on its own account, without undergoing any special transformation, in our apprehension of it, due to the experience we are having. Likewise, some physical entity may have helped in an outstanding way to induce the religious mood and prompt its distinctive insights; or, again, the natural scene, in whole or in part, may have some affinity, for example by its vastness, its wildness, its remoteness or its calm, with the enlivened religious awareness. In these ways also an association may be established and the experience as a whole signalized and enriched by this identification with natural fact.

This, in large measure, is how some localities become holy places, as in the story of Jacob at Peniel, and objects sacred, as in the case of Buddha and the Bo Tree. A predisposition, due to association and history, for certain kinds of places or objects to acquire such status would help, and in this a prominent part would no doubt be played by the importance which certain kinds of things or places would have independently; they might be dominating features of the natural background against which life is lived, like some remote and mysterious mountain peak, or factors indispensable in some way for survival or prosperity, a river or spring or some centre or condition of favourable or sinister seasonal change. But these would usually become properly sacred, in the first instance, when there was superimposed on their natural impressiveness a properly religious character due to their becoming the focus of religious experience and helping to hold together more firmly the meaning of the whole.

Due regard to this and kindred considerations would have prevented a great many loose and highly misleading allusions to the alleged numinous quality of certain things and places. Popularizers of Otto's work are the main culprits here, but the master is not altogether exempt from blame. Some of Otto's observations could be taken as if he meant the 'numinous' in nature to be some quality inhering objectively in things or places;[1] and it has become widely the fashion for others to speak in the same way, although I do not think Otto himself seriously meant this. But whatever is a quality of objects in this way the numinous is not. We may speak if we like of sensing the numinous quality of some awe-inspiring scene or some hallowed spot, and students of the early paintings discovered in caves may tell us of the almost tangibly numinous character of remote parts of

[1] For example when he speaks, in *The Idea of the Holy*, p. 68, of gigantic monoliths being erected in order 'to store up the numen in solid presence by magic', and of being 'confronted with the numinous itself', p. 69. He writes also: 'The tower of the Cathedral of Ulm is emphatically not "magical", it is *numinous*', p. 70.

the subterranean places they explore. But this is still metaphor. The 'numinous' does not haunt a place like a smell or mist. We may 'sense an atmosphere' but atmosphere in this context has no existence apart from ourselves. The natural qualities of objects and places, whatever the independence our epistemology allows them, do not include religiously more than a predisposition to elicit religious experiences in which a peculiar mode of apprehending those objects and places has a prominent part.

It is not, however, merely by their function within an experience in which they themselves figure that material things have a symbolic role in religion; they may be representative in yet another way, one not altogether detached from the first but connected more with the ripening of religion into the fullness of articulated knowledge of God. For almost from the very first incursion of religion proper into human experience the occasions of distinctive religious illumination will begin to coalesce in our total impression of them and yield in due course the sense of a significant pattern by which God becomes known to men and deals with them. Individual occasions will combine into a total picture, sustained by mutual enrichment of one another's insights in the continuing life of society. This, as we have seen, will be further extended and enriched by the deliberate reflections upon the course which religious experience takes in such ways as to yield dogmatic formulations of belief. At all these levels the developing pattern of religious awareness will be directed and made a more complete possession of the whole personality, and morally more creative, by imaginative representations of itself. And in this process also outward forms, including the contemplation and manipulation of material entities, will have an important role to play.

One important determinant of this will be the part which material things have played in initial and other formative religious experiences. Certain kinds of entity, rivers and trees for example, will tend to acquire a recognized religious status on the basis of which they can be made to serve in more elaborate representative functions. To the latter personal idiosyncrasies and turns of fortune, including outstanding and formative events in the history of peoples, will have much to contribute; and within these, and within the imaginative representation of them, items of men's physical environment will have much prominence. They may either have some outstanding place in the stories which take shape in the play of men's imaginations, individually or co-operatively, about their lives as religiously orientated, or they may be seized upon directly, on account of some inherent appropriateness, by creative imagination as required. In the renewal of religious experience, enriched by the accumulation of experience in the past and the shape it is given in particular traditions, the outward symbols of religion will have gained new associations and depths of meaning which heighten their potency and make their role more precise. In this their inherent suitability to present our developing sense of God, as in the case of buildings contrived to give a feeling of lofty spaciousness, will have a place throughout.

In a religion like Christianity, where the beliefs which experience yields acquire a very determinate form, certain material things, notably the bread and wine of the sacrament of holy communion and the vessels and instruments used in administering it, will have a precise symbolic meaning derived from the Christian sense of the way God has been active in the life of the world.

The point that has to be especially stressed for our purpose is that material items have no proper place in worship except in the causal sense considered earlier or in representation of experience, either directly by providing a focus for what matters most in a particular experience or more generally by bringing to the enrichment of particular experiences, and to the maintenance of religious dispositions, the accumulated and patterned impressions of the past in imaginative forms.

It might be thought that there are general notions about God which some may entertain in a way detached from the determinate course of our experience of God. But I have already adduced reasons for doubting the possibility of acquiring any substantial knowledge of God in this way. The doctrine of analogy is the strongest candidate. But even if this does, on its own account, yield some constructive knowledge of God, which I much doubt, it will be of a very tenuous kind; and if it calls at all for further images to represent it, which seems again unlikely unless they are very deliberately contrived to justify preconceived notions, they are not likely to have the potency and persistence of the images which have been more spontaneously produced in the warmth of vital and shared experience. The images prominent in the great religions are of the latter sort.

An equally mistaken notion, if anyone seriously entertains it, is that material entities and certain manipulations of them have some kind of spiritual significance or efficacy on their own account. To believe this is to degrade religion to magic, or even to less than magic— since it seems certain that belief in magic, when it is genuine and persistent, contains a good deal more, including some religious elements, than the ascription of abnormal causal properties to things. I shall add a word on magic shortly, but to suppose that there is some virtue or merit in mere physical configurations of things or physical performances as such is altogether absurd. We may of course sentimentally invest things with some kind of personality, as in our veneration for an old house. But in no other way than a metaphorical one can material things be significant on their own account, for religion or ethics.

It is probably some form of the doctrine of transubstantiation, in the Christian religion, that comes nearest to outrightly contravening the principle just advanced. If it is held that the bread and wine literally change their physical properties in holy communion and that this, although not sensibly discernible in any observable properties, is a vital or appreciably important part of the sacrament and of its fulfilment of its purpose religiously, then we are certainly straying far from the view advanced in this book, namely that no material elements in religion can matter except as they help to induce or direct and maintain the personal awareness of God and extend it to our lives as a whole. There are difficulties enough in the notion of transubstantiation in itself, not least those which concern the relation of a substance to its attributes. But these, in the context of the religious import of the doctrine, seem hardly worth contending with, since it appears to me inconceivable that changes of a physical nature can matter in religion except as they help to form the experience of individuals; even if the changes are known to occur, their religious import is nil except in relation to what they help us to think and feel and do in our relations with God.

I am well aware that few, if any, would detach the efficacy of the Christian sacraments from some kind of mental or spiritual condition. On the cruder forms, as they frankly seem to me, of the doctrine of *ex opere operato*, it is certainly held that an unworthy and religiously torpid frame of mind on the part of those who officiate would not invalidate the sacrament provided there was the minimum requirement of an intention to perform it. Most would add penitence on the part of those who are to participate effectively. But this falls very far short of the requirements as they seem to me. For it is not enough to attach certain spiritual conditions to the efficacy of the material performances; we must also insist that the efficacy must itself be

understood entirely in terms of changes in the mind
or personality of those who participate in the sacrament
—or perhaps those they may influence.

It also appears to have been held—to adduce one
further instance of the view I tilt at here—that if, in
the sacrament of baptism, the water to be sprinkled on
the brow, or other part of the body, of infant or adult
for some reason missed its mark and the error went
unnoticed and were not repaired, then the validity or
efficacy of the sacrament would be lost. This seems to
me to be again an entirely untenable position which is
deprived of all plausibility by its detachment of material
operations in religious ritual and sacraments from their
function of ministering to the religious state of mind
of those who participate.

I do not wish to insist that profound and moving
renewals of religious apprehension and feeling must invariably accompany a religious sacrament, if it is to be
worthy and efficacious. A sacrament can have other
functions, a solemn commitment to the implications of
one's belief for example and a reinforcement of the
bonds which hold a religious fellowship together. It
may again be thought of as a discipline which has
mainly a long-term effect in the perpetuation of insight
and understanding. But unless it is somehow related to
the perpetuation and deepening of insight and the cultivation and expression of the attitude and conduct
appropriate to these, it seems hard to ascribe to it any
religious function at all. In addition, the more it is
accompanied by deep and moving renewals of personal
understanding, not necessarily at a very abstract level,
the better; and in all these regards I should be reluctant
to draw any absolute distinction between the ceremonies
which are definitely sacramental and other forms of
religious ritual.

The performatory side of religious ritual loses nothing
of its force and significance on the views advanced here.

For religion is by no means exhausted by contemplation of God, it is a many-sided living relationship to a personal being maintained in the whole of life, and ritual must reflect this and induce in moments of disciplined meditation an adequate representation of God's initiative and man's response. Historically, the performatory side has been very prominent in most religions, especially at the point, a very central one, where men's response is sealed by sacrifice of some kind, and this reason alone would incline us, in availing ourselves at all points of the help which the past can give us, to have due place for performance and response in ritual and liturgical practice. But there are psychological reasons also for that policy, for the more we involve ourselves, by participation, in some ceremony, the more, normally, especially in respect of oft-repeated ceremonies, do they become significant for us.

It seems also very likely that the germinative effect of a ritual in maintaining a certain attitude or belief generally in life is much heightened if the performatory side is strong and significant. For, if anything is lost in efficacy and concentration at the time, it may be compensated for to some degree by the greater firmness with which the ceremony persists in subsequent thought and subtly sustains or modifies disposition and practice.

This will have had much to do with the perpetuation of religion in early stages, and recent students of religion have emphasized in particular the prominence of the performatory element in early religious practice. In doing so they have been influenced by the generally practical and empiricist character of thought today, and I believe there is a very misguided tendency among anthropologists to make undue concessions to the *Zeitgeist* here and also, in being down to earth and empirical, to make their own tasks in some respects more manageable than they are. In some ways at least the study of religion is easier if we confine ourselves to what men actually *do* in their religious practices, how they bury their dead and build their temples and perform their dances. But doing is never merely outward doing, and avoidance of all speculation about the meaning of various practices and their place in a properly religious consciousness may lead us far astray. How deeply I believe this will be evident from most that I have said. On the other hand, it would be idle to deny the insight that is brought us by better appreciation of the highly performatory character of early religion. The observations made in the preceding passages will provide some indication of the way this should be fitted into views commended in this book.

That is, however, far from exhausting the interest the topic has for us or providing, even in outline, an adequate account of it. The truth is, as repeatedly stressed, that religious activities are very closely integrated with others; and once the association is established between, on the one hand, the mystery of religion and our dependence in it on a power which extends and activizes our own experience, and, on the other, certain historical situations and material entities and types of entities, the latter tend to become invested, in men's general impression of them, with some inherent potency, beyond their normal causal efficacy, which they tend to retain on their own account. To attempt to control or exploit this power is a very natural step which is next taken, and, when it is combined with much ignorance and credulity and wishful thinking or suggestion, the scene is set for taboo and totem and all manner of superstitious practices and beliefs whose hold is deepened by being institutionalized and given the further sanction of religion, not least by being merged in properly religious practices or having a properly religious significance and function superimposed on their magical one. Subtle supernormal powers of which we are beginning to learn more today attach themselves to this situation, and give, in measures of which little can as yet be ascertained, a further causal efficacy alike to magical and properly religious rites which in turn again confirms the belief in them.

Yet other features no doubt contribute to superstition and magic. The crudest mistake would be to assume that certain objects or places acquire alleged magical properties fortuitously, or that we may not probe in any way into the process by which such properties are acquired, but merely accept the fact and proceed on that basis to such further understanding as the subject allows. One suspects that some anthropologists come dangerously near frustrating and misleading themselves in this way. But the situation with which they have to cope is full of subtleties and complications which need to be untangled for a fruitful interpretation of the facts, and to some extent to know what the facts are; and the most that I venture to do here is to give an indication of where, in my opinion, the main religious clue to the subject may be found.

That early religious rites and attitudes of worship admit of confusion and distortion in the way indicated is a matter of no mean importance for us in the conduct of our own religious life. For not only are we helped, by judicious consideration of these aspects of religion in the past, to be more discriminating in bringing the past to the succour and enrichment of the present, but we are also put on our guard against the persistence or recrudescence of magic and superstition in our present practices. For in subtle ways these may still make their way into our religion; and just as the outward manifestations of religion may degenerate into magic, so are they also open to the other forms of the corruption of religion which we have noted, idolatry being made more powerful, and thereby more sinister, when further charged with the dynamism of belief in the magical properties of things or persons.

Indeed it is in respect to outward practices, and the

entities which have most prominence in them, that idolatry gains its easiest entry into the minds of sophisticated as well as simple-minded worshippers. For an outward object has a solidity and independence which makes it easier for it to attract and absorb into itself the glory which belongs to a reality which has as one of its characteristics that it should be very certainly and completely outside ourselves. The beyondness of sensible things is not the beyondness of transcendent being, but it is externality of one sort; and we need thus to be on our guard against the insidiousness with which, in being accorded an almost indispensable function in signalizing our religious experiences and giving them a focus, outward symbols insinuate themselves into the position of real and final instead of representative and transitional bearers of the glory.

The need to be heedful of this danger is heightened because the relationship in which we stand to external objects much facilitates a transition from the idolatry in which such objects have the central place themselves to the more vicious and devastating form of idolatry in which the regard we have for ourselves has the dominant role. For the power we have to manipulate objects and our ownership of them, or a custodianship in respect to some office, helps the identification with ourselves of any power or magnificence we may find in objects and speeds us to the end in which idolatry normally culminates of according divine status and honours to ourselves. Of the sad progress of this kind of idolatry, especially among profoundly religious people and in places where the institutions and rites of religion elicit deep respect and devotion, we can find no better or more instructive examples than in the Bible. But I suggest that it is far from being altogether a thing of the past.

To save ourselves from these perils, whose grimness is not invariably reduced by the subtler forms they assume in conditions of high culture and enlightenment or even by the greater admixture within them of genuine devotion, we need to have constantly in mind that our outward practices have no meaning or any proper role in religion which is not derived, directly or indirectly, from religious experience and the course it has taken in history. Likewise it is in ministering to a religious life in which enlivened individual awareness of God is the central concern that all our rites and 'instruments' have their justification.

CHAPTER 12

SYMBOLISM AND TRADITION

The views I have been advancing about various forms of symbolism in religion have a close bearing on the difficult and much debated question which has rightly been the subject of much concern to anxious leaders of religion today, namely the extent to which religious ceremonial and language have become too antiquated or out of relevance to man's normal experience and outlook in an age of such rapid and extensive transitions as ours. This problem is so familiar that it needs little exemplification from me. What, it may be asked, is the role of kingship in modern society, when the traditional and largely hereditary monarchies are either giving place altogether to newer forms of democratic or despotic rule, or being shorn of their properly political functions and made to serve in a different and less awe-inspiring way in the maintenance of the ethos of societies through ceremonial performances which often require royal personages to become fairly familiar figures to all and sundry? What is left here of the majesty and mystery of kingship and the divinity that hedges it round? What significance has the idea of a shepherd and his traditional crook in highly industrialized communities where even agriculture is extensively mechanized and where values and interests are so much shaped by motion-pictures and television? What can it mean to a Western child to read of being comforted by a 'rod' and 'staff' and have one's head anointed with oil? Should we not seek the modern counterparts of these expressions which were so charged with significance and so moving at one time?

No one confronted with the colossal ignorance of Biblical and religious matters which prevails in most Western countries today can fail to feel the force of the present suggestion. Religion cannot live on its past or survive in a healthy state if it is largely divorced from life as we know it now. If not made relevant to modern concerns it is bound to wither or become the unhealthy preoccupation of a few. It has indeed to do with things 'not of this world' but it must be discovered by us 'within us' and within our main present preoccupations. How is this to be achieved? Can it be achieved without extensive modernizing of our ritual practices and language?

Part of the answer, and much the most important one, is that we certainly need to bring the whole of what religion means for us to life in relating it to moral, social and cultural and personal issues of the greatest importance for us. Realism in this sense is essential for religion, and there can be few undertakings of greater importance for the promoters of religion today than to find adequate means of making it relevant to the mind and conditions of our times, for example by accepting more boldly the general ethical implications of the Christian faith and seeking with more confidence the renewal of special religious insights in coping with new problems and the adjustments required of us within and without our national life. But it is another matter to modify the language and formal practices of religion. There are reasons here for being fairly conservative.

These do not preclude, but rather require, the fullest instruction about the origin and history of religious imagery and formal practices, and especially about the Scriptures from which they derive; and in making this possible some judicious modernization of terms and usages will be helpful, as in some well-known and highly valuable renderings of Scriptures in contemporary idiom. Scientific imagination may also find extensions of traditional images or bring new ones to birth which are authentically religious and stimulating. But the latter cannot altogether supersede traditional imagery, they must grow out of it, and out of the full religious life in which the past, sustained by traditional forms, is germinative in the present. To attempt too deliberately to contrive new forms and images, when these do not present themselves spontaneously in the kindling of imagination within the renewal of religion in its fullness in modern life, will be artificial and probably most frustrating. Imagination must not, in art or religion, be subjected too rigidly to rule or made to conform closely to preconceived ideas. It must be coaxed and come to life in its own way, and the likelihood is that if we move too impetuously ahead of the spirit in matters of this sort we shall encumber ourselves with a pseudo-imagery which has no real power and cut ourselves adrift from the true sources of the imaginative sustenance of the spiritual life in the past. Our aim on the contrary should be, while maintaining a rounded and vigorous religious life in the present, to seek in traditional imagery and forms a means of maintaining the continuity of religion through which the wealth of its content has been accumulated and made available to us and our successors.

It is here that the insistence on the relation of religious imagery, in its sensible or outward forms as in other regards, to experience is most relevant, and we need again to remind ourselves that the experience in question involves the coalescing of particular experiences into recognizable patterns within the full context of individual and social existence. In attempting to devise new images to suit contemporary needs we may only too easily find ourselves seeking to provide imaginative embodiment, probably of a very unconvincing kind, for formal notions whose proper substance has been lost already in detaching them from their appropriate historical context. The traditional images are meaningful in relation to a significant past, and this is why they cannot be easily replaced, although they may be supplemented or extended as religious life progresses. Attempts to give our images too sharp a 'new look' may only lead to a detachment from the past which deprives them of substance and power.

Nor should we be unduly daunted by the seemingly archaic or antiquated character of much religious language and imagery. For the task of appreciating this and entering into the meaning it had originally is not quite so stupendous as might seem at first. The main condition is that we should sympathetically reconstruct the context in which such language and imagery first appeared, and, for this, exceptionally detailed information is not required. The more the scholar enhances our vision the better, but simple and ignorant people, placed in circumstances and conditions of life very different from those of the countries and times of the Bible, have in fact been able to nourish themselves culturally and spiritually most effectively on Biblical history. They certainly could not do this without knowing some things about the Bible and without making themselves very much at home in its contents. But granted the minimal factual clues, it does not seem to strain our normal potentialities unduly to bring to life in our own way, and possibly with much inaccuracy of detail, the substance of alien literary allusions. We may have a most inaccurate impression of what a desert is like, or what it means to tend goats or camels, our mental pictures of a well or spring may conform little to the realities in hot or desolate countries and the emotions they naturally stir may be weak or far removed from those of the peoples of whom we read, the shelter of a great rock may not naturally mean much to us, we may never have seen cedars of Lebanon or lived in the proximity of wild beasts, we may not even have seen wild beasts in captivity. But none of this seriously hinders us from effectively appreciating Biblical literature in which all these, and much of like nature, are the normal accompaniments of life. Children enter easily into folk-lore and fairy tale, and even if imagination becomes more sluggish later it rarely atrophies completely—as the unfailingly high vogue of fiction of some sort even in more mundane times like the present amply proves. In point of fact the Bible has taken its place comfortably, not only in Western countries where geographical and historical conditions differ much from those of Palestine, but even in places much remoter and more different geographically and with little continuity of history with the Middle East—North America, Lapland, equatorial jungles and tropical islands of the southern seas. It is in much the same way that great literature generally travels from one land or civilization to another and becomes the inspiration of peoples in very different circumstances, and indeed the very possibility of abiding great literature presupposes our being able to recreate, in the present, certain allusions to things and conditions which have undergone drastic change or of which we have no first hand acquaintance at all. The popularity of Shakespeare was probably never so great as it is today. But this is in no way due to attempts to perform him in modern dress, however interesting that may be occasionally; least of all is it due to attempts to modernize his themes. No one needs to have shot with bows and arrows or wielded a sword to appreciate *Henry V* or have any superstition about witches to enter into the spirit of the opening scene of *Macbeth*. Familiarity with Shakespeare and an initial aptitude for the enjoyment of drama and poetry on the stage or in books will amply compensate for lack of factually correct impression of details in the Elizabethan scene or of familiarity with it. In some ways our detachment from reality in this respect may assist us to recreate the dramatic essentials all the more effectively. What matters here, as in sacred literature, is that the substance of literary situations should be reproduced and made alive in terms which our imaginations may extensively manipulate in their own way. Granted some initial understanding at the ordinary level, we can derive the imaginative literary meaning from the context. It is due appreciation of the context that matters most.

Historians of Welsh literature have often remarked upon the exceptionally extensive influence of Biblical terms and imagery on Welsh life and literature. Many simple Welsh folk, whose main, and sometimes sole, literary diet was the Bible, have often been more at home in Biblical allusions quite alien to their own environment (and more moved by them) than in terms of more familiar scenes quite near to them. Battles, until recent times, had long ceased to be a reality for them, but they had fought the Scriptural battles many times over, in simple bethels they entered into the splendour and solemnity of temple worship, they faced fiery furnaces and languished in dungeons, they wept by the waters of Babylon, often without the least notion of what they were like, they sat in the shelter of palms, they met in 'upper rooms' and entered into all the solemnity and nostalgia of Passover feasts, they travelled in ships and were wrecked; and they made their own spiritual pilgrimages in much the same terms, sustained by experiences 'as sweet as the wine' from which in actuality, notwithstanding the frequency of its appearance in their hymns, their teetotal consciences would have recoiled in horror; they spent the evening of their days traversing the plains of Moab to the river of Jordan, which had far greater significance for them than any real or imaginary stream that drained their own hills. They drew their lives together in solemn worship at the foot of a hill where an execution occurred in a form completely unfamiliar to them.

And not to them only, but almost to all who have found the idea of a cross far and away the greatest religious symbol for them. This has lost nothing of its potency because no longer a familiar instrument of terrible punishment. It is the meanings that have accrued to it in the age-long contemplation of the spiritual significance of a particular crucifixion at the culminating point of certain historical occurrences that matter and the further figurative and emotional associations of the image and the word derived from the many situations and contexts in which it has been central. How many people really think of blood when they talk or sing about 'the Blood of the Lamb'? Does the Lamb of God appear in our imaginations as a lamb at all, or the Good Shepherd as a shepherd? If it does, is that what matters for sanctified imagination rather than the infinite subtle associations of the terms accumulated in the variety of profound and moving contexts in which they have drawn together deep and moving spiritual experiences? There is, no doubt, a very grave danger in all this, the danger namely that subsidiary accumulations of meaning and emotional associations distilled into moving words or splendid and beautiful art of some other sort should take a course of their own or overlay the initial and proper symbolic significance of the image. And this is again where we need to keep the symbol to its true purport by renewing, with its aid, the context which first gave it life, the patterned events to which it was initially organic.

This was very vividly brought to mind for me in a recent incident which I may perhaps recount without undue digression. I was on a visit to Glasgow soon after the celebrated picture of Christ by Dali had been ac-

quired for the Glasgow Art Gallery. It was the special
exhibit there for the time. It had received much publicity
and there had been sharp controversy about it in the
press. Had it the artistic merit initially ascribed to it,
and was it proper to spend as lavishly as had been done
to secure the picture in this way for the public? There
is no need, even had I the competence, to enter into
this controversy, but it had all aroused my curiosity and
keenness to see the picture. In addition, as is well known,
the picture has a fascinating history. That takes us back
over many centuries to the days of St John of the Cross.
In one of his mystical states St John had a vision of
Christ on the Cross and afterwards made a sketch of
what he had seen which was happily preserved over the
years and served as the basis of Dali's masterpiece.
This link, having regard to the affinity of temperament
between the saint and the painter, notwithstanding
differences of another sort, is itself of interest to the
student of the life of images, and it certainly heightens
the expectancy of those who view the picture.

The special exhibit had been accorded a room to itself,
and when the visitor entered, it faced him impressively on
the wall opposite. There was good taste and reverence in
this arrangement, and when we do find ourselves discussing ways of extending religious symbolism into the
fullest context of modern life and making it significant
and arresting for the lay mind of today, often out of
touch with traditional religious institutions, there is
clearly something for us to ponder in this action of the
Glasgow Art Gallery. Very probably, hundreds of persons
who rarely attend a church and make no regular practice
of reading the Scriptures, and many perhaps with no
religious allegiance, viewed the Dali picture of Christ
undistracted in the quiet room that housed it. They
might catch something of the reverence of other on-
lookers and know enough about Christianity in a general
way for the picture to speak to their condition and give

them something they might take away to ponder in their hearts. It certainly spoke to me.

That is not, however, the main reason why I allude to it here. I should indeed find it hard to say just what the sight of this picture had meant to me. For it was certainly not a case of crystallizing merely abstract notions, although much recent wrestling with problems of the Christian religion would come into it. My experience was more like adding a further touch to a picture I had already or setting it in a new light. Earlier experiences and impressions, and the travail of much thinking, were drawn together and extended in the way appropriate to religious symbolism, and while I might single out certain things that had become more sharply defined for me through this experience (much more so than I had anticipated in the somewhat cautious and critical mood in which public interest and controversy had left me), no attempt to unpack the experience could do it proper justice. It meant much more than I could easily tell. But I allude to it here mainly for a sequel to it.

On leaving the museum I bought a number of postcard copies of the picture which were for sale in the building, and one of these I sent to a very aged and devout friend at home. On my return I visited my friend and fully expected that reference would be made to the replica of Dali's picture. But there was no mention of it, and at last I made bold to enquire on my own account. My friend had received the card but he was plainly reluctant to refer to it, and the truth eventually came out; he had sensed my own feeling about the picture and was loath to hurt me, but he had not cared for it at all. It made Jesus look *ugly*.

I am not sure that 'ugly' was quite the word he wanted. There are certainly more horrible realistic pictures than Dali's 'Christ'. Dali's picture is certainly realistic, and with the rugged implacable realism of art so much more effective than mere reconstruction. There is a real crucifixion in the picture, and if this were not so I doubt whether it could be a success at all. The young body draws away from the nails. But there is more than realism, and for some tastes the realism has been ruined or unduly overlaid by the more ethereal and mystical quality of the picture. To my mind, on the contrary, the impressiveness of the picture and its power is due to the inspired centring of a wealth of subtle and deep additional meaning on the realism of it. It is certainly hard to see how it could be offensive, and yet in point of fact my friend, a not wholly unsophisticated one, had found it so to the point of irreverence. It hardly conformed to the picture of Jesus which he carried about in his mind.

And is not this by now the case for many? Our impressions of the crucifixion have been so overlaid by centuries of praise and adoration, of making the 'Cross', in words or sensible design, so much a symbol of triumph and glory, that actuality and horror have gone out of it. It has been so much the centre of reverent esteem, of power and triumphant approbation, that the scandal and offence is lost. Men may be on their guard today against cheap sentimentalism of the 'gentle Jesus' variety, 'gentle' being incidentally not an inapposite word when properly used, but we may nonetheless be so idealizing the stark and severe features of our Christianity, under the influence partly of accumulations of subsidiary symbolic meaning, that rawness and horror and shame are lost at least to its symbolism. This is not of course due solely to subsidiary associations. For what the 'Cross' should mean most of all is triumph and glory, and it is not unnatural for this to become a sole preoccupation. If it stayed at the level of shame and offence it would not be a symbol for religion, least of all the Christian one. But it is not any triumph, not any glory. The scandal is inexpungeable, and the danger is, it seems to me, that accents of joy and praise and triumph should have been so distilled into the contexts in which they were sounded, and preserved there by association and symbolism which reflect more the context and matters incidental to it, that the particular quality of the triumph or joy should be muffled in the transmission of it.

There are of course other reasons for the escapism and evasion which is a besetting temptation for Christians. The moral exactions of Christianity are very severe for all who take them seriously, and there is a strenuous side to the cultivation in a rounded life of the right sort of piety, and Christian salvation has in addition its own costing character. These stresses also may induce us to divert our religious life to the more incidental and less disturbing features of it. At the moment my concern is with the encouragement these failings may have in the proneness of much of our symbolism to edge away from the centre of the course along which it is proper for it to develop. The moving words of our hymns, the places and times in which they have meant most to us, associations with home and dear personal relationships, religious artistry and literary splendour, the extension of religious joy and comfort into appropriate secular concerns, these may come to occupy the centre of the stage too much on their own account. But provided we are mindful of this peril, we may properly and helpfully appropriate much of traditional imagery, in its incidentals, into the contexts in which our own imaginations can best manipulate them. Provided the substance is retained, by keeping our symbols in healthy relation to their initial context, we may give them life *for us* in our own way, and that will normally serve us much better than trying artificially to fabricate new ones.

CHAPTER 13

ART AND RELIGION

The situation I have just been describing has its close parallel in art. The artist too must find ever new modes of expression. If he ceases to be novel his art fails him. But the newness must not be merely that of new things to say, or new material to shape. The art is in the saying and shaping too, and the essence of it lies in providing some new experience of things through symbolic presentation. But the symbols which serve the purpose here do not come out of the void, they grow out of other ones. The bid which some artists, including recent ones, have made to detach themselves, in the quest for newness, almost wholly from an artistic past is a most delusory one. Art requires always that some past be alive in the present, and this past must itself be art. It will benefit the new art if the old is so completely absorbed into it as not to be easily detected, and the old art which is in this way to nourish the new need not be the most readily identifiable or familiar sort. But no one can find artistically significant forms or expressions which do not involve manipulation of turns of phrases or kindred symbols which are already artistically expressive. The artist must skilfully exploit the old to make it new.

The artist who neglects this may yet produce an effect of some kind. He may startle or astonish or impress us by a certain virtuosity in reproducing carefully observed situations in real life. But not every effect is an artistic one. A noise may startle and a threat cause panic or fear, the reproduction of a sad situation may cause grief or pity. But there may be no difference in principle between reproduction of the latter kind and actually witnessing or experiencing events. To be overwhelmed with grief or filled with joy is not art. Else we should all be artists. The artist must illuminate in a very special way, he must present the common experience in a new light, we must see it and appreciate it as we do not normally do; and the secret of the particular illumination in question here is the subtle manipulation in new ways and new contexts of terms already initiated into these uses.

It should be remembered that not all art is that which wins public laurels and open acclamation. There is much art, although not the highest, in some common procedures, sprouting up in our ordinary exchanges to enliven and extend them—a joke or a gesture perhaps, or odd figure of speech; and one of the things, it may be, which we have not sufficiently considered in aesthetics is the interweaving of art and life in this way, and the problem where art properly begins. But subject to qualifications of this kind, and noting that there are art forms, some more overt than others, besides the cultivated and sustained ones which gifted conscious artists produce, we may regard art as the transmuting of old art into new.

This suggests an infinite regress, and the question how art could begin. But questions of origins in matters of this sort are bound to be shrouded for us in great obscurity and involve barely perceptible gradations from the rawness of the initial impetuses to other remote forms of the sophisticated procedures with which we are familiar. In any but the most initial stages, the artist requires some conventions and the creations of others within which to create; in no other way could he make an impact as artist or communicate anything, least of all of an elaborate kind, which others will be able to apprehend artistically. If an artist neglects this we are not able, in our present maturity, to know how to take him and he, in turn, deprives himself of the associations and recognized significance of certain conventions, for example, to note a simple instance, certain accepted exaggerations or distortions in mimicry to which we spontaneously respond. Tones of voice, postures and gestures come into art with a subtle licence of the same sort acquired already, however little obvious this will be in good art.

Much of the evident malaise of modern art, and its failure to create a proper public for itself, may be traced to this source. Artists feel rightly that they must break with the past and launch on new ventures if they are to flourish. They must say a new thing in a new way. If there is no novelty we have at best virtuosity and imitation, but not the startling disclosures with which art must surprise us, the newness which casts its spell and makes us gasp. But in apprehending this and being weary of mere accomplished variations on familiar modes and themes, artists have tried to break away altogether, to spring upon us creations out of the void, claiming to be complete and fully articulate on their own account without ancestry or recognizable affiliations, and the result of this is to fail to be articulate at all, as in some plays where the absence of convention leaves only banality and an audience desperately and a little snobbishly trying to persuade itself that it is not bored.

In this situation the recognition of genuine new art is exceptionally difficult, and confusion abounds, exploited by the charlatan. For creative work, in its newness, is always hard to recognize and we may do it injustice just because it is unfamiliar and calls for adaptations we have not made. But it is very much harder when artists are prone to lapse into modes of activity which are not properly art but only borrow some of its trappings, where effects are produced which only resemble art in being unusual, and where some artists, out of fear of speaking in too familiar terms, are reduced to near silence. But my concern at the moment is not with the way out of the uncertainties of the twilight world in which our culture leaves us to stumble in matters of art today. Suffice it to insist that new art must be parasitic on the old, and that we forget this much at our peril today.

It must not be supposed that, as art develops, it becomes more discernibly complicated all the time. That in some sense it is certainly complicated in its higher forms is true. But its complexities need not be in any way obtrusive or disconcerting. They are compatible with, and may be included within, great simplicity, as when some very simple structure in plastics, or forms in painting, or some almost, but not quite, trite words in poetry, may provide an effective focus for a very wide range of artistic meaning.

In substance what we find in art as in religion is that the new forms are not thrust upon us wholly unannounced in a totally unqualified newness, much less are they deliberately manufactured to meet a contemporary need; they grow out of earlier forms, not in a random way which calls for no particular tending, but with a subtlety which makes its own most exacting demands on attention. And this, in both cases, involves much besides the spontaneous generation of form out of form. For the latter activity can not proceed effectively, even if it can occur at all, apart from the novel apprehensions or experience of a further content which they mediate. A lack, in modern art, parallel to the one noted, is the absence of new insight and effective relevant new experience of the world. We are all realists in a sense, forced to be so in the exigencies of new and alarming situations thrust upon us; and yet we may view the changing scene obtusely and be stunned by its crudities and clamour, so that we do not draw our new experiences together into the perspectives which can make them artistically and religiously significant. We need, in art, to live in a certain way in the present, without evasions and undaunted; and at the same time to cherish and sustain the art of the past, not in a dilettante fashion but as a rounded way of experiencing the world by people not afraid of the impact of the world. In this way the art of the past is enabled to pierce the present and produce within it new art forms by which the world of today is illumined.

These resemblances of art and religion are not accidental. There is much affinity of substance between the two. In art as in religion there is an alertness of mind by which we become aware of features of our mental or physical environment which we should not otherwise notice. Objects and situations acquire a starkness and character which they do not normally exhibit, they are placed in new perspectives and thrust into contexts which give them new interest and significance. Ideas and things are coaxed out of their normal background and made to impress us more in this way on their own acount, while at the same time being put in suggestive juxtaposition to others. The world is viewed thus without the gloss which habit and personal interest put upon it and assessed more objectively on its own account; the worth and interest it ought properly to have for us are better displayed, and in this respect the artist, however averse to the title in some moods, is bound to be a moralist. He is not the teacher of precepts, and in the matters which fall outside his main or immediate purview his own practice may be lax, although much less so in essentials, I suspect, than is often assumed in many cases; the morality he inculcates need not be conventional, and it may not be co-ordinated. As a creator and innovator in his proper role, he may be unduly attracted to novelty in manners and morals, and not be appreciative enough of established practice and humdrum, but often indispensable, services of the normal round. But when every allowance of this sort is made—and the finer the artist the less in the main is there need for it—the artist, in the particular illumination he brings *qua* artist, presents the world in a way which exhibits better its worth and claims. In the process which engages our interests and emotions more completely, we are also enabled to view things in greater detachment from ourselves, in more arresting outline and truer perspectives.

The artist accomplishes this by various devices, exploiting the links of association, comparing and contrasting and following out partial resemblances in novel situations by simile or metaphor or unusual allusion. But when these and kindred devices, and subtle variations of these, on which the artist hits by living in the world of art, and on which he need not reflect in an abstract way—when these yield the images which give us the appropriate new impressions of things, these images generate others out of themselves and add to the available store or repertoire of the artist on which he may draw in further disclosures of reality. The immediate generation of image out of image must however be checked, as we have seen, and subdued to the process of producing the patterned imagery which continues to be revelatory of experience and the world. Images will thus expand and merge into others, not merely by their own momentum but under the impact of new experience which they help to make possible and direct.

This happens in religion also, but this *and more*. For there the merging of symbol into symbol and the patterning of imagery has a basic principle of its own which is not present in art as such. In art we need only the insights and appropriate symbolism which provide best on their own account a peculiar disclosure of what some facts or situations are like, together with the fusion and extension of the experiences in which this happens, and their sustaining symbols, into others in a way which is naturally required or inherent in this process in itself. There is mystery here and newness, but only that which is involved in coming to know our finite environment in this extraordinary way. The artistic devices are effective in themselves and combine in their own ways under the impact of fresh experience. But this is not what happens initially in religion.

In religion, as we have seen, we have a new impression of our environment due to the apprehension we acquire of the world as a created world and all that is within it as deriving from an unconditioned source quite different in nature from all finite being, complete or perfect in the most absolute way and irreducibly mysterious to us. This awareness, the shock it administers to us and the sense that all things are made new to us in consequence of it, does not depend essentially or in the first place on special techniques as in art, or require familiarity with the techniques of art, least of all in their more cultivated form. It comes about in its own way, and there is inherent in it as a rule an insistent or summoning character of its own, not derived, as in art, from the content disclosed and our interest. This is bound up with the situation in which we find ourselves, but with a sense, not wholly derived from the situation, of there being something radically irresistible in our having this experience here and now, of its being imposed even if also sought, and imposed more from outside ourselves than in the compulsions to which the artist is subject. The inherent character of this experience points also in its own way to the appropriate focusing of it and predisposes it to a certain representation. This is where art is taken up into religion and serves to give firmer form and continuity to the religious insights, just as it may also predispose us to have them by the character it gives to the antecedent situation.

The similarities of art and religious experience make it

easy to confuse them, as they also make it hard to disentangle the properly religious process from any artistic
activities, incipient perhaps or unsophisticated, which
may be included within it. This also makes it hard to
determine how far some kind of art is indispensable in
religion. The vision which the artist has is moreover
always on the point of passing over into a religious one,
for in having the individual character of things displayed
in the strangeness and mystery of their being just what
they are, in being caught up in their finality in the
impact they make in art, we are impinging closely on
the ultimate mystery of all things in the inevitability of
their having a transcendent source. The reference
'beyond' which objects have is not something around
them, or attached to them; they wear it in being what
they are. In his own exhibition of the world, to himself
and others, the artist comes thus very close to the
religious visionary or prophet, and the one role may
thus the more easily and imperceptibly pass into the
other. Through misunderstanding, as indicated earlier,
this may not always be evident to artists or to religious
persons; both may affix to themselves wrong labels. But
in point of fact art is made all the more readily available to the religious process it serves because it is always
on the point of transmuting itself into religion proper;
the associations it sets up vibrate in close harmony with
those of religion and help the transmutation of artistic
symbols into religious ones.

Kindred affinities are present in the patterning of
religious experiences. This is again determined in the
first instance by the inherent nature of those experiences
and the occasions on which they occur; they are merged
into one another and are renewed and extended and
take on their own account some significant course determined by the transcendental reference at the centre.
This is quite different from the spontaneous interweaving of artistic images at their own level. The controlling

factor, the drive or impulse, is different in the two cases, and the meaning we cull from a religious course of events is an expressly religious one. But art may not only help to focus individual items of this, it also brings its own momentum and the confluence of its terms to help in exhibiting and sustaining the inherent patterns of the religious occurrences; and here again the affinities of art and religion are important, for they help to keep the former subservient to the latter and ensure its more effective absorption into the inherent dialectic of the religious process itself.

There are then these close affinities of art and religion, and art in the service of religion, most of all at the level of shaping the creative religious images, has been of extreme importance and contributed extensively to religion out of what it is in itself; it has merged into the religious process, but it has not dominated it. The danger is indeed always present, as stressed, that the artistic imagery should pull religion out of its proper course into other paths, or become an end in itself in religion and corrupt the whole. But one of the marks of great prophecy, and of the religious life which is closest to it, is its avoidance of this danger and the triumphant absorbing of creative artistic activity into its own processes. Religion has in turn provided a corrective to the proneness of art to lapse from its own course.

These are matters which seem to have been much overlooked by Dr Austin Farrer in the discussion of religious images to which I have already referred. In one chapter Dr Farrer considers expressly the relation of poetry to prophecy. He urges, very properly, that what the poet 'says is said in the poem' and 'cannot be put into other words',[1] that it is a mistake to suppose 'that the symbolical sense can be *stated*, in a number of sentences other than those of the poem itself'.[2] But Dr Farrer seems to have failed altogether to appreciate

[1] *The Glass of Vision*, p. 127.   [2] *Op. cit.*, p. 120.

the reason for this. He distinguishes sharply between 'great or serious poetry' and other poetry. The latter would include 'simple love-ditties, or simple dirges, or drinking songs'.[3] It is 'a free play of the mind, a delight : and if some people have taken it in deadly earnest, what of it? Some people have taken football in earnest, and some people never grow up'.[4] 'Language, being repetitive noise, is capable of musical arrangement',[5] and it is possible for the 'musical game' to become 'the expression of the imaginative game. Such a joint form of game may not seem any more inevitable than other mixed forms, say opera or polo. And even granting that men will mount upon the crests of verbal rhythms to play at imaginative creation, it is, again, in no way inevitable that anything serious should come of it'.[6]

This is more elusive than one would like. Just what view of 'musical arrangement', for example, is entertained here? The suggestion seems to be that it is a game to be classed with polo or football, and this suggestion is itself not easy to assess. We must not dismiss it too light-heartedly. For originally art would have a great deal in common with play or mimic conflict and could not perhaps be easily separated from it. But, then, that would in turn be due to the fact that play was originally much more than play as we know it, especially in the highly organized forms of polo or football. Art and play would be much fused at the start, and both would be largely part of other activities. Poetry as play is in short a very special sort of play. Dr Farrer seems to imply this when he talks of 'imaginative creation', but he also leaves us wondering when he assimilates poetry to any 'joint form of game' and classes opera with polo.

The upshot is at least that Dr Farrer is convinced that no light can be thrown on the nature of the poetry

[3] *Op. cit.*, p. 117.   [4] *Op. cit.*, p. 114.   [5] *Op. cit.*, p. 114.
[6] *Op. cit.*, p. 115.

which is of most worth or interest to us by considering the proneness of men to spin verse light-heartedly, to write simple love-ditties or semi-doggerel like 'Sing a Song of Sixpence'—to take Dr Farrer's own example. For it seems that these, whatever they involve, have little in common with great or serious poetry and may be dismissed when we consider the relations of poetry and prophecy.

This seems to me most mistaken. The approach of Mr Day Lewis is sounder when he regards 'O Waly Waly up the Bank' or some similar nonsense rhyme as not without relevance to what poetry is in itself at all levels. We may of course properly, and with good precedent, speak of great poetry, although 'serious' is not quite a word one would care for here—it has associations which make it inappropriate and it tends to suggest that other poetry is bogus. How we should define great poetry is another question. Presumably range and richness would count a great deal, but it would be wrong to suppose that only the more obviously elaborate or complex poetry could qualify. For some very simple terms may hold a whole world of meaning in art. I suspect that Dr Farrer tends to overlook this in some of his allusions to 'simple' poetry. But where he seems more obviously mistaken is in the sharpness of the distinction he draws between the 'serious' poetry which merits attention and poetry which is mere play and of no account. For the demarcations are fluid and uncertain here, and there are niceties of distinction which we need to handle very circumspectly. We may find that the 'sort of thing which has been going on since men and blackbirds first began to sing'[7] is not without place in our enjoyment of great poetry.

These faults become plainer when we note how Dr Farrer himself defines 'serious' poetry. He declares : 'What the poem presents to us is simply two things—

[7] *Op. cit.*, p. 115.

first, the literal and obvious sense, whatever that may be, and second, whatever echoes of human nature or destiny or the like the poetry does in fact evoke'.[8] Now it is certainly right to distinguish between the 'literal' meaning of a poem and its full poetic meaning, although the former has its place in the poem as art. But we draw this distinction just because the poem has something distinctive to say in its own way and is thus particular in a fashion which makes it implausible to speak here of 'echoes of human nature or destiny'. This, however, occasions Dr Farrer no misgiving. He goes boldly on his course and writes of the poet :

'Consciously, perhaps, he is only setting images in motion by rhythmical incantation, and then appreciating a certain way in which they "ought" to develop and to express themselves. It is this "ought" which is the heart of the riddle. The poet does not know what sort of an "ought" it is, except that it is the "ought" with which his craft is concerned, and that he is able to feel and acknowledge it. But what the poet assumes, the philosopher investigates. We need not here, perhaps, take the investigation very far. It may be enough to say that since, by our hypothesis, the poet is going to produce a symbol powerfully expressive of a deep quality in human existence, what he must feel in the "ought" is the quality of human existence clamouring for expression and, as it were, pressing upon his mind and directing the manipulation of the poetical symbols. The poet's imagination is responsive to the possibilities of destiny in general as well as to the particular possibility realized in Hamlet.'[9]

What matters for the poet is to be 'responsive to qualities or patterns of human existence'.[10] 'Qualities and possibilities of human existence, vaguely felt or anticipated in many parts of our minds, find expression

[8] *Op. cit.*, p. 120.   [9] *Op. cit.*, p. 122.
[10] *Op. cit.*, p. 122.

in the poem.'[11] Great poetry 'is supposed to express the texture of human existence, or the predicament of man'.[12] 'It is a sort of focus into which is drawn together much that seems to us most important in the common essence of our human existence.'[13] It is such 'essences' which constitute 'the subject of poetry'.[14]

In terms of this a sharp distinction is again drawn between the 'novelists, elaborating the simply particular' and the 'poets, expressing a common essence extending through multiple experience'.[15] In classical culture, we are told, 'the poets cease to write about the gods as real persons who govern or intervene, and must be served and propitiated : they become names for the aspects of human destiny. Aphrodite is no longer anything but the passion of love itself. But in so far as this passion is still personified and divinized, a common essence is felt to be expressed in all loving'.[16] 'Keats wrote an ode to the god Autumnus, not a description of an autumn day; the personification holds together the various autumnal features in a single essence which, without the personification, would fall to pieces.'[17] It is doubtful whether 'the poets have now got any essences to write, about, and whether, in the lack of them, they will be driven either into prose, nursery rhymes, or true religion'.[18]

I have quoted at some length, for Dr Farrer seems to go off the rails here in a way that should be a warning to us all. The differences between novelists and poets may be many and sharp, but they are certainly not the kind suggested here, and we must not forget that fiction is no less genuine art because it is prose and not poetry. Narrative poems would obviously have much in common with novels, and it seems very strained to suggest that they nonetheless have the radical difference that one

[11] *Op. cit.*, p. 127. [12] *Op. cit.*, p. 117. [13] *Op. cit.*, p. 119.
[14] *Op. cit.*, p. 118. [15] *Op. cit.*, p. 118. [16] *Op. cit.*, p. 118.
[17] *Op. cit.*, p. 118. [18] *Op. cit.*, p. 118.

deals with essences while the other elaborates particulars. Whether classical culture took the course suggested seems to me also very doubtful, but if it did we should have to say then—so much the worse for it. Keats may not be describing an autumn day, but whatever he was doing, it seems certain that he did not triumph by trafficking in essences, and it is quite incidental, in my view, to Shelley's poetic achievement that Dr Farrer can quote him as referring to 'the spirit of this, and the spirit of that'.[19]

'Elaborating the particular' is a phrase of which Dr Farrer might have made a great deal more, and it applies to the poet, or any other artist, so it seems to me, quite as much as to the novelist. The particular need not exist in the world of actualities; it plainly does not in fiction. But the poet nonetheless goes straying down some particular way which his images illumine for him, and he makes possible for us a novel experience. This is not detached from other experience. We can hardly enjoy Keats's poem without some impressions— at least at second hand—of autumn in these lands, but these issue in a very special experience in reading the poem or calling it to mind, an experience we should be very bold to attempt to analyse; for what is distinctive of it may easily elude us. It is like, but not quite like, enjoying a real autumn day; and its being not 'quite like' is not mainly due to the personified God in the background, it is due to the poetry. The poetry takes us into its own world or transforms the present world, but it is certainly not a world of qualities and essences, but of things very real to us in their way.

If it were the alleged essences that mattered in poetry it is not very evident that poetry would be the best way of getting at them. Philosophical analyses might serve us better. Dr Farrer assures us that we must grasp the essences 'in a richer and more confused way'.[20] But there

[19] *Op. cit.*, p. 118.   [20] *Op. cit.*, p. 121.

is surely no merit in confusion in itself. And is the artist really confused? Is there confusion in the 'Ode to Autumn'? It might well be truer to say that the poet is the least confused person, that he sees things with particular clarity, although he has to see and present them in a very special way.

This links the topic again with revelation and prophecy. What Dr Farrer says directly about prophecy here seems on quite the right lines. The case of the prophet, we are told, is not at all like that of the poet. For what the prophet 'has got to say is determinate and particular, it is what the Lord God declares and requires on the day on which He speaks. It is designed to evoke not an exquisite and contemplative realization of human existence, but particular practical responses to God'.[21] Dr Farrer will interpret this further in his own way in which the authority vested in images as such will be paramount. But on the main issue I am quite at one with him here, giving centrality, as I do, to the illumination obtained on particular occasions and peculiarly pertinent to them. The prophet is alight and aflame with this, much though that may be due to the burning within him of earlier fires. He is also apt to express himself in poetry or its like. This also Dr Farrer stresses, noting the closeness in practice of the relation of poetry to prophecy—'poetry, for the prophet, is a technique of divination, in the poetic process he gets his message'.[22] But it is not easy to see how this comes about if it is also the case that 'the whole nature and purpose of the two utterances go widely apart'.[23] Admittedly religion has its own course and drive, and it is much more than poetry, but if poetry were so alien to it in nature as the contrast drawn by Dr Farrer suggests, it is not easy to see how they could combine to such good effect. Dr Farrer declares that the poet is a 'maker' while the

[21] *Op. cit.*, p. 128. [22] *Op. cit.*, p. 128. [23] *Op. cit.*, p. 129.

prophet is a 'mouthpiece'.[24] The contrast is not, I feel, helpful and the terms of it not peculiarly happy. The poet is certainly more than maker, as the terms we often apply to him show—he is a seer and visionary too. And if the prophet is a mouthpiece, he is not a mechanical one, he does not 'move images' under a blind control, but through apprehensions he himself acquires as a whole person, his own character and personality having a significant part to play. But if, as against Dr Farrer, we hold that there are close affinities between poetry and religion, that both have to do with the particular and its symbolic presentation, we can understand more readily how religion could merge itself in poetry and other art forms or absorb so completely into itself the natural creative processes on which it supervenes.

[24] *Op. cit.*, p. 129.

CHAPTER 14

RELIGION AND THE PRETERNATURAL

Not very far removed from the function of art in religion is that of certain extraordinary or preternatural experiences which men appear to have. Some people, including sophisticated writers on religion, ascribe great importance to these. Indeed the mention of religious experience suggests to some persons at once situations or occurrences which fall altogether outside the range of normal human experience. In one regard this is quite sound. I have been at pains already to oppose the attempts which are sometimes made to account for religion entirely in human terms. There must be a reference 'beyond', the object of religious experience is God, a transcendent being. At the same time we come to know God from within our situation as finite beings, and the occurrences by which this normally happens are those which ordinarily constitute the lot of human beings in this life, some of course being much more important of their kind and crucial for us than others. For many people, probably for most of us, religion never involves more than this.

There is nothing to be especially regretted here. Religion is not markedly impoverished if it fails to provide us with experiences which are, in respect of their initial or natural content, in some way more elevated than those we normally enjoy. That is not its main business, but to disclose to us the character of God, and His mind towards us. For this there is ample scope in conditions of life as we normally find them, as love can be as genuine and deep between the simple-minded as between the wisest. Thus it has happened that the simple-minded, when sensitive to the course of God's dealings with men, have achieved as much, and sometimes more, in the way of genuine spirituality and devoutness as the wise. They are in some regards less self-centred than the wise, who have to resist the tendency to be preoccupied with their own achievements. 'Weak things and things that are despised hath God called.' And for the same reasons the genuineness and the depth of our religious lives and insights are not to be measured directly in terms of any powers to surmount the conditions of human existence as we normally find them. It is the transmutation of the latter and the shaping of them into the significant patterns of a divine intervention in the world that matter.

Some parallel may be found here with morality. The strength of temptations and the worth of moral endeavour to surmount them do not vary with the outward splendour of our achievement or the material scope of our responsibilities. Morality is the same in a cottage as in a palace, in the duties of the artisan as in those of the minister of state. The difference between these two in other regards is not for that reason trivial, the burden the minister of state must bear is obviously in one sense much weightier than those of ordinary citizens, and there is much which he must heed and undergo for that reason which is peculiar to his lot. But duty is no different for him than for others. Likewise, the core or substance of religion is no different in some extraordinary triumphs to which it may lead from what it is in the religious life which shapes itself in normal human conditions, such as those in which religion is usually found.

The objection may be made here that the religion which appears in the ordinary round of human activities is not strictly religion at all, it is the mere habitual observance of certain practices and the adoption of attitudes and beliefs in a derivative way without any infusion of genuine religious insight. That this *may* happen, and that it is a situation fraught with the gravest perils against which we should always be on our guard, has already been stressed. It has been a major theme of this book. On the other hand it does not by any means follow that the alternative is the sort of experience which disrupts the basic conditions of present existence altogether. Religious experience may certainly be disruptive, and in the case of conversion from a non-religious state cannot fail to be so. It puts all things in a new perspective and it brings an enrichment of life and deepening of responsibilities in all respects. But falling in love may do something like this also, and in neither case is the preternatural normally involved. The disturbing character of religion comes from the reference to the transcendent and its manifestation of itself in an astonishing intimacy with us in the here and now of things as we usually find them. There is all the world of difference between being religiously alive and religiously sluggish or dead, but it does not turn essentially on our surmounting the normal limitations of our existence.

These are the matters which give some plausibility to the humanist account of religion and help to explain the attractiveness for some persons of a position so patently absurd. Such persons feel themselves effectively within the stream of our religious life, but are not aware of any experience which, in its material content, lifts them obviously to a supernatural sphere. They have known nothing of a preternatural character, and thus, reinforced as they are today by a militant empiricist philosophy, they attempt the desperate task of describing their religion exhaustively in humanist terms. Others who might well feel the force of religion and appreciate its claims are repelled or made unsympathetic because they assume that religion must involve peculiar states or powers which they do not detect at all in themselves. They affirm that they have no religious experiences, and while prepared, in some instances, to allow that others may be differently placed in that regard, they confess themselves wholly unable to make anything of the claims put forward in the name of religion by others. In this they may be correct. On the other hand it may also be that they have the wrong expectations and predispositions and that, if they knew better where and how to look for religious experience, they would find or acquire it.

The suggestion has sometimes been made that all our experience involves subtle elements of a paranormal kind, unrecognized telepathy for example between man and wife. But this cannot affect our present contention, for whether such factors are in truth commoner than we had assumed, or more pervasive, does not affect my present main submission that it is in the round of human experience as it normally occurs, in the ups and downs of life, in moral struggle and failure, in art and intellectual pursuits, in personal and social relationships, in all that normally makes up human life and history, that religious experience usually forms itself and takes a course of its own. A devout person of profound religious insight need not have had any preternatural experience.

Nevertheless such experiences are possible and they have from time to time had much prominence in religion. Before we comment further on them, and try to assess their importance, it may be well to distinguish two forms of such experiences between which the line is not usually drawn as clearly as it should be.

There are, in the first place, experiences which are causally paranormal or which come about in some paranormal way without deviating, in any other respect, from the normal, for example the usual forms of precognition. If I have precognition of the card the experimenter is about to turn up, the content of which I become aware is, in this case, quite simple, indeed trivial. Those who arrange the cards or turn them up also know it, and so may anyone who cares to look or ask. There is nothing unusual in my knowledge other than the way I come by it, although that does not make the phenomenon less astonishing or suggestive to the student of mental processes. Likewise if I learn by telepathy and clairvoyance that an acquaintance is drowning hundreds of miles away. Others may know this, for example by being in the vicinity, and I might have known it in a perfectly normal way myself if I had known that my friend was engaged on a perilous undertaking and had arranged to have an account of it radioed to me. There is nothing strictly out of the run of ordinary experience in knowing that a man is drowning, but only in knowing this independently of normal observation and means of communication. If, again, someone had reliable premonitions of earthquakes, his knowledge might be of momentous importance in saving life and property, but it is the kind of knowledge we might all acquire after the event or which a sufficiently clever seismographist might acquire in due course in a strictly scientific manner. Its being paranormal lies in the dispensability of ordinary data, although that in itself would be quite extraordinary.

We have substantially the same situation in regard to certain extraordinary powers men may display in the control of their own bodies or of other physical objects. There are reports of Tibetan monks who are able to put themselves into some sort of trance and travel considerable distances rapidly and without rest by means of elaborate hops. This certainly goes well beyond anything which human beings normally attain, and yet it is substantially comprehensible to us on the basis of natural performances. We can all hop and move about in space, or be moved, in some fashion. The performance of the monks can be described in simple terms to anyone familiar with human life at all. It is peculiar only in being out of accord with the usual determination of physical processes and the control of mind over body. The how of it may baffle us but not the what.

This would be equally true if some persons had powers, as it is indeed claimed they have, which depart much more sharply from those we now enjoy, if, for example, we could effect considerable changes at a distance, or make ourselves invisible and materialize at will elsewhere, or immediately read one another's thoughts. These powers, whether acquired by systematically wresting more of her secrets out of 'nature', that is by science, or in some more random or relatively accidental way and thus less understood, would still be some kind of extension or variation of powers which do not go beyond the orbit of the kind of experience of the world which we all have. They are extraordinary, but they are intelligible to us on the basis of what we all find the world to be like and what anyone can do. I have never witnessed levitation, and find it astonishing that it should occur. But I have no difficulty in understanding what it means.

The claim is sometimes made, however, that men may have experiences which are not describable at all in terms of the experiences we normally have. They are not special dispositions of the sort of things we all of us find in the world, but altogether different. In illustration of this let us suppose that the majority of men were blind, or at least colour-blind, but that a few had acquired powers of vision of the sort we now enjoy. Then the few could give no proper indication to the many of the sort of experience they were having. They could of course describe it obliquely, or, as Evelyn Underhill put it in a related context, 'slantwise'. They might find analogies in the powers of touch they have, and speak of variations of colour in terms of the smoothness or roughness of surfaces, they could speak of the delight they have in certain colours or of the general pleasure of vision or of the aesthetic character of other sights, provided, in the latter case, that the more limited experiences of others allowed of some aesthetic quality. If vision were co-ordinated as now with other sensations, much could also be made of that to report on the new experience, and in this way some intelligent discourse might be possible about sight between those who had it and those who did not, and the latter might discuss it among themselves. But the essential thing would still elude the sightless many and they could only take on trust the report of the privileged few, having much heed naturally to the general reliability of their witnesses, the consistency of the reports of witnesses and their behaviour in matters presumed to be affected by the peculiar new experience.

There appear in fact to be situations similar to this in respect of their contrast with the sort of experiences which mankind generally enjoys. It seems that some persons have been privileged to exceed the sort of limitations and conditions of existence to which most men are confined. But they can naturally tell us very little about this, since they must attempt to describe it for us in terms of the experiences we already have or negatively by contrast with those. They can speak of exquisite delight or transports of joy, of wonder and novelty, of clarity and the dispelling of mysteries, of freedom and unimpeded activity, or of the superseding of activity, of the shedding of gross physical limitations and the discarding of present concerns—or many of them—of purity, and rest and light, and so forth. For we can make something of all this. We may be persuaded that these novel experiences should be cultivated, but of what they are like in themselves we can have no conception until we achieve them. We cannot cash the analogies and general terms of commendation, and we have to decide on purely circumstantial evidence, such as the importance we ascribe to the credibility and character of the witnesses, whether they are totally deluding themselves, or perhaps having experiences sharply, but not quite radically, different from the normal, or imposing on us.

The view which it seems to me reasonable for those who have never had the experiences in question—and that covers most of us—to adopt is this. In the first place, there are no doubt many bogus or fraudulent claims in this field as in others where the impostor has usually much to gain. Some of these will be easily detected, but others may not be easily winnowed from the claims which are sincerely advanced. Of the latter, however, many will be misconceived. They will concern occurrences sharply at variance, indeed, with normal events but not altogether different in substance from matters familiar to men in the ordinary course of life as we find it. We shall, in fact, have varieties here, some more odd and extreme than others, of the first kind of supernormal experience I noted. But some of these will be exceptionally hard to describe, and in trying to cope with the strangeness of his experience, and the contrast with normal states, the witness may have recourse to terms more suggestive of the second and more absolute kind of supernormal experience, most of all if the distinction between the two is rarely drawn or heeded, as usually happens. It is thus not easy to know from the description just what is the status of the phenomena in question and the claims made about them.

Suppose, for example, that dreams were extremely rare or rarely remembered when we awoke. Then any one who had a dream and recalled it might well be led by the strangeness of his experience to describe it in terms which took little account of the many features which are common to dreams and waking consciousness. The stuff of dreams is normally much the same as the stuff of other experiences. Various entities, including

ourselves, behave oddly and wildly, but what we observe
and do is similar in substance to the things we encounter
when awake, and we find no difficulty in roughly describing a dream if we remember it. I may dream that I was
chased by a many-headed beast and that I defeated it by
changing myself into an enormous giant able to crush
the beast in the palm of its hand. This would be a very
extraordinary dream, and, for other reasons not relevant
here, not very probable, I should imagine. But we can
compound in imagination a many-headed beast out of
the impressions we have of the animals or other objects
we normally see and we need only to know what our
bodies are like to think of their being vastly enlarged.
On the other hand, if I had this or some kindred dream,
involving things and persons as they truly are or in
distorted forms, and had this quite by surprise on some
one occasion only, I might well say that things had been
happening to me in this extraordinary state altogether
different from ordinary occurrences, that I had been
carried right out of the present world and seen things
impossible to tell or comprehend. In one sense this would
be proper, for we cannot, by ordinary standards and
expectations, comprehend how a body could have one
head one second and another the next. Hence the ambi-
guity. We might suggest that we were dealing with
things altogether incomprehensible in terms of our
present normal experiences.

The case of dreams is suggestive for us in another way.
For an obvious and major difficulty about reporting and
understanding dreams is that they fade. What seemed so
clear and easy to remember one moment is gone the
next, and we are left in this way to fumble much
more than we otherwise might for the right description.
We are often reduced to generalities. If it is a nightmare
we have had, all we can do perhaps is to speak of our
insane terror or recall something of the atmosphere of
the dream, and that probably in terms which we know

will convey little to others of what we actually felt. If the dream was enjoyable we may speak of the entrancing experience we have had, and it is quite likely that we have extremes of terror or delight in dreams which few could otherwise have. The detachment of the dream from the normal continuity of experience, the relaxing of control, together with physiological conditions, will give a special quality or flavour to the experiences we have in it; and when we come to describe the dream, already rapidly fading and normal emotional states reaffirming themselves, we may well be reduced to the vaguest terms and allusions when we should not be nearly so baffled if we could report the dream as we had it. May it not be that persons who enter into various preternatural states are likewise at a loss, and apt to be misleading, in reporting their experience, when they need not make quite such a mystery of it if the return to normality allowed them to retain a clearer impression of what it had been like?

It is at any rate much to be expected that the terms which have one meaning in one such context should be made to fill a somewhat different role in another. An experience which is beyond normal comprehension in a fairly partial sense, or owing to incidental reasons, may be spoken of as if it were mysterious and incomprehensible in a much more complete or absolute way. This makes it hard to assess some of the claims that are made about preternatural occurrences and to appreciate what may have actually happened. A witness impressed and overwhelmed by what has occurred to him is apt to use extravagant terms, and, since his imagination will have been inflamed, to have recourse also to colourful language. In being emphatic he will be reluctant to modify or qualify his claims, and his mood will not usually be that of the detached investigator or the philosopher drawing careful distinctions.

For these reasons I think we should view with caution

any claims that are made to have had experiences which are paranormal, not only in the causal sense, but in being in some very radical way different in character from ordinary experience, the second kind of preternatural experience I noted. At the same time we must not allow caution to degenerate into dogmatic incredulity. There is nothing inherently impossible in some persons having experiences at least as different from those we now enjoy as are those of people with sight from the experience of the blind. We cannot conceive what such experiences would be like, except in the incidentals which we can understand, such as their being pleasant or unpleasant, caused in certain ways and so forth. But if persons outstandingly honest and reliable in other regards persistently claim to have had such experiences, we must at the very least retain an open mind about it, and I am prepared to go further and allow that it is likely, in view of all that has been claimed in this regard down the ages, often by persons whose credentials are in other respects of the highest and whose unusual personalities and attainments might well be thought to qualify them for a singular role, that there must be well-founded claims to the more absolute sort of preternatural experience in question. Very few nowadays doubt that the less extreme forms of paranormal or psychic experiences occur, notwithstanding much fraud and superstition to which these have given rise, and this should tend in turn to soften further the scepticism which has already been shown in one respect to have been unduly dogmatic.

It does not follow that we should accept all that is said about the extremer forms of supernormal experience as it stands. We may accept the reports as being substantially sound while finding much to query in detail or semi-detail. The claim is sometimes made, for example, that a person has been 'out of time' or in some peculiar temporal order. The truth in such cases may be that the sequence of events has been peculiar and the sense of the passage of time exceptional; and we are all familiar with the latter case, time may 'fly' or be 'long-drawn' or 'stand still' for most of us, according as we are going like 'a thief to the gallows' or awaiting a verdict or listening entranced to a concert. The situation would no doubt be more complicated than this in preternatural states, and some of the circumstances in which the temporal sequence seems to have been disrupted or superseded take a great deal of explaining if the facts are well attested. Precognition and the equivalent paranormal cognition of the past do not of course in themselves imply any disruption of the temporal sequence as such; other explanations are possible, but if someone, under the influence of drugs, is able at the time to record his own performances in a sequence other than the one they have taken, this is certainly upsetting for our ordinary notions of time. But I imagine it is not impossible to bring the harder cases under some explanation which leaves the temporal sequence of things as such unaffected. Many things that have been said in this connection have in any case been confused, and theories of time have been rather too lightly left to proliferate, not least by philosophers. All this should induce us to be cautious in assessing claims that have to do with time or being 'out' of time. But it does not seem to follow, from any understanding we now have of this exceptionally difficult subject, that it is inherently impossible for a being normally subject to the temporal order to cease to be so, and here again we must not be dogmatic on the basis of what is incomprehensible *to us*. I would merely add that the absolute character of time seems to me so fundamental and irreducible a feature of finite experience as such that I remain proportionally sceptical of the likelihood or possibility of its being in suspense for ourselves or any other finite beings. All the same, the claims which are made to the contrary need not be entirely bogus, much less fraudulent. *Something* beyond our normal comprehension may be happening, and almost certainly does so in some cases, whether 'in' or 'out' of time.

A further question which arises here is whether there is some limit to the transformation of our normal environment which we can stand. Presumably a very drastic change would involve a shock which might impair our equilibrium or derange our mental system altogether. Our normal existence and consciousness of ourselves and other persons involves some stability of our environment, and one wonders whether even the temporary suspension of this, if sufficiently extensive or sharp, might not be unendurable in some way or prevent the subsequent adjustment to normal conditions. The danger, we should again suppose, would be aggravated if there were involved extremes of horror, on the one hand, or of splendour and glory on the other. There are special reasons why we cannot conceive it possible literally to know God as He is : we should need to surpass all the bounds of finitude to do so, to be ourselves the one absolute God. But may it not also be the case, without involving the contradiction of the many created beings becoming the one creator, that there are extremes of attainment, or of degradation or of diminution of being, beyond which we could not go without violence to the sort of finite status we have? Believers in doctrines of transmigration have not, I think, sufficiently considered this and do not seem to have been much daunted by it, having in any case, as a rule, notions of self-identity fairly accommodating to their view. But it is highly questionable, however delightfully our imagination may play with the possibilities and change a 'Lady into Fox', whether identity could be preserved in metamorphoses of human beings into beasts. May not this hold at upper levels of the scale also? Would I be myself if I became an archangel? Against this we have the considerable changes we do in fact undergo, notwithstanding their bewildering character to anyone who ponders them, in our progress from infancy to maturity. The latter is, however, gradual and consistent of its kind, and involves nothing, even in the so-called second childhood of senility, like a strict reversal; the changes which come to us with the years are not sudden or intermittent. We find closer parallels to preternatural states in dreams, delirium, or insanity, and it certainly is remarkable how complete and undisturbed the resumption of normal states can be in these instances. The mind has probably defence mechanisms, like forgetfulness or the suspension of some processes when others are intensified, which help the alternation of one condition with others, and it may be that, if we but knew it, we are only faintly screened from variations and complexities of experience which we do not in fact enjoy.

All this is highly speculative, and now that we are acquiring new techniques for the investigation of paranormal phenomena of various kinds, the topic presents a very stimulating challenge to the philosopher. But for the present all I wish to note is the likelihood that the natures we do have set some limits to the novel modes of experience or existence which are possible for us. This may be relevant to religion in many ways, notably to discussions of immortality. I suspect that our notions of the latter are often much more imprecise and unenterprising than they need be, and that it would much advance the subject and give it more interest and worth if we approached it more boldly on the basis of such anticipations of future states as we can most plausibly form, notwithstanding that Christian resurrection means more than survival. But this is by the way, as the subject of immortality does not come within the scope of this book. For the present it is enough to note the likelihood of the limitations just envisaged and their bearing on the general question of preternatural experience.

Closely related to the last point, and very vital to the relevance the present topic has for us, is the fact that the incomprehensible character for us of the experiences which are of a sort radically different from any we have enjoyed is not in the same class at all as the incomprehensibility of God as absolute or unconditioned being. There is nothing in principle to preclude our having experiences vastly different from our present ones or undergoing drastic change or development, but we can never be God, or fathom the ultimate mystery of His being. This limitation is not a peculiarity of our present existence only, but of all finite existence. Notwithstanding that the glory of God may shine for us with a radiance, of which we have but a faint notion now, when, in some future state, we have shuffled off our mortal coils, and that with this and similar contrasts in mind we may expect then to see 'face to face' and live in the continual presence of God, yet in one sense, and that the most fundamental, the Face of God will always be veiled and His glory more than we can bear. This is ultimate and absolute and not relative to the sort of finite nature we or any others actually have.

In consequence, the description which mystics have often given of the extraordinary states they have entered is in one regard very misleading. We may not doubt that they have broken the bonds of our finitude as we know them and seen the glory of God in ways far surpassing our own. But, whatever concessions we make on this score, we cannot allow that the mystical union with God, in a Christian or in any other form, is complete in the sense of dispensing with mediation of any sort from within our own experience. No one, saint and mystic or any other, can ever be literally at one with God and have all veils torn apart, however perfect or final the union may be in all other regards. It is not surprising that the experience of the mystic should have been described in confusing and misleading terms, or that he should misunderstand it himself. For the contrasts he has to cope with are overwhelming, and the language designed for more limited purposes inadequate. But, for that reason, we must insist all the more firmly that, from the nature of the case and quite independently of what our own attainments might have been or lack, completely unqualified union of any being with God is impossible.

This would, I think, be admitted by most Western mystics, and that reflects the better appreciation of the Creator-creature relation of God to man which we owe mainly to the Hebrew-Christian tradition. General religious thought and practice, especially again in the West, seems with us here. For in referring to superhuman beings, like seraphs and archangels, they speak even more pointedly of their veiling themselves from the glory they cannot otherwise bear; and this is doubly suggestive, for may it not be that the closer we come to God, and the more we are metamorphosed to know Him more fully, the more we may need in other ways to be veiled from Him?

A further consideration converges here on the central issue. It is that the sort of paranormal phenomena of which we hear most from psychologists today, those which wall into the first main division we made, do not seem to have an inherent or outstanding religious character. They naturally interest religious people if they involve some communication with the dead or bear in some other way on the question of survival. But the facts, as they appear hitherto, do not suggest that psychic power is a peculiarity of exceptionally religious people, much less that these have a monopoly of it. Little seems to be known of the reasons why certain persons should be endowed with paranormal gifts. Mediums just come to be discovered in the display of their powers, they are not found merely among special types of people. I suppose some day it may be possible to improve on this and anticipate the exercise of mediumistic gifts, but there is little to encourage the expectation hitherto or to suggest that at any time a medium could be independently spotted more easily than, say, a poet or a mathematician. Precognitive powers of some sort, the ability to score in the card-guessing game for example, seem to go with the most humdrum attainments in other respects. And if it transpired that the exercise of paranormal powers in general called for no special intellectual attainment or gifts of a kindred sort, and did not involve any unsual qualities of character, there would seem to be little warrant, solely on account of the unusual nature of such powers, to assimilate them expressly to religion.

This subject is admittedly still in its infancy, we know the bare facts and little else, we know little how to explain them and co-ordinate them with others; such theories as we advance are very general and tentative, but it seems perfectly fair to say from the start that a mere extension of our powers, however considerable, is not in itself religious. To know things by telepathy or clairvoyance is no more religious in itself than to know by observation. If we had more clairvoyant power, the sort of things we discovered thereby would still be further finite phenomena, and there would be nothing in the mode of discovery other than a gift which, as finite beings, we found we had. It would not be materially different in this regard from sight or reason; and in addition the evidence hitherto available makes it almost certain that paranormal powers may be exercised without any specifically religious repercussions or conditions.

Indeed, the case is not unlike other advances we make, for example in science. The mastery we have over nature, in driving things by electric or atomic power, rather than by dragging them along or training animals to do so, does not in itself exhibit to us anything of a peculiarly religious character. It creates a novel situation for religion, boding good in some ways and ill in others. But that is quite another matter. Are 'the miracles of science', as we understandably if rather misleadingly call them, very much more astonishing ultimately than our ability to walk or swim? In one sense they are, as involving a greater intellectual feat. But what we discover in science, even at highly elaborate levels, are the relations of some finite facts to others. This is not as such religious, and one can be a brilliant scientist without being religious. If the powers which science confers could be exercised without special intellectual triumph, as in the case of our natural aptitudes (we learn to walk without knowing physiology), if we were so made that we could, for example, move about at tremendous speeds or move and live much further from the earth than hitherto, there is no obvious reason why that in itself should bring us closer to God. Birds and insects, and most other animals, surpass us in some ways already. The range of our aptitudes as such, least of all when not involving special insight and knowledge, has little to do with religion.

If therefore there are people who exercise powers very different from those we have normally, levitation, precognition, clairvoyance, telepathy and so forth, even when these involve certain disciplines and techniques, nothing of a peculiarly religious character is attained, and there need not be anything obviously and invariably predisposing us to religion in them.

But if this holds of the more tractable sort of paranormal phenomena which we are best able to study at present, those which involve unusual ways of attaining things which we might, in principle, attain in line with our usual performance, is there any reason why the case should be substantially different in respect of powers or experiences which men, or other beings, may have which are more radically at variance with our normal lot? If such experiences are *merely* different the answer seems plainly, no. But even if our powers were vastly enhanced and much richer modes of experience made possible and our understanding much extended, that in itself would not give us anything expressly religious, and there may be other conditions appertaining to these attainments which hinder or inhibit religion. Our powers might, for example, be exercised so smoothly and our lot be so unvaried as not to prompt the peculiar sort of reflection by which religion begins nor to provoke the toil and uncertainties through which it develops and is deepened.

This would hold also of some occasional incursions into other modes of being or experience. To have some present limitation, a temporal one for example, rent away or to penetrate realms, as it were, entirely unknown to us normally, to have sight where we were formerly blind, again need not involve any special vision of God. It may be dazzling but it need not be expressly divine glory. The language in which we might attempt to describe it may assimilate itself to religion, but perhaps because no other language is available. We must thus be cautious in considering the properly religious character or worth of alleged preternatural or occult experiences. For merely rending the veils of our present existence or passing 'beyond' is not enough, whether it comes about by accident or in some other way. Even if there is reason to believe that such things happen, their religious worth is another matter. At the same time the subject cannot quite rest there. It has a more positive side which I must now attempt to exhibit.

CHAPTER 15

RELIGION AND THE PRETERNATURAL
(continued)

There has traditionally been a close association of the occult and religion. This has not always been a happy one. Fear, conservatism, palpable evidence of fraud or abuse or of peculiar perversions of religion have often brought strain and conflict. If it had not been for the ill repute of necromancy we might know much more today about psychic phenomena. But in one way or another the occult has been closely linked with religion in the past, and this is not merely because most activities were merged in religion at first. The linkage seems much closer than that.

This may be ascribed in part to certain resemblances between religion and the occult; they both thrust us out of the ordinary course of experience and confront us with a disconcerting 'unknown' which we are not sure how to manage; they are both sources of exceptional power and influence and call for unusual disciplines. That alone would account for their being much confused and merged in each other. But the resemblances which could have that effect might be the basis also of more substantial relationships and integrations; and this also happened.

It happened because the kind of 'unknown' with which men were confronted in occult or preternatural occurrences, and the discipline and reactions which went with this, produced situations exceptionally favourable to the apprehension of the religious 'unknown', the ultimate mystery of the being of anything, the transcendent from which all is derived. The view has already been advanced that properly religious awareness is prompted, most of all in the first onset of it, by circumstances which disturb or thwart us and break the routine of our normal existence, and some indication of what these might be was given. But few things would be more likely to have these effects than to be confronted with powers and events not even partially comprehensible on the basis of our normal understanding of the world. Storms and upheavals in nature are not wholly unlike the occurrences which go on all the time. A gale only blows more strongly than a gentle wind, and an eruption is not very unlike the kind of boiling over which is a common occurrence. Simple people may not think of the matter in these terms, and may have recourse to more mysterious agencies. But if they find that things may occur which do not even in themselves, to say nothing of remoter causes, fit even partially into the normal sequences, if there is causation at a distance and other consummations altogether at odds with usual expectations, if there is knowledge and communication without normal evidence and media, and most of all if this is used in disconcerting and threatening ways, the reflection is easily induced which leads beyond all regularity and comprehensibility to a source of things which is not bound or limited at all.

The emotions which accompany paranormal occurrences, when encountered among credulous and unscientific people, together with various behavioural reactions to these occurrences, would also help to induce the general frame of mind favourable to religion, and this would be intensified as associations with religion were firmly established. The linkages would in these ways become closer again.

When there are preternatural experiences of the more

extreme kind I noted, those which involve not only disruptions of ordinary sequences but some entirely new modes of experience, the repercussions would naturally be greater, the disruption of ordinary notions would be more complete and the contingency of the matters we are most apt to take for granted unreflectively made evident. There is also, I suppose, the possibility here that minds initiated into some entirely new modes of reality, and these in some fashion immensely impressive, might stop short there and ascribe what eludes our understanding of the usual world to some operation of these further newly discovered realities. This may have something to do with some forms of polytheism, but I do not wish to pursue this very tentative suggestion further now. For it seems to me evident that the most likely and common reaction would be to lose the sense of the finality of finite explanations altogether and come all the more surely and humbly to the realization of the irreducibly mysterious character of all existence and the transcendent of which it tells.

This display of the transcendent may also have a peculiar richness as it shines in some sphere of splendour and worth far beyond what we normally know, or even if it merely invests with its own absolute wonder the relative wonder of a radically new experience. Those who tell us of such experiences often ascribe to them surpassing beauty and worth, they speak in terms of ecstasies and ravishment and overwhelming joy, of great radiance and brilliance. This may of course be due solely to the fact that in these cases the sense of God as such is firmer, more overwhelmingly obvious, and more profound, and to the effect of this on the total experience. But it seems to me likely also, if we give credence to these claims at all, that the alleged new union with God is closer, not only in the sense that the inevitability of the being of God as involved in all things is plainer, but also in the association of this with experiences of surpassing worth in themselves. The language of mysticism strongly suggests that.

It seems very likely therefore that some experiences in which men have been lifted out of the normal human situation and afforded glimpses of matters otherwise hidden, although not in themselves expressly religious, have in fact stimulated genuine religious awareness and brought it enrichment. The extent of this cannot easily be gauged, because the communication of matters which exceed our normal comprehension must be oblique and settle into the normal modes of religion. The student of religion, when he comes to heed this aspect of it, and especially if he hopes to consider it closely, has thus a peculiarly difficult task but also one which affords a stimulating challenge to his ingenuity and resourcefulness and imaginative understanding.

One matter which may be put in a new light on this basis is a common criticism of Otto, namely that he assimilates the uncanny, the eerie, the ghostly too readily to religion. For, while these things are not in themselves religious, they may well have had a great deal to do with the development of properly religious awareness and have contributed to it.

The relationship would, moreover, almost certainly be two-fold. For while certain attainments stimulate religion, it is the nature of religion, as we have seen, to articulate itself and develop in animating and directing other propensities. The relation of religion to the occult may well owe much to this factor also. Religion involves inevitably putting things in a new perspective and breaking the routine of our habitual outlook, it accustoms us to look beyond the world as we usually find it and may thus predispose us generally to entertain novel possibilities; and if men have powers of passing beyond their normal limitations and enjoying new modes of experience, these seem thus very likely candidates for the enlivening of appropriate faculties by which so much of the progress of religion is made. Consumed by the sense of God and burning with convictions at odds with normal evaluations, the inspired religious person may find himself liberated also in other ways and exercising gifts of a supernormal kind which might otherwise be dormant; new worlds may be opened out for him which, in a sense, only religion discloses.

How far this is possible for all, given the appropriate religious inspiration, or for a few endowed with peculiar gifts, is a very moot point, and it may well be a point where the co-operation of psychical research—assessing for example the spread of psychic processes accounted paranormal and how far we all have them mildly— and religious studies may have the most fruitful results for both.

A further difficulty encountered in the study of this topic is that imagination has so prominent a part, as has been stressed, in sustaining and extending religious experience. Vivid metaphorical terms and colourful descriptions will thus appear and be important in religion, but it will not then be easy, if we allow that religion may involve awareness of a supernormal kind, to determine always whether imaginative language which refers vividly to new levels of experience and surprising insights is to be understood in terms of extensions of normal experience and the religious transmutation of it in itself, or in terms of experiences radically different in substance from our normal ones. How much, in some of the vivid language of religion, is metaphor and normal poetical hyperbole, and how much is due to supernormal vision, and how extensive in the latter case is the departure from normality?

Let anyone consider, in terms of these possibilities, the celebrated celestial journeys of some religions, their visions and transfigurations. If a man is said to be 'borne up into heaven', just how do we understand this? If the claim is not totally fraudulent, would dreams afford our best approach to it? Just how do we understand the visions of Isaiah and Ezekiel, are they imaginative presentations of profound impressions of God's dealings with His people, or were there literally visions? If, as seems to me much the most likely case, we say there were visions, of what sort? Would their substance, in distinction from their religious import, be very unlike extraordinary dreams? Quite likely not, and yet there may be more to it. The difficulty is that the same language would be appropriate in either case. The vision of the Apocalypse provide an even better example, for they come in a context more generally concerned with the superseding or cancellation of our present conditions of existence. What does the writer mean here by a city that has 'no need of the sun, neither of the moon, to shine in it, for the glory of God did lighten it, and the lamb is the light thereof'? When St John was 'in the Spirit of the Lord's day', what was happening to him? How precisely do we get the reference of his imaginative language? The question may in no way be decisive for faith or the abiding import of apocalyptic literature. But it is worth asking and may throw much light on the main concerns of religion. I ask it now, not to attempt an answer, but to indicate the difficulty of assessing the scope and intention of imaginative terms in religion. Kindred problems arise when we think of the light from heaven which shone around St Paul and the voice which commissioned him, or of the opening of the heavens at the baptism of our Lord and the Spirit of God descending like a dove.

If there are in religion experiences of a sharply supernormal kind it is highly likely that this would stimulate imagination and summon to the articulation of such experiences, and even more to the perpetuation and communication of them, the imaginative forms current already. It is also likely that the latter would be extended and supplemented by new imaginative notions precipitated in the excitation of the moment and its novelty. These would not come mainly, if at all, by manipulations of the novelties of the peculiar experience, partly because these would be limited, partly through the need for effective contrast, partly because a mind already subjected to strain would be disposed to take the line of least resistance, but even more because imagination naturally orientates itself towards the needs of communication. The new currency would be minted out of normal experience, and thus, in its imaginative presentation and perpetuation of experience, the new and the normal would be much intermingled. The task of assessing the possibility and scope of the paranormal factor in religion is proportionately harder. Communication would have to be in terms of normal experience, and the main concern in many cases, outstandingly in that of the prophets, would be, not to establish one's credentials and status as a visionary, but to present the religious substance of the message.

It may well be—I am certainly disposed to think so—that some of the imaginative forms most valuable to religion are due to paranormal occurrences of some sort, and if this should be the case we owe to such occurrences the multiple debt of not only stimulating properly religious awareness and affording extension of it, but also of supplying some of the apparatus by which religion maintains and enriches itself. The paranormal as such is not religion—at any level—but it seems to have place in the service of religion.

Not everything, however, goes to the credit side here. Reasons have already been noted for the ill repute of the occult in much religion, and for the suspicion under which it has often lain. The esoteric rarely finds its course easy, and the normal, understandably, is apt to show some resentment or aversion towards the abnormal. But the hostilities engendered in the relations of the occult and normal religion seem deeper than this, and the core of them may be found, I believe, in the scope which occult and esoteric elements in religion afford for the idolatrous perversion of religion.

His commerce with the occult sets a man apart, and it also endows him with exceptional power, it enhances his sense of achievement and of triumph over common limitations. But when this occurs, as it is most likely to do, in the setting of enlivened religious awareness, any disposition we have to divert the significance and splendour of the transcendent to more manageable channels, to retain it in forms not too obviously and grossly inconsistent with it but, at the same time, less overwhelming and exacting in their impact, will find scope exceptionally apt in achievements, on the one hand, rare and pecular, and, on the other, an enhancement of ourselves. Occult practices have, I think, often taken that form, and even led to the explicit conferment by men of a divine status on themselves or on one of their leaders.

Once set on its course this diversifies itself into many further forms of impiety, including much defiance of moral principle; for once men set themselves up as divine they are not very likely to be patient of restraint. They will also feel it imperative to sustain their new status, and if their peculiar powers lapse or, as seems inevitable, the properly religious inspiration fails, substitutes will need to be provided, pseudo-occult practices no longer directed by modest and pious aims and subdued in the wonder of a world infused with the divine; excessive and unnatural strains will be imposed on mind and body, not relieved by high aspiration and the serenity of a heart at peace with itself; unusual states will be sought regardless of their content and worth; the accompaniments of exalted states, strange physical conditions and derivative emotional disturbances, will be cultivated for their own sakes, and, lacking the control of genuine ecstatic vision, these will encourage extravagant impulses to disport themselves at will and tear personalities apart; frenzies and orgies will proceed, inflaming one another and other perverted practices to which men are prone, not least those which thrive best under the cover of secrecy and the affectation of mystery—cruelties, mutilations and obscenity.

This situation can in turn be readily exploited by the seekers after power, sometimes crudely and naïvely, and sometimes on a large scale and persistently; and like other perversions of religion it will continue to have subtle repercussions in enlightened cultures and may be revived in times of strain and confusion, as happened lately in the releasing of daemonic power in Europe.

To all this the answer is control, not suppression. The Church has not always understood that, and in its zeal, most pardonable if not sound, to keep all manifestations of religion within severely rationalized schemes, it has not always shown the necessary patience towards peculiar outpourings of the Spirit of God whose credentials were not immediately evident. It has been sometimes grimly resentful of seemingly pathological forms of religion. But today, while remaining critical of unco-ordinated and disorganized outbursts of religion, we also appreciate better how much the Spirit bloweth where it listeth and how many more things there may be in heaven and earth than are dreamed of in our more mundane and commonplace systems. Only we hold to criticism and prove the spirits by the direction they take and their accordance with the central disclosures of our faith.

It is the latter which finally count. Occasional manifestations of peculiar power can never supersede them. Supernormal experience may show us the glory of God in a new way and give a new dimension to our praise. But what is most impressive and humbling of all is not that God is great and wonderful in Himself, or that

His light shines in whatever realms the spirit traverses, and with radiance proportionate to them, not that God is God and supreme everywhere, but that He deals with us as we are and at the heart of our essentially human concerns. It is in His will for us and the intimacy of His dealings with us that the essentials of a particular faith are found, and it is here that God, being God and supreme, is also most wonderful and, in His holiness, most compellingly Lord of all. This does not depend on the modes in which we discover Him, but on the character disclosed and the quality of what is done; it is not the setting that matters but the scene enacted in it, and this we observe primarily, not in moments of exalted detachment from our normal lot, but as we become inheritors of the patterning of divine intervention in history which displays its significance and brings it to its overwhelming redeeming climax.

Those who have had extraordinary visions granted them and been blessed with unusual gifts have themselves been often the first to bring these to the test of accordance with the prevailing course of God's dealings with men and the points where they find that crucial. This is pre-eminently true of Christianity; ecstatic experience, however authoritative for itself, is in due course brought to the test of the permanent deposit of faith in the live experience of a Christian community and the doctrinal pronouncements which buttress it. This is how the Church, impressed and tolerant as it has been in some outstanding cases, has understood the matter; and with becoming and holy humility the saints have usually so understood it themselves.

Moreover, the exalted vision, opening out vistas of reality normally veiled, will appear as a rule in the firm context of accepted belief and as an extension of it; and the more surely faith has been formed in significant accumulations of patterned experience, the more in short we have an explicit faith, the more will the visionary interlude be fashioned in accordance with faith and reflect its triumph. The visions of the Christian will be those appertaining to his belief. The comment has occasionally been made, with a sceptical intention, that saints have visions which blend with the preconceptions they derive from their particular brand of religion, the Catholic being thus more prone to visions of the Madonna than the Protestant. But there is nothing to disconcert us here; it is just as it should be, for the vision, whether it be strictly a vision, like those of St John of the Cross or St Theresa, or some other strange and exalted experience of which 'vision' is the nearest rough description we can give, has its main worth, not in what it is in relative detachment, but in the extension (and concentration too) of what has become significant in our own experience through appropriation into the fullness of our own life of what we find most distinctive in the religiously animated social existence of which we are a part.

The accounts we have of some supernormal occurrences suggest very strikingly that they may have an exceptional suitability for the purpose of enlivening religious awareness and providing a focus for it. It appears from some reports of paranormal states artificially induced, and thus subject to more deliberate and designed inspection, that they involve a very sharp impact on the mind of real objects in one's vicinity or of hallucinatory ones. This has interesting affinities with art and religion, and if these should be confirmed and seen to affect imaginative power in general, it would give us reason to expect exceptional states of consciousness to have a function, not unlike that of art and in combination with it, of focusing and sustaining and extending our religious life as a whole. But if this should be the case, we come back again to the integration of individual occurrences, however extraordinary, with our total religious impressions as they disclose to

us the character of God and of His dealings with us
which are much more vital for our relationship with
God than any incidental feature of the setting in which
they appear.

Nowhere is this more evident than in the Book of
Revelation. Whatever vivid flights of imagination or of
supernormal perceptions we find there, however overwhelming and insistent the impression of 'the last things'
and the surpassing of limited terrestial and temporal
conditions, however much the years may fall away and
the Alpha and Omega be one, in the midst, at the throne
of God and dominating the whole scene, is 'the lamb
as it had been slain'. What this meant in the Apocalypse
it meant also for the apostles, and what it meant for
them comes from the actual life and death of one Jesus,
killed in his early manhood. The significance this has
for Christians is open to all who see it in its context,
and however much it may enlarge all other visions we
may have and open the seals of all the mysteries, yet
it may be apprehended by any, however dim their
powers and drab their lot, if in the simplicity of their
hearts and the sincerity and devotion of their lives they
know what it means to speak of 'the lamb that was
slain'.

In the Book of Revelation we have also, incidentally,
the complication of yet another kind of symbolism. This
does not bear very closely on the main problem of this
book, and for that reason no mention has been made
of it hitherto. But it will be well, for the record, to
take the present opportunity of noting this further kind
of symbolism, the more so as it has considerable interest
on its own account in some contexts and is not devoid
of relevance to our theme.

I refer to the ascription of unusual meanings to terms
already in use or the coining of new ones. In modern
times this usually comes about through the need for

technical terms in science and other studies where new conceptions and distinctions are important. But the motives have often been different in religion, in particular the need to disguise rather than to clarify meaning. Initiates into practices and notions reserved for the few, a priestly order for example, may have to devise ways of communicating readily without giving away their common secrets, especially in contexts which involve other members of the community. A minority liable to be persecuted has the same need. It is thus not surprising that apocalyptic literature should much reflect the use of religious codes of this kind. For a great deal of it started among esoteric sects with their own secrets to guard, and in the stages with which we are most familiar it is the product of minorities subject to intense persecution.

We thus find many allusions in the Book of Revelation itself which scholarship has since decoded as references to historical events and persons, Babylon representing Rome and the heads of the beasts in Chapters XIII and XVII standing for Roman emperors, 'the wounded head' referring to Nero and the legend about him. Much which we might hasten thus to ascribe to the spontaneous generation of vivid imagination or preternatural experience must be understood in the first instance more prosaically in terms of contemporary designations of facts or persons, some of these having a wider or more public currency than others.

There is nothing peculiarly religious about the adoption of a semi-private language of this kind, although in the case of apocalyptic writings, religion would be the source from which it was drawn. But the special allusions and terms of it would of course rarely be matter of fact and coldly deliberate (it is not often that even modern technological terms are quite that); they would be the product of colourful imagination in minds at work under various stresses and pressures, and they would be taken up into distinctively religious imaginative meanings in the special use to which they were put. They would provide ready counters out of which religious imagination would coin its own currency.

But the nearer we come to the heart of religion the greater is the inherently religious need for symbolism, as we have seen already; and when we encounter preternatural experiences or mystical states peculiarly hard to communicate, there may be found here also a set of symbols restricted to peculiar people sharing an experience which gives the symbols their meaning, various mystic signs and numbers and so forth. The difficulty, for the outsider, is to know when he must confess defeat as not having the requisite qualifications to understand the signs, and when the symbols are obscure merely because they are in a code to which he has not in fact been given the key. Much that is studied under the name of mystical symbolism appears in fact to be of the latter kind and thus capable of being explained or translated in ordinary terms. At the same time we must beware of being too cavalier in such matters. For in religion the ordinary is often being subtly baptized into extraordinary uses, and poetic imagination is always at hand to transmute the commonplace into the exalted.

In dealing with signs and imagery which we find in mystical writings and apocalyptic literature, we have thus to avoid the extremes of ascribing all to sheer imagination or preternatural insight, on the one hand, and, on the other, of seeking factual clues which will provide us with exhaustive explanations in normal terms. We must avail ourselves of all that exact historical scholarship can tell us, but we must not forget that we are dealing with matters where powerful imaginations and prophetic religious insights are also at work. The specific reference of visions need not diminish their visionary quality—it may give them greater body.

This seems to be peculiarly well illustrated in the reference to Nero in Revelation XVII as the beasts that 'was, and is not, and shall come'. If we like we may treat this as a conundrum, and merely remind ourselves of the belief that Nero had been falsely reported dead by his own hand but was actually alive and expected to return. But we should do this at our peril, for the very adoption of language used normally of Christ throws the whole into an entirely different dimension. It is a reference to Nero in the context of cataclysmic events and of the religious transmutation of the situation in which Nero figures which brings it under the light of eternity and 'the life of the world to come'.

CHAPTER 16

MIRACLE AND PRAYER

Embedded in the observations already made about the preternatural element in religion, although in many ways extending beyond it, are the vexatious questions of miracle and the answer to prayer. Some indications of the bearing of our theme on these latter questions will now be given.

From time to time, the attempt has been made by theologians and philosophers of religion to present the idea of miracle in ways which did not involve any ultimate rupture of the sort of sequence we normally presuppose in our explanations of events. Some would maintain, for example, that miraculous occurrences in the external world would admit, in the last analysis, of as exhaustive a scientific explanation as any other physical event. Jerusalem was saved by a miracle from the onslaught of Sennacherib, but the destruction of the invading host may also, it is argued, be ascribed to a sudden violent plague of the sort which has often wrought the ruin of great armies. The difficulty with this view is obviously to see what room is left for the miraculous element in the story. Some apologists seek to cope with this situation by subterfuges which deserve little respect, as when the turning of water into wine is brought within the natural course of things by regarding it as merely 'the acceleration of natural processes', as if that did not raise all our questions afresh. Others ascribe miracles to some extraordinary power of mind over matter. Now there is nothing incredible about the exercise of such power, as we have seen already. We find we have certain limited powers of affecting physical events, and there is nothing to rule out the possibility that these should be varied in certain states of mind, at least not for anyone who can admit genuine inter-action of mind and body. Only exhaustive physical determinism could rule this out, and such a theory would have to accommodate somehow the well-attested facts of levitation and kindred phenomena. The real difficulty is again to see just where the element of miracle comes in. The exercise of supernormal power need not, in principle, fall outside the explanations we offer of other mental events and their consequences. They would only be miracles if some expressly religious factor were required to account for them; short of that they would at best be freaks which we might find pecu-liarly hard to explain in terms of some relation to other phenomena. Even if we thought they had no such rela-tion, they would still not be miracles, any more than undetermined choices would be. The word 'miracle' must surely involve some reference to a religious factor in the determination of events if we are to keep at all to its normal use and association. To speak of a 'miracle' is not just to say that an event was extraordinary or bewildering, it is expressly to ascribe the event to a religious source, to offer one kind of explanation, albeit a very special one.

To meet this, some religious thinkers have described a miracle as any event with a supernatural or religious significance. But this, as it stands, is obviously too wide. For those who hold a religious view, everything may be said to have some religious significance, in as much as everything depends upon God or is sustained in being by God. There have indeed been thinkers not averse from accepting this consequence and who would thus

maintain that properly viewed everything is a miracle
—it is in the last analysis a wonder that anything should
be what it is; the rising sun and the changing seasons,
lovely sights and sounds, and even things that are not
outstandingly impressive, the most commonplace occurrences from moment to moment, ought properly to be
considered as miraculous as any : to see them properly is
to see the wonder of God in them.

This, however, just will not do. It is quite true, as has
been stressed throughout, that God may be made manifest
in anything, but to see all things in this very general
way as the work of God does not justify us in regarding
all things as miracles. For if we take this line the idea of
miracle loses all its distinctiveness. We shall have shown
that miracles happen, but only in a sense so attenuated
as to be largely, if not wholly, unhelpful. If we claim
that miracles occur we should normally be understood
to affirm something distinctive about particular occurrences and not merely to be expressing or eliciting the
general truth that all things bear in themselves the
wonder of God as their creator or transcendent source;
and if this is how we should normally be understood, if
a miracle is usually thought to be quite different from
ordinary occurrences, it would be misleading not to heed
this in our use of the term. 'Miracle' in other words,
becomes otiose unless it means more than an event
which has some religious significance.

Apprehending this, some writers have tried to meet
the case by regarding miracles as occurrences of an unusual or unexpected nature in the course of which men
have also acquired some distinctive religious insight. It
might thus be possible to retain the prospect of some
scientific or rational account of allegedly miraculous
events. If, for example, the crossing of the Red Sea be
considered a miracle, the present requirement would be
met if we thought the event capable of explanation in
terms of an extraordinary combination of tides and

winds at the time when the Israelites, in flight from Egypt, needed to cross. The coincidence would indeed be overwhelming, and it would be the occasion of solemn thought about God and occur in the context of deep searching for the will of God by the people or their leader and the sense of being granted special religious illumination. I am convinced in fact that all this happened and that the occasion is one which provides an outstanding and most instructive instance of the process of divine disclosure and of the communication of God with man in a pre-eminently personal way. But if no more were involved I should still think it fell short of being miraculous.

For, again, if 'miracle' be extended to every occasion of divine disclosure or even only to cases of live and impressive religious experience in circumstances of a very exceptional nature, it remains otiose or misleading. However important in the process of Moses's apprehension of the mind of God, and however decisive the parting of the waters and the attendant circumstances may have been for the subsequent religious life of the Hebrews, not many persons who were convinced that the occurrence admitted of as full a scientific explanation as any other natural event would continue to regard it as a miracle. Something further is needed, and I submit that what is required to yield the distinctive factor which sets miracles apart from other events is that there should be some deviation from the course which events would have taken due to some religious factor and yet other than the process of revelation itself and the effect this has naturally on other events. A church may reflect the piety of those who caused it to be built, but we should not for that reason say that its appearance was a miracle. But if, in express consequence of their religious state, persons without any instruction or training in building had been enabled to set up a faultless elaborate edifice, or just to summon it into existence, then we should certainly count that as a miracle. I have urged already that live religion enhances our powers in various ways, but we should not regard that as miraculous. If my moral sense or my grasp of some particular problem is sharpened by my religious experience, or by its effects, in the way and measure in which this normally happens, that is not a miracle. But if in consequence of being religious I acquired immediately an understanding of complicated mathematical matters of which I had no previous knowledge, this would be miraculous. It may be hard in practice to know where exactly the line should be drawn but this holds also of some paranormal events. If my achievement went markedly beyond anything that would normally be expected, then, in the circumstances noted, it should count as a miracle.

Some would avoid the problem of where exactly we draw the line between miracles and the normal enhancement of human powers in religion by taking 'miracle' in a stronger or stricter sense than the one noted, namely by requiring that there should be some express or direct intervention by God in the course of events (much as we ourselves may modify natural processes) other than divine disclosure in revelation. This, it seems to me, simplifies the notion of what a miracle is, but at the same time presents us with a situation where it is much harder to know whether a miracle has occurred. We can see in general how we might establish a connection between certain preternatural occurrences and religious states of mind or dispositions, especially in cases where the former had some consistent association with the latter. But it would be another matter to ascribe an occurrence to the direct intervention of God in some way quite different from the ultimate dependence of all things on Him.

Before saying more about this latter question, it may be well to interpolate the remark that in the case of miracles, in either the weaker or the stricter sense indicated, there would of course remain much in the total situation capable of the sort of explanation, a scientific one perhaps, we might normally attempt of any occurrence. If this were not the case, if all determination or system were suspended, it is hard to see how anything could occur. The position here is like that of undetermined choice; if all continuity were suspended I could not act or survive at all. What is postulated is some sphere within which the continuity which makes events intelligible and capable of manipulation is broken. There might thus be much which could be naturally explained in the case of the crossing of the Red Sea, but at some point, perhaps in some remote conditions which produced a high wind, there would have to be some occurrence not merely unusual and exceptionally hard to explain, but not capable at all of scientific explanation. In the case of miracles in the strong sense the explanation would be in terms of direct divine intervention.

The problems which this presents are sharply displayed in the claim that God answers prayer. The practice of prayer is central to most religions, and some would claim that prayer is an indispensable ingredient of all religion. The soundness of this latter claim turns in part on how the idea of prayer is understood. I have been maintaining earlier that all religion involves some reference to a transcendent being and that, from the earliest stages, this begins to take the form of a personal relationship which ripening religion makes more explicit and refines. If prayer is defined as communion with God, this might be understood in a way that makes prayer and religion, as I view religion, co-extensive. For although the live and reflective sense of the presence of God and of His dealings with us will be occasional, this vital core of religion will dominate the rest and give it its meaning. So that at every stage, including the conduct which religion instigates and regulates, religion can be regarded as some extension of a personal relationship of which we have awareness, much as a friendship may extend into matters which do not expressly involve the regard we have for our friends or the cultivation of it. This, I believe, is one of the main ways in which some people have been disposed to equate prayer and religion, or at least prayer and worship.

The same tendency has been reinforced by concern for consistency in religion and the right relating of its parts. Thus Coleridge, in the person of the Ancient Mariner, says:

> He prayeth best who loveth best
> All things both great and small.

Jesus, like the prophets before Him, was vigorous and unsparing in His denunciation of devotional practices which did not carry with them appropriate conduct; and, in being thus emphatic about the right relationship of prayer to conduct, we may find ourselves saying, not only that proper prayer involves right living, but that true prayer is to be just and selfless in our dealings with each other. For rhetorical purposes this may be proper, but it can also be highly misleading; for however deplorable the show of piety may be without the conduct that is in keeping with it, right conduct as such does not amount to any form of religion. We must thus be careful not to obliterate essential distinctions or conceive of prayer in so loose a fashion as to miss its significance.

This holds also if we equate prayer with the whole of religion, even when religion is properly seen to involve much more than ethics. For, as in the case of 'miracle', the term 'prayer' becomes otiose if it becomes synonymous with 'religion', and in the same way the peculiar practices which we may want to extol in this connection, or to signalize for a theoretical purpose as outstanding features of religion, lose the distinctiveness by which

we can appreciate them. If we say that prayer is important, we surely have in mind some particular feature
of religion.

Two courses present themselves here. One would be to
define 'prayer' in terms of certain outward or physical
features of devotional practice, for example to say that
we pray when, in the course of our devotions, we kneel
or bow the head or clasp the hands or shut our eyes
and so forth. In themselves these distinctions can have
very little importance, but they are also associated with
differences of meaning and centrality in the ordering
of devotional services. These vary much from one sect
or denomination to another, and in some cases the
linkage with certain physical postures would be much
closer than in others. But until we look at the properly
spiritual meaning of such distinctions, and thus raise
questions of a more ultimate character about the nature
of prayer, we find nothing very illuminating for our
understanding of the substance of religion.

A pedant might object that it is not in accordance
with ordinary practice to designate anything as 'prayer'
which does not involve customary physical postures, and
it would certainly be very misleading to say that some
incident happened in church in the course of the prayer
when we knew that the congregation was standing up to
sing at the time. But these are very rough and ready
distinctions which we draw for purposes largely incidental to the proper practice of religion, and which do
not prescribe the more serious use of the word 'prayer'
in other religious contexts.

This does not imply that the varied physical performances in worship have little importance. They may,
on the contrary, be charged with great symbolic significance, and in considering this we may find it expedient
to follow the conventional divisions of worship into
reading, singing, praying, and so forth. But there is no
uniformity in these divisions even within the religions and

denominations that hold more strictly to them. A prayer may be sung as well as recited, and a 'reading' may take the form of collective reading of a psalm which is also a recognized prayer. Nor does it seem to me likely that many Christians, at any rate, would deny that the whole of a religious service is a prayer, many complete services being expressly so called. Nor would it be very plausible to say that in singing :

> 'Take my life and let it be
> Consecrated, Lord, to Thee'

one would be doing something radically different religiously from kneeling to say 'Make clean our hearts within us'. In both cases we have surely a form of prayer, and consideration of what prayer is in its more substantial and universal sense is our best guide to the distinctions to be drawn at the level where 'prayer' has its more limited application in distinction from a 'reading' or 'singing'.

The other course which presents itself is to identify prayer with all religious experience or what I have designated earlier the live moments of religious awareness. This, I think, comes very near the mark, but I suspect that it is still too wide. For while prayer could certainly include private meditation about God, I do not think we should extend the word to the sort of religious illumination in which the initiative of the recipient of it was slight or nil. One would hardly say that the infant Samuel or St Paul were praying when they were summoned to God's work, although prayerful responses speedily followed. A strict demarcation may not be possible in these or other cases, but I should think that the sort of distinction within live experience of God which we have in mind in the more serious use of the word 'prayer' is that whereby we single out within religious experience as a whole that form of it in which

the action or the initiative of the worshipper has prominence. Prayer is not what happens to us, but what we
do, notwithstanding that it is in a context in which
much is being done to us.

The objection may be made here that it is possible to
pray without the enlivened religious awareness of which
I have spoken, namely when prayers are offered or 'said'
in a formal or habitual way, as when we say a regular
daily prayer or ask blessing on a meal. But even a formal
or regular prayer needs to be said heedfully, and the
fact of its being brief does not preclude its involving a
live awareness of God. Short ceremonial prayers can
often be solemn and moving, and we normally so dispose
ourselves, by bowing the head or shutting our eyes, as to
induce a devout and attentive frame of mind. When
prayers are not said in these ways they are in grave
danger of becoming empty formalities or of being
practised as magic. The well-known picture of the
peasant pausing in the field with bowed head at prayer
suggests effectively how rich the momentary pause for
prayer can be. Our customary prayers need not bring
a blinding sense of the holiness and nearness of God,
nor issue in new insights, although they may sometimes
do that. But they may, without this, stir the mind
gently and touch the heart. And it seems to me they
should do so.

In saying this I do not overlook the extensive dispositional factor in life and belief. There are things we
do in the context of our dispositional attitudes as a
matter of course and appropriate response without much
new reflection, and these will include some ceremonial
matters as well as practical response to various situations. But prayer has not the function of social formalities by which status and position are marked, it is not
observed initially for one another's benefit but addressed
directly to God; and it seems to have no point therefore
as the more formal token of a disposition. A case for

prayer which is not itself an enlivening of faith could more plausibly be made on the ground that the practice and discipline of the mental and physical motions of prayer, of uttering and entertaining certain thoughts in a special way, help us generally to sustain the religious life and to cultivate and make easier the moment of true and reflective awareness: I do not deny the im-. portance of the cultivation of religion in these ways. On the other hand there are limitations to what we can properly do or say as a discipline, even on the basis of firm dispositional convictions. How much can be said to God if it cannot be said as live conviction at the time? And is not the 'prayer' which fails to bring a dispositional belief to life best described as an attempt to pray? It may be necessary to persevere much in the attempt, and this is part of what we mean by 'wrestling with God'. But what is sought is the quickened conviction; and prayer, it seems to me, has little point apart from the expectation of its involving a live awareness of our relation to God.

Indeed, if our dispositions, on due reflection on the facts which most sustain them, fail to become alive in the way noted, it must be doubted whether we retain them. The alternation of despair and assurance is a well-known feature of religion, and one which need not much disconcert us. It is in this way that religion ripens into its finer forms of personal conviction and commitment. But temporary darkness is not light, and religious insensitivity is not altered in itself when offset by a firm hope of its dissolution; and thus when our faith becomes faint, through some special circumstance or through besetting staleness, is it not more correct to say, when we think closely, that we have tried but failed to pray? At a certain level, and in exhorting one another to strengthen our faith through prayer, we may indiscriminately use the same term for the attempted and the successful prayer. But this does not dim what seems to be at any rate the dominant aim of prayer, namely to address God in the enlivened and reflective conviction of our relationship to Him.

This, most of all, is why prayer is so central to religion and why prayer becomes increasingly important in the maturing of religion into the firm sense of a personal relation with God and the awareness of His presence. In such states there is much that we do, and not all of it can be formalized or easily designated. Praise and the expression of contrition will be prominent. So will petition which is, in some contexts, the most specific meaning of prayer; and with this we return to the point where consideration of prayer has most affinity with the question of miracle on which I have already commented. Indeed, notwithstanding the difficulty of specifying the most distinctive and regulative uses of the word 'prayer' from among the admitted varieties of its applications, much the hardest philosophical problems present themselves when we consider the petitionary aspect of prayer.

These are so severe that many find themselves reluctant to allow to petitionary prayer a proper place in religion. They admit that the form of prayer is markedly petitionary, it involves asking for specific things; and they do not wish to discourage this. The petitionary form they find to be so fundamental and familiar that it would be highly and needlessly disruptive to modify or surrender it. We must continue to make supplication to God, but at the same time we must make it plain to ourselves and others that this is not to be taken at its face value; the real intention is different, for example to bring ourselves to the appropriate religious frame of mind, to remind ourselves that we owe all to God and accept the good and the bad in a spirit of devout thanksgiving and resignation, to bring our own will to due accord with the will of God.

These last suggestions are not exhaustive, but the

course they follow is familiar, and its attractiveness is evident. At the same time it seems to me also gravely mistaken and little likely in the end to further the cause of true religion. There is much, admittedly, in religion which we do not take at its face value, but to persist in the practice of petitionary prayer as some kind of spiritual discipline, when we no longer believe in its possible efficacy, seems spiritually very frustrating and to present so sharp a conflict between form and substance as to impair the integrity of the spiritual life, both for ourselves and for those who observe us. The proper procedure, it seems to me, for those who find the notion of petitionary prayer repugnant or in some way unacceptable is to forswear the practice and thus undertake a radical modification of their prayers at the point where the petitionary factor is most pronounced. Drastic reforms are sometimes unavoidable, and however great the sacrifice of matter rich in associative power and consecrated literary forms, and however sharp the new orientation, the price must be paid and a new course followed. Religion will survive this more healthily in the long run than the loss of fundamental integrity.

To give point to this, consider the case of the minister who prays with an anxious parent at the bedside of a gravely sick child. He will, among other things, ask that the child be restored to health. This will not be asked without qualification, there will be humble acceptance of the will of God as taught to all Christians expressly in the Lord's Prayer. But the plea for the recovery of the child will be specific and if this is not to be taken in substance at its face value, I submit that, in harrowing circumstances of this sort, the making of it is a mockery which we cannot but abhor when we recognize it. Could we really pray earnestly for the recovery of the child and at the same time instruct the parent that this is only one of the ways—a very roundabout one, he may think —in which we may bring ourselves to meet this crisis in the proper religious way? Most parents would prefer greater frankness and simplicity.

One reason why we are able to hold basically sceptical beliefs about the efficacy of petitionary prayer and, at the same time, continue in the practice of it, is that, in religion, we are in many regards prone to departmentalize our thoughts. The strain which one aspect of religion imposes on others is eased by keeping them apart. But this is a counsel of despair, and nothing but ill can eventually come of it, in respect both of the quality of the religious life itself and of its reputation. Religion, more than anything, should make us whole and produce balanced personalities able to bear the truth about themselves and the world.

It would certainly be peculiarly objectionable to persist in the general practice of petitionary and intercessory prayer without faith in its efficacy and also without making it explicit, to all affected by the practice or likely to observe and emulate it, that we are only seeking, under the outward guise of petition, to produce certain incidental effects in ourselves and others. For the priest who does not believe that his prayer may 'make a difference', other than its psychological effect, to leave his distracted hearer under a totally different impression seems altogether indefensible; it involves an extension of the notion of 'the dual standard' which cannot fail to become increasingly sinister in a society struggling to be more effectively democratic. But to make earnest supplication and at the same time be at pains to show that our procedure has none of its apparent purpose seems to call for the sort of spiritual agility with which few are endowed and which is perhaps not much to be coveted. It may lead to presumptuous and perilous practice.

Someone may interpose here the remark that I have earlier insisted myself on the highly figurative language of religious practice and the ease with which we may perpetuate this in new and changing situations; am I not now disposed to forget this and take things too literally? Symbolism need not be confined to affirmation, and may not those who discard the petitionary aspect of prayer still put the form of it to good use in a figurative or symbolic way without hurt to their spiritual state and integrity? My reply is that we have to do here not with the novel extensions of symbolism but with forms and beliefs too irreconcilable for them effectively and safely to serve each other. There is a point at which figurative forms and practices stray so far from fact as to leave nothing but tenuous and dangerous sophistry.

If then we encounter insuperable difficulties in the notion of petitionary prayer, the proper course seems to be to abandon it altogether, not to retain the shadow without the substance; for that could be very misleading and injurious to ourselves as well as others. In some religions, some forms of Buddhism for example, petitionary prayer has no place, while other religions, Islam in particular, in giving prayer a very prominent place sharply reduce the importance of petitionary prayer. In Christianity, for the most part, the position is very different. Prayer is very central and the petitionary aspect of it takes its place easily within the whole. From time to time, but mostly in recent days, some Christians have been daunted by the difficulties and attempted, by various expedients, to avoid committing themselves to explicit acceptance of the petitionary and intercessory forms of prayer. But generally, in the teaching and practice of Christians, there has been a very complete acceptance of petitionary prayer.

This seems closely in accordance with the explicit teaching of the Scriptures and the implications of the procedures it commends. In particular, Jesus seems clearly to have commended, and even required, petitionary prayer. A very strange gloss would need to be put on the relevant passages, including 'The Lord's

Prayer', to elicit any interpretation of them other than the explicit exhortation to petition God for material or spiritual benefits in the confident faith that He may grant them. This is, moreover, fully in accord with the implications of the Christian conception of God and His dealings with us. For what is pre-eminent here is the personal character of God and the intimacy of His relationship to us as disclosed and extended in distinctively Christian occurrences and the events which prepared the way for those. It is no accident that prayer in general is peculiarly important for Christianity, nor that explicit and confident supplications to God should have a firm place within Christian prayer; for if these supplications are proper at all one would expect them to be seen to the best advantage and be most prominent where the dominant theme is that of God dwelling amongst us.

But in that case what shall we say of the difficulties? Let us now take a look at these and consider how they may be met.

CHAPTER 17

PETITIONARY PRAYER

The difficulties involved in the notion of petitionary prayer divide themselves roughly into two sorts. The first of these may be said to be the most expressly theological ones. I refer to the difficulties of reconciling belief in petitionary prayer with other things we feel impelled to believe about God, especially His justice and wisdom. These difficulties are sometimes made to centre on the idea of God's foreknowledge and may also arise out of some beliefs about predestination. I do not think we need, for our purpose, to look closely into beliefs of this kind; it will suffice to say that the right approach to them lies along the way of better understanding of the uniqueness of God and the highly qualified way in which we may speak of foreknowledge as applied to Him. In other words, I believe the sting can be taken out of our difficulties at this point if we take to heart the lesson which recent religious thought in particular has taught us about the way in which we must think about God and refer to Him. I shall not undertake that operation here, but the hint I have given may be enough to justify us in taking as the central type of the difficulties in question now the simpler one of the problem which occurs most readily to the layman, namely, how God in His infinite goodness and wisdom can see fit to be swayed by the petition of limited and imperfect creatures. In other words, God clearly knows what is best and will do it : my prayer can hardly make a difference.

A subsidiary form of this question consists in noting the apparent unfairness of allowing some to benefit because a prayer has been uttered by them or on their behalf. Ought not God to benefit men according to their needs or merits and not in terms of the rather haphazard and arbitrary condition of being the subject of prayer? Should momentous things, like recovery from sickness, depend on someone's asking God? Will not God, if He has the nature we ascribe to Him, succour men without waiting to be asked?

So the questions run, and it must be admitted that, whatever the theologian may feel about them in his study, they are very real problems to the layman and the priest he consults. They cannot fail to set up a continuous strain or tension within the religious life and to accentuate the general problem of unmerited and seemingly pointless suffering.

Part of the answer here must be that our well-being in physical or spiritual ways does not depend solely on prayer. This seems most obvious in the physical sphere, but it is also true where prayer is most directly involved, namely in receiving spiritual gifts like forgiveness and new spiritual life. The divine beneficence is the most fundamental in both these respects. It is only in some limited ways that prayer can be expected to make a difference. The over-riding control does not pass from God's hands.

We have next to recall that the case of prayer is not altogether peculiar here. There are a great many ways in which the well-being of my neighbour depends on me— in some regards his life is in my hands. I may cause him untold harm by negligence or malice. Children may suffer throughout their lives by the negligence or cruelty of their parents, folly and villainy may lead to war or social disaster. Whether we like it or not, we are, in a

great many ways, one another's keepers. That is the
world God, in His wisdom, has made, and we can,
in very large measure, see the wisdom of it ourselves.
A world in which we could do no harm to others or
seriously affect their lives would not be the world in
which we could exist and develop as moral beings and
have the personal relations open to us now. This is far
from solving the whole of the problem of evil, and we
are not expressly concerned with that problem now. But
if it can be seen that we need to be left for certain
purposes at one another's mercy, and if we deem this
to be not inconsistent with the goodness and power of
God, it becomes easier to see how, in some situations,
our prayers, or failure to pray, could affect others.

It may be thought, however, that prayer must be in a
class of its own here. It is one thing to provide opportunities for us to fend for ourselves and succour, or
neglect, one another. This provides the opportunity and
inducement to right behaviour. That another should be
allowed to suffer or lack because I neglect him or
purposely cause him harm is one thing, and it expressly
involves the relations we have with one another. But my
praying for myself or others, or my neglecting to do so,
seems so far removed from the normal conditions of
well-being and mutual help as to seem a rather pointless
or irrelevant condition. To leave scope for me to help
people is one thing, to allow their fortunes to turn on
whether I pray for them another.

In some moods, this will no doubt appear a formid-
able point, and for the sceptic, viewing the situation from
without, it is certain to carry much weight. For, in these
cases, prayer may well seem a rather trivial matter. But
it is quite otherwise for the religious person, and especially for the Christian, for here prayer is the very heart
of things. It is the live centre of our relation to God,
and that it should have ramifications extending into the
whole of life and our relations with one another is not

surprising. It is when we know or meet one another in our prayers and prayerful living that we have the finest relationship with one another, bound together in the union of our bond with God. But that this should affect our lives, not only where the mutual relationships we have with each other in expressly religious ways spill over into other concerns and conditions of existence, but also in further more direct or subtle ways, will not appear strange to those who appreciate properly what prayer is. We may not understand at all points what power it has and how that operates. But that it should carry with it profound, and sometimes extraordinary, consequences will surprise no one who appreciates its momentousness. Prayer is not pressing a button or listing our requirements; it is live communion with God.

We have to recall especially here that prayer has most prominence where the personal relation of God to men is stressed. In the Christian religion God is known as a Father who so loved the world that He gave His only begotten Son. Where the relation of God to men is so close and where God may be known to be peculiarly present to us in Christ, then it is not very strange that the extension and sanctification of this in the whole of life should lead to the granting of certain things simply because they are brought before God, in humility and resignation and faith, in our most sacred communion with Him.

By right understanding of religion, and especially of our live and personal relation to God, the way is open for us, at any rate, to deal with the more expressly theological difficulties concerning prayer such as the consistency of belief in petitionary prayer with the character of God. In the light of the way in which God is known to deal with us and His involvement of Himself in exceptional ways in the world He has created, we may find it credible that in some circumstances our petitions, if properly made, should affect what is ultimately for the best or what God in His infinite wisdom will do. The problem would be more intractable if we thought of God as an 'unmoved mover' after the fashion of some Greek thinkers, or merely as a mysterious ground of being which could not be brought into closer relation to ourselves or thought of in any way other than irreducible mystery. The peculiarity of the Christian religion is that it retains the sense of the absolute perfection and trans-cendence of God and yet is able, in the sharpest contra-distinction to the dominant view of the Greek philoso-phers, to think it consistent with the perfection and sublimity of God, indeed an articulation of it, that He could also concern Himself with the affairs of men as to dwell amongst them and suffer at their hands. If we find ourselves able to accept this we ought not to find insuperable difficulties in the notion of petitionary prayer at the level which I have called for convenience the theological one.

I shall not pursue this further, as my concern is only to indicate how my main theme would bear on the present issue. But what of the other aspects of the question? Suppose we admit that it is consistent with what we believe about God, in His dealings with men, that He should answer prayer in the strict interpreta-tion of the terms; but do we know that in fact He ever does so? If so just how do we know? Is it a matter of evidence, or of appeal to some other considerations independently known? It is in regard to this question above all, it seems to me, that the theme of this book bears most closely on the subject of prayer.

At this point our topic has also exceptional contem-porary relevance. A great deal has recently been said about verification and the way in which evidence would be relevant to the truth of religious statements. Much of the controversy so engendered has centred on the question of the existence of God or of very general attributes of God such as His love or the dependence of the world upon Him as creator. The reply which the religious apologist makes at this point refers, as already noted, to an intuition of the necessity of the being of God which does not involve us in any specific considerations of what we find the world to be like. But on the face of it at least the question of petitionary prayer is in quite a different category. It would be very hard to press some procedure like the use made of the doctrine of analogy to the point of its yielding so specific an affirmation as that God answers prayer, and for this reason I have been not a little surprised that our positivist opponents have not made more of this particular matter. It may not make sense to ask what would count for or against the existence of God, but it seems not unreasonable to ask for some evidence that prayers are answered.

Can we meet this challenge at all on its own ground, or must we fall back again on more general reflections? Some apologists take up the challenge in a very cavalier spirit, and there has probably been as much tantalizing evasion of the issue here as anywhere in religious apologetics. One common line is to identify whatever happens with the proper answer to a prayer. I prayed for health, my health was not restored, but I gained great serenity of mind, and that was how God answered my prayer. But that does not advance the subject one whit unless it can be shown at least that the serenity in question could not be attained in any way other than, in this instance, by my praying for health, and it is in any case a most unusual answer to a prayer for health. If the answer *is* serenity, we have to press the question of cases, like the present prayer for health, where serenity was not forthcoming. If we find that disappointment is never disconcerting, that we can persist in our claim whatever happens, we seem to be exposing our claim very perilously indeed to the notorious 'death by a thousand qualifications' which our opponents hold over us.

Indeed, some seem disposed quite deliberately to fall on their swords in this way. They say that the person who asks, 'Well, did God answer your prayer?', is forgetting that the answer may be 'No'. This has certainly been said from time to time in pulpits, and of course there is no objection in the least to supposing that God might say 'No'. As I shall note again, we certainly should not expect every request to be conceded. But if the claim that our petitions are granted is based on some appeal to evidence, we clearly cannot shuffle out of our difficulties by supposing that however things go the prayer will have been answered in this way.

Others believe they have a way out of their difficulties here by supposing that we should only pray for spiritual benefits, for grace and repentance and the will to live well. But however important it may be to make these matters uppermost in our prayers, that does not help us at this point. For even if we did hold that the efficacy of prayer was restricted to spiritual matters such as those listed (and this would be much out of accord with the main pronouncements on the question) the initial difficulty would present itself quite as formidably at this level as at any other. The evidence might be more elusive, but it is evidence that we should need : something would 'have to be different'.

An evasion characteristic of much popular apologetics —and of some that is not merely popular—is typified well in a story which had considerable circulation in our pulpits at one time. The story is about a small boy who much desired a toy which he could not buy. He had been taught to pray in a pious home, and so one day he decided to kneel by the hedge at the side of the road and ask God for the toy. As it happened a kindly farmer was working in the field on the other side and heard the prayer. He was much moved by the earnestness and faith of the boy and he hurried ahead and made his way into the road in time to intercept him. He engaged the boy in conversation, leading up to the subject of the games in vogue at that season and so to the boy's longing for his toy, and then he made him a gift of the money needed to buy it. The boy's faith in prayer, we are told, was much confirmed, the farmer tactfully keeping silent about his part in the story.

Now it is not surprising that an occurrence of this sort should have a great psychological effect, especially in the case of a susceptible child brought up in an atmosphere of unquestioning faith. We need not concern ourselves with the propriety or otherwise of the farmer's alleged tact. But what is very plain is that the logic of belief in prayer is not strengthened at all in a case of this kind. The intention is plain enough. It is to show that prayer can be answered without spectacular intervention in the course of events or ruptures in the normal continuity of our lives, this in turn being intended to make acceptance of prayer easier to persons inclined to be sceptical of strictly miraculous occurrences. But the attempt fails and exposes itself to the charge of 'double-think' which would normally be expressed in dismissal of the story as a coincidence of a sort not exceptionally rare.

To this the reply may be made that it was God in fact who had arranged for the farmer to be at the right place at the right time. The force of this turns on how seriously it is meant and how it could be supported. If God had arranged the event merely in the sense that all occurrences are in some way under God's control, then we have no reason to regard the occasion as being more than any other occasion whatsoever an answer to prayer. The most that we might get in this way is some warrant for belief in general providence—and not even that in my own view. But if God had brought the farmer to the proper part of the field in some special way, then our questions repeat themselves. How do we recognize this sort of intervention; how do we ascribe it to God?

It seems that we should at least need to be shown that it was not the farmer's original intention to work where he found himself that day at the relevant time. But that would also not be enough. If he had changed his mind, by 'taking a look at the weather', then the charge of coincidence looms up again. On the other hand, suppose the farmer had felt instead some compulsion or urge, which he did not understand, to change his plans and work near the hedge which bordered the boy's road to school : what should we say of this?

Various possibilities present themselves. The sanest and most purposeful of us are sometimes liable to act oddly at the behest of some irrational whim, and perhaps a sufficiently clever psychologist might uncover the causes of this in some particular case. One also thinks of paranormal possibilities, clairvoyance, telepathy, precognition. These would present special difficulties in this case, for presumably the farmer would have to change his plans before the prayer began, unless we postulate that the boy had formed a clear intention beforehand to pray at a certain spot. But if we can overcome generally the difficulties of precognition (perhaps by not regarding it as direct knowledge of the future), we might have available to us an explanation in terms of some paranormal factor not expressly religious.

I am aware that the phrase 'mere telepathy', for example, has not the explanatory value that is sometimes accorded to it, any more than 'instinct' explains the curious phenomena of which it is often the label. But if we do find, as seems in fact to be the case, that some persons have paranormal powers or that there are certain paranormal events, then we might find reason to include the strange occurrence posited now among those; and to do that would not in itself accord it any religious status, unless a firm connection were otherwise established between the paranormal and religion.

To be sure that a prayer is being answered we should need more than the materialization, even in very extraordinary circumstances, of the good prayed for; and this appears fatal to many ways in which belief in the practical efficacy of prayer is commended. The procedure adopted often is merely to recite astonishing examples of alleged answers to prayer. Someone was desperately ill, the ablest doctors were convinced that there was no hope of his recovery and 'gave him up', but he himself, or perhaps his friends unknown to him, prayed for his recovery, and lo, contrary to all expectation he began to mend, and a situation which seemed irretrievable was restored. The difficulty which presents itself at once when this sort of case is cited, is that of the many seemingly similar circumstances in which the prayer has not been answered. There seem to be enough negative examples to leave the explanation open, to attribute the recovery of the patient, if not to some subtle psychological influence, at least to some unknown factor which may, or *may not*, be religious.

It was in the spirit of this sort of scepticism that one person, according to Bacon, on being shown a picture of those who had paid their vows as having escaped shipwreck, observed, 'But where are they painted that were drowned after their vows?'[1]

Can we then redeem the situation in any way? As part of the attempt to do so let me note first certain ways in which the sting of the 'negative instances' can be much reduced in the case of prayer.

In the first place, not every prayer is for a sufficiently worthy end. Men do indeed sometimes pray for ends which it is preposterous to expect God to bless in any way. If I pray for terrible destruction to fall on my enemy or request that fire from heaven should consume

[1] *Novum Organum*, Bk. I, Section XLVI.

those who oppose me, then I am seeking God's co-operation in matters not consistent with His character and declared purpose. The corrective to malevolent prayer of this kind is found in the express teaching and example of Jesus. Even if I am being opposed in a good cause there are very severe limits to the hindrances which I may ask to be placed upon my adversary. One certainly ought not to pray for preferential treatment which would place others at an unjust disadvantage. If I am competing for a post I ought not to pray that my rival be ill or fail to do himself justice when he meets the electors. Nor, if I have been idle, should I pray that I pass my examination.

Instances need not be multiplied. A vast number of unanswered prayers will fall into the class of prayers for radically unworthy ends which it is wrong, indeed blasphemous and not merely ill-judged, to make the subject of prayer. To these we may add prayers for trivial ends or things we can quite properly provide for ourselves. We have been set to live in a certain kind of world, and to ask at every point that the normal conditions of existence be altered to suit our immediate convenience is to rebel against the wisdom of God in creating just this sort of world and to repudiate our own responsibilities. It only needs ordinary human wisdom to realize how impossible the sort of life we now lead would be if we could immediately implement any purpose or satisfy any wish at will and without effort. The order of nature must have reasonable stability for us to inhabit the world at all, and much of the worth and interest of what we do depends on contriving to achieve our ends under certain limitations and with obstacles to overcome—co-operation has its worth in the same way. It would be very far from being to our advantage to have accorded to us an Aladdin's lamp or a spiritual button to press to rid us of the slightest inconvenience.

This does not mean that simple and ordinary concerns should have no place in prayer. We ought, on the contrary, to bring our whole lives to be consecrated in the most solemn and sustaining and closest of our relationships to God. We may ask His blessing on all we undertake and commit our friends and others in their normal pursuits to the loving care of God. But this is not the sort of case where we should normally expect special divine intervention. At most we should expect it in some exceptional unforeseen situation. Normally the prayer for blessing on ourselves and what we and others undertake would be understood elliptically as a way of bringing our lives and mutual relationships as fully as possible within the orbit of our relation to God in all its forms. This will certainly 'make a difference', but the sort of difference we normally expect from the intertwining of lives religiously lived. No one expects more except in extraordinary contingencies—and it is with these that we are concerned now.

All that I have just said bears very closely on another reason, not in the least embarrassing to religious faith, why many prayers are not answered, namely the way prayers must be offered and the conditions of their acceptability to God. Prayers made in a casual and light-hearted or thoughtless manner are hardly likely to avail at all. To suppose they can is again to equate prayer with magic, to make it an Aladdin's lamp which anyone could work at will, once told the correct formal procedures. But it cannot be stressed too much how far removed prayer in the proper sense is from magic. It is not a standard way of manipulating either things or God, but communion based on a rounded personal relationship, the most solemn and sacred of all; and the petitionary side of prayer must be considered in the closest relation to the whole of it.

Mention has already been made of the mistaken view that the efficacy of religious rites does not depend much on the spirit in which they are performed, and that it is possible, in some cases, for the rite to be observed by unworthy persons or in very unworthy frames of mind, and yet achieve its purpose; and I expressed my profound lack of sympathy with this formalization of religion and noted its extreme perils. The case of prayer is the same. It does not follow that all prayer must be spontaneous and never be practised except as it wells up within us. A religious life needs formality and discipline. But if there is any soundness in the theme of this book, centred as it is on the notion of live religious awareness, it must be plain that prayer is not genuine at all in the absence of certain moral and spiritual conditions.

I do not mean that the only persons entitled to pray are highly moral ones—and that only in highly moral states of mind or will. If that were the case prayer would need to be very sporadic, and not what we are commanded to do without ceasing. We have, in fact, the highest authority for the propriety of the sinner's prayer. On the other hand, what is most commended in that particular context is the contrition and repentance of the sinner. Where there is no evidence of contrition or any acknowledgement of sin, or any other moral concern, it does not seem likely that proper prayer is possible— a desperate cry sent echoing into the void perhaps, but not the prayer which religious enlightenment teaches us to address to a just and holy God. If there is not at least genuine repentance we can hardly expect to be made free of the power of prayer, and the more there is positive moral attainment the more we should expect, other things being equal, that the union we achieve with God should release exceptional powers or be accompanied by extraordinary incidents.

But the condition of efficacious prayer which is most stressed is faith. This includes moral factors and much besides. I shall not consider carefully here how 'faith' must be understood in this context. It is much more than having a confident attitude, and, if I were to include close consideration of the subject within the scope of this book, it is to the enlivening of religious awareness that I should turn again for my clue to the sort of faith which has most relevance to the answer to prayer. But however we understand faith, in a close analysis of it, and however much dispositional as well as occurrent factors enter into it, it is a spiritual condition not always easy to achieve or maintain. Even those most fortunately placed to achieve it have often lamentably failed, as the Christian Gospels and the lives and confessions of good and devout persons fully demonstrate. A very small amount of genuine faith may bring astonishing results, but the faith which moves mountains is yet of a quality which very few achieve.

There are then conditions attaching to prayer, although we need only give a brief indication of them here. And, in addition, we have to remember that belief in the efficacy of petitionary prayer does not involve the expectation that such prayers will invariably receive an explicit answer. The Christian usually prefaces his petitions with the words, 'Thy will be done', and to all that he asks of God he adds the proviso, sometimes but not always expressly uttered—'if it be in accordance with Thy will'. Now we have suggested that our relationship to God may be such that our making prayerful requests will, on occasion, affect what is best for us and others to receive. But there is no reason to suppose that this will happen in all cases where petitions are sincerely and worthily made. God in His wisdom may know and dispose otherwise.

The advocate of petitionary prayer need not therefore be altogether daunted by the fact that there seem to be so many prayers not answered—at least in the sense of granting our explicit petitions. On the other hand the case that he has to make is obviously complicated and made harder by the impossibility of finding an obvious and close correlation between petitions seemingly made devoutly and sincerely and the granting of them. And it is just at this point that the theme of the present volume seems to me to bear on this vexing question and the closely connected question of miracle in general. For I submit that the correlation which we need may perhaps be found after all if we bring in a further factor, namely the enlivened experience to which I have referred. If we look to reputed cases of answers to prayer in the present sense, and especially to notable ones such as those which have prominence in sacred scriptures and the lives of conspicuously holy men, we may indeed find that there is much which may be treated as coincidence or superstitious legend; but we may nonetheless also find an impressive correlation of such occurrences and the peculiar enlivening of the sense of God reflecting itself in the way described already into the situation in which this happens. Some relation of this kind between petitionary prayer and religious experience may take us a long way, and this may be strengthened for certain individuals by finding that some prayer of their own seems expressly efficacious in some circumstance of that kind.

My own view is that the firm conviction which some devout persons have that their prayers, for material or spiritual benefit or for guidance, have been directly answered, should be understood in this way, although no doubt many bogus claims will be made through unreason, arrogance and credulity. But the case will not rest entirely on these experiential and quasi-empirical grounds. It will depend also in part on the view we generally form of the character of God and the way in which we find that He deals with us, a view in turn also derived from the course of God's intervention in the experiences of men. The closeness of the personal character of God's relation to us should make us at least fairly open to the expectation that this may sometimes take the extraordinary form of answers to petitionary prayer.

Into the final reckoning there must also be put the explicit teaching on this subject of outstanding religious leaders, and especially for Christians of Jesus. It seems to me very hard not to understand the teaching of Jesus as involving the injunction to include in prayer petitions which we expect to be granted. To this it may be replied that the limitations to which Jesus was subject as a human being, whatever further view we may hold of His 'person', prevent His views from being infallible on all matters. We do not, for example, credit Him with perfect foreknowledge or exact historical knowledge or understanding of science. Nonetheless, when all allowances are made for these limitations and the circumstances of His time, the belief in miracle and petitionary prayer seems sufficiently near the centre of the teaching which is inseparable from the mission and status of Jesus, however precisely a Christian understands this, to carry special weight with those who accord exceptional authority to Jesus.

This does not render the sort of considerations I have advanced about prayer redundant. For, in the first place, the views we may hold about Jesus, as about other outstanding persons in religion, are not to be detached from our understanding of what religion and the process of divine disclosure in general are like; and we have likewise to draw on the same source for our correct interpretation of all religious teaching. My recommendation would be that we regard the place we find we can accord in a general way to petitionary prayer and miracle as having a reciprocal or organic relation to views independently arrived at about the teaching and authority of Jesus, the two thus tending, subject to possible misinterpretations and error, to support one another. One may thus look to views which for independent reasons we esteem or trust for support of the

approval and confidence with which we may regard
the practice of petitionary prayer.

If this position can be maintained, it will in turn
afford us our point of departure for the discussion of
miracles in general. I do not in fact think there is much
to be added on the subject of miracles which does not
come into any adequate discussion of petitionary prayer,
and I have singled out this latter subject for discussion
as the best way of exhibiting the general bearing which
the theme of this book has on questions of this kind.
Miracle and prayer are not easily detached, but, to the
extent that there may be miracles which are not answers
to prayers inwardly or outwardly uttered in some form,
our reason for accepting them, unless it be derived from
some other teaching which we consider independently
to be authoritative, must turn much, I submit, on
correlations with distinctive and exceptional religious
experiences of the kind already described.

This enables me to add that I do not ascribe to
miracle, the altogether vital position which it takes in
some forms of Christianity. In some traditions, and they
are as live today as ever, the view to be held about the
work and person of Christ depends, in an almost mechanical fashion, on acceptance of miracle; and this is
sometimes coupled with desperate efforts to establish the
credibility of the miracles of Jesus on historical evidence
in which there is little admixture of independent religious
factors. I do not think the case for miracles can be made
in this way, and I do not consider that the essential
things which a Christian has to believe about the work
and person of Christ have the belief in miracle at their
core.

To this I shall return, albeit very briefly for the purpose of this book. But in the meantime I have to
comment further on an aspect of the personal character
of God's relation to us and His intervention in the world.
The latter, as I have urged, becomes apparent as the

pattern of men's religious experiences in the past, extending into the whole of their lives and the life of their society, becomes evident to us, and especially as it displays its significance within the enlivening of a like experience in the present. But within this process a special place is to be accorded to morality.

CHAPTER 18

RELIGION AND MORALITY

The relation of morality to religion is a subject that has been widely and frequently discussed, and there are few issues of great importance which have been more bedevilled by misunderstandings. Of these no proper account can be attempted here. But there is one point which we must make plain, namely that there is no immediate argument from the objectivity of ethics to the existence of God or to other truths about Him. The view has often been advanced, firstly that there can be no morality in the proper sense unless worth and obligation are independent of our own inclinations and reactions, and secondly that there cannot be this independence in the way required unless our standards are imposed or established by God or in some other way due to Him. The attractiveness of this view is obvious. It provides for morality the firmest possible foundation, and, at the same time it gives to morality that central place in religion which seems to be its due. Morality and religion we feel to be closely intertwined, and the account of them just noted seems best fitted to do this justice.

Nonetheless I think the argument a specious and misleading one. There is certainly some sense in which morality, like everything else, depends on God. The universe is one universe, and all there is within it leads out eventually to one mysterious and transcendent source by which all is sustained in some way of which we have no conception. But this is in no way peculiar to morality. It is as true of the most insignificant speck of dust as of the principles of highest worth or of lives in conformity with them. It is as true of arithmetic as of ethics. This does not mean that moral worth and other norms and values retain their significance merely at the finite level, and are of no direct account when we think of God. They are what they are in a transcendent reference as much as anywhere else, but they have no monopoly of the reference to the transcendent and expressly exhibit to us nothing in this connection beyond what they are or mean in themselves and the dignity or awesomeness which invests them when seen to share with all things an ultimate absolute source. One consequence of this is that it is in no way preposterous to believe in objective ethical principles while denying or doubting the truth of religion. The atheist does not believe in God, but that is no reason why he should not believe that certain things have worth in themselves and that he has duties. Nor is he committed in any way to degrade his duty to some kind of enlightened self-interest. Duty is duty for him as for another, we admire his conformity with it and censure his lapses. If he feels remorse for wrongdoing, that is as it should be. We regret that he does not *also* see the necessity by which God exists, and we try to enlighten him on this and other religious matters. But that he should fail to follow us in this further step is no reason for suspecting that he does not apprehend properly other things which he claims to apprehend in common with religious believers.

We should rejoice in fact when common ground is found for atheists or agnostics and religious believers, and the strategy for the latter, most of all in the menacing and confused state of the world today, is to seek all the co-operation possible with enlightened and idealistic humanists. To deny that humanists can be actuated by the same motives as ourselves, or that they have the same understanding as religious folk have of justice and compassion in themselves, seems preposterous. Do we not all know admirable humanists whose idealism it were well for others to emulate? Dare we in seriousness impugn their motives? And why should we? We do not question their understanding of arithmetic or their knowledge of ordinary facts or of science. We do not discredit a scientist or a logician as such by declaring him an agnostic; it is not impossible for a brilliant scientific discovery to be made by an atheist. Why should ethics be in a different case? If the atheist can see the truth of the one, without also seeing what is true about God, can he not do this of the other? Where is the difference, at this stage, between ethics and arithmetic?

We should remember also that the most instructive discussions of the objectivity of morals (including, in the case of books like G. E. Moore's *Principia Ethica* and W. D. Ross's *Foundations of Ethics*, what seem to me the best defences ever offered of moral objectivity) make no mention of any expressly religious argument. That does not preclude their authors from having religious views, but, if they do, that is a further matter. We do not require to know their religion to endorse their arguments about ethics.

The view has sometimes been put forward, even by high-minded theologians, that if one loses one's religious faith there is nothing other than expediency to restrain one from any nefarious action or to discourage alliance with oppressive and evil movements. Professor Leonard Hodgson, for example, writes: 'If this space-time universe, this developing process, be the whole of reality, I do not see how we can ever get beyond acknowledging it as a brute fact . . . I do not see how our judgements of value could ever be more than the expression of our own subjective tastes. . . . In theory, the last word would

be with the existentialist; in practice, with the dictator.'[1]
Now Professor Hodgson is a notably humane and rational
person, and I submit that if he were to cease to be a
Christian, he would still hold the practices of dictators
in moral abhorrence and not dream of allying himself
with oppressors.

Moreover the force which ideas of worth and duty
have in a transcendent reference, and in religion generally, would be lost if we emptied them of the meaning
they have in ordinary or secular contexts. To put this
very simply, if we are to say that God is good we must
give 'good' some meaning not expressly derived from
'God'.

But from the religious point of view there is an even
more serious objection to thinking of religion and
morality in terms of the present argument from moral
objectivity to religion, namely that it tends to present the
relation of God to the world, most of all at the vital point
of morality, in a very remote, rather deistic and impersonal manner. God is relegated to the limits of experience
without also bringing Him to the live centre of it,
He functions as a foundation or scaffolding for moral
principles instead of being Himself encountered as the
living voice of individual conscience, a real person
disclosing Himself in moral experience and expressly
concerned about our conduct above all.

By contrast with the view which is rejected here,
and which I have attempted to criticize in much greater
detail elsewhere, the account of religious experience and
revelation offered above finds the distinctive relation
of religion to morality not in some peculiar dependence
of morality as such on religion nor in extrapolations
of morality in a transcendent reference open to our
understanding, but in the provision by morality of the
sphere *par excellence* where finite experience is transmuted into the disclosures and operations of the trans-

[1] *For Faith and Freedom*, p. 131.

cendent within the world we know. It is not merely in
the moral life that God speaks—we find Him in other
interests and in by-ways where we sometimes least expect
Him. But the centrality of ethics for other human concerns, and the difficulty of engaging in any activity
without some implicit assessment of worth, make these
extensions and intensifications of ethical insights which
are due especially to religion of paramount importance
in the religious conditioning or toning of human experience and progress.

We discover, moreover, that the course which distinctively religious occurrences have shaped for themselves within the general life of mankind has in point of
fact determined itself especially in relation to moments
of moral tension and crisis, such as the abandonment of
established practices in favour of new and more enlightened ones or the strains and exactions of some specific
personal or social moral dilemma. The sense of the
transcendent becoming compelling in a striking and
significant fashion, and providing truer and refined
understanding of a present situation, has come to men
especially in circumstances set for them by moral
issues; and this has recurred, in countless obscure cases
as in more momentous occurrences, in such a fashion
as to establish the dealing of God with men in these
ways as a concern He pre-eminently has for the moral
quality of our lives, with respect both to moral understanding and to performance.

It is furthermore in our responses or failures at this
ethical level that the relation in which we find ourselves
standing to God completes its personal character. For
there is not only the illumination from within the normal
functioning of our own faculties which is also signifi-
cantly initiated from without, but also the requirement
of our own co-operation, not only in the way of heedful
and sustained attention but also in the inclination of
our wills to the exactions of a new way of life. Through-

out there is this reciprocal, dynamic and often dramatic
character within our experience which is much affected
by the adaptations we make, or fail to make, ourselves.
And the persistence with which this process renews
itself, in spite of betrayal or neglect on our part, and
the modifications of it to counter neglect or resistance,
the exhibition of a variable strategy of seeking and grace,
render exceptionally evident the character and purpose
of divine intervention as pre-eminently a loving care for
the rounded perfection of our characters, a perfection
in which moral integrity moulds the rest into the form
which this communion of man with God requires for its
fulfilment.

One consequence, but not the only one, of holding
this view is that the dignity of man as a responsible
being is much enhanced. One of the extraordinary
features of some highly influential and persistent theological views is the equanimity with which their authors
seem able to discard the notion of man's genuine capacity for responsible action, notwithstanding some half-
hearted lip-service to freedom. In opposition to these
views, I have been maintaining in earlier writings that
nothing but harm can come to the cause of religion
from dimming or depressing our sense of the soundness
of moral distinctions and the freedom of choice which
they presuppose. But if the view I have outlined is the
true one, and if we think of God genuinely at work
in the experience of men, it is this basic condition of
moral activity, namely the freedom by which we function most distinctively as individuals, that needs to be
stressed.

Moral freedom is not the only freedom we have. There
is an important sense in which intellectual activity and
art are free. But this is not the freedom of choice between genuinely open alternatives. The latter choice
is not determined in any fashion, not even by our own

characters, much less by circumstances. The occasion
for it is set by conditions, within and without ourselves, which we do not finally control, and its scope
is limited in the same way. What we are and the situation in which we find ourselves determine how far
inclination and duty are in accord, and the occasion
for properly moral choice presents itself, not at all times
nor freakishly in any and every direction, but when our
strongest inclinations at a particular time deviate from
the course we take to be obligatory upon us. Further
analysis of these conditions of moral responsibility
falls outside the scope of this book. My concern at the
moment is to insist that it is in his capacity of an agent
capable of exercising such a choice that a man has his
most distinctive part to play in the drama of intervention and response by which the purpose of God is
achieved.

But at this point we seem bound to face one of our
stiffest hurdles in the form of the alleged dilemma of
grace and freedom. If our reading of divine disclosure
and intervention is correct in exhibiting these as pre-
eminently showing concern for our moral welfare,
should we not expect our own moral improvement to
have a prominent place in the process by which God
thus takes us into fellowship with Himself? This is how
the matter is commonly understood; if God's concern
is especially for our moral well-being, that is presumably
an end He promotes, and grace comes thus to be
regarded as an influence by which we become morally
worthy or are enabled to do what is proper. There are
other reasons for holding this view, concerned with
beliefs about God's foreknowledge and omnipotence. I
shall not enter into these now, but confine myself to
expressing my own inability to reconcile these widely
accepted ideas of grace with what we feel is bound to be
true about our responsibility as moral agents and with
the notions of distinctively moral worth and evil and

of the guilt and remorse associated with responsible action.

There may indeed be a 'double determination' of our activities at certain levels, poets or musicians may owe as much to the influence and inspiration which their friends or others provide as to their own talents and effort, their work is pre-eminently their own and also that for which they are particularly indebted to others. But this can hardly hold of moral activity in the strict sense; and our moral experience, I submit, is the one sphere where we are thrown altogether on our own resources and required to function in a way which owes nothing directly to either man or God. The difficulties involved in the notion of our morally good actions being themselves the action of God within us are fairly evident, for is it not implied, among other things, that God must also be held to account for our failures? And whatever view we hold in general about the exceedingly difficult problem of evil, we can hardly ascribe *moral* evil to God. There are difficulties also in the libertarian view which I commend instead, but I shall not attempt to supplement here the admirable discussions of the subject in recent philosophical literature.[2]

But if we are not to regard the operation of grace as an influence directly inducing us to do what we ought, how shall we think of it? In the first place, it is not, in my view, wise to include in the idea of the grace of God all the good influences to which we are subject. We do indeed sometimes speak in a way which implies that wide connotation of the term, we ascribe a fortunate upbringing or the care of wise teachers to the bountifulness of God's grace. But I should think it better on

---

[2] For example in chapters IV and V of C. A. Campbell's *Scepticism and Construction* and chapter IX of the same author's *Selfhood and Godhood*; cf. also 'Freedom and Punishment', by J. D. Mabbott, in *Contemporary British Philosophy*, Third Series.

the whole not to extend the term in this fashion to all the good things in our lot which we must ultimately ascribe to God. We need a term for the distinctive influence of God upon us which comes through special religious channels, and, as the word 'grace' has mainly been used in that sense, there seems to be much to be gained by confining it to his more restricted use.

In this more determinate sense, the operation of grace appears in more than one form. One of these is the illumination of our minds about worth and duty, and especially about the course to be followed on particular occasions. We have seen that this does not happen independently of our ordinary faculties, but by the heightening and correcting of these in the enlivening of religious awareness; but there is nonetheless provided in this way an insight not otherwise obtainable which we may thus properly ascribe to a distinctively religious influence. But in the same way our characters are modified and our interests transformed and elevated. Many temptations which might normally assail us lose their force, ends which might turn us from the course of duty lose the attraction they might otherwise have and our lives will in this as in other ways be different and better because we are subject to the operation of grace within us. But what we attain in this way is not strictly moral worth, it is virtue perhaps, there being good precedent for using the word 'virtue' to designate admirable traits of character, such as a brave or charitable disposition. But moral excellence, in the strict sense, is attained when we do right on the occasions when our formed characters, subject as they may be to the refining influence of grace, are not of the strength to ensure that we do right or find our firmest inclinations in accord with our conssciences. Grace is not at work here, for this is the point *par excellence* where God leaves it to us to co-operate with Him and respond in a way that is wholly our own. It does not follow that a person subject

to the influence of grace lives no better than another,
or than he would do himself if left merely to secular
influences. He will, on the contrary, exhibit virtuous
qualities of character which are not only noble in themselves but which will also keep his conduct outwardly
more seemly and serviceable to his fellows.

We may thus properly ascribe to the influence of
grace a gain in sensitivity and insight, most of all in
moral matters, and the refinement of character. It is
likewise by grace that we come to view our obligations
as the will of God for us and the discharge of them as
service by which our fellowship with Him is deepened.
Other pursuits which do not derive their worth expressly
from being undertaken as duties acquire likewise the
additional significance of activities we consecrate in the
fullness of fellowship with God. But we have yet to
exhibit the point where grace acquires the form and
significance which the religious consciousness has come
to consider most distinctive of it and its special function
in the developing process of religion as a whole.

This is where grace brings about a sense of repentance
and sorrow at wrongful action, as not merely morally
wrong, but also a rupture and betrayal of our fellowship
with God and contempt of the claims of that supreme
blessing. Most that we find to be of worth is tied up in
some way with personal relationships, and among the
things most valuable in themselves are intimate personal
relationships, our loves and friendships. Nor are there
many greater causes of sorrow and distress than the
rupture of such relations, especially when this is known
to be due to some avoidable fault or offence of our own.
But by far the richest and most enthralling relationship
we can have is our fellowship with God, little though the
fullness and wonder of this may dwell in our minds. Even
the most devout do not sustain at its height the triumphant sense of the glory and wonder of the presence of
God, but the more God's presence is made evident to us

the more we treasure it as our richest prize extending its own inestimable worth to all other gains; and at the very heart of this lies the knowledge that it comes about by the initiative of God, it is His own gift of Himself to us. But if we also know that, by negligence or wilful wrong, we have dimmed and strained this relationship and made ourselves unworthy of it by setting our own lesser concerns above its claims, then this is the most searing and tragic agony of spirit we can ever know. It brings the sense of irretrievable loss and of despair made the more hopeless by guilt. And this, in the course of renewed awareness of God, sometimes brought about in turns of events we can trace and sometimes more mysteriously, is what grace accentuates and keeps open, bringing the sinner to the despair where repentance begins.

But the process does not stop there. For that very hope which helps to convert the extremity of despair into repentance exhibits the work of grace as being from the start to restore and reconcile at the same time as it induces despair and shame. The sense of shame is an advance into reconciliation which is made more complete with the deepening assurance of God's abiding concern, humiliating and costing though it may be to Him as to ourselves; and this is displayed to us in renewals of the sense of His haunting presence still seeking us out with the gift of Himself. This crowning work of grace, in reconciling men with God and perfecting them anew in their union with Him, brings no immunity from further lapses, least of all when the superseding of old temptations exposes us to new ones. The experience of the saints, afflicted as the most devout continue to be with the distresses and anxieties of our present lot, shows that there is no laying down of arms in the battle to be waged with their own weaknesses; and the more they have advanced in the knowledge of God's all-encompassing and reconciling love, the greater also is the horror and despair with which they view their own lapses, enabling us again to understand better how devout and estimable persons come sincerely to describe themselves as the chief of sinners. It is not in immunities that grace 'abounds' but in the inexhaustible possibilities of reconciliation, it does not eliminate sin but reclaims the sinner; and that is its work *par excellence*.

The centrality of moral conceptions in the dealings of God with men and in the modes of His presence to them is that which has caused some religious writers of exceptional insight and sensitivity to come very near equating God with the moral order itself. An instructive example of this may be found in Professor John Baillie's justifiably celebrated work, *Our Knowledge of God*. One of the main themes of this book is that religious belief is universal, the seeming atheist 'really' believing 'at the bottom of his heart' that there is a God; and, to sustain this view, in the face of obvious difficulties, Professor Baillie is inclined to write as if the presence of 'an uneasy conscience' were all that he had to establish, thereby gaining his point at the cost of a very grave attenuation of what Christians would normally understand by being 'confronted by the challenge of God in Christ'.[8] But Professor Baillie is not alone among theologians and philosophers today in tending to identify God with duty. I think these writers are wrong, but we can see how their view may seem true when God comes to us so much in the demands of conscience and in the exhibition of His concern about our moral worth and the mending of the breach caused by our lapses, mending them in ways consistent with our status and freedom as moral beings and without diminishing the sanctity of duty, overcoming sin, not by abrogating or reducing the claims of justice, not by minimizing the gravity of sin, but in the costing humiliations of a love that makes itself 'of no reputation'.

[8] *Our Knowledge of God*, p. 8.

This is the context in which the claims which Christians make about Jesus are properly viewed. Christians affirm that Jesus has a crucial role to play in the process by which God makes Himself known to men and wins them to Himself. All that had been religiously astir before Jesus, and all that came after, finds its fulfilment and ultimate meaning in Him. He is the centre of the story of religiously determined events and presents a unique and decisive mode of divine seeking and reconciliation. All other forms and occasions of divine intervention, both within and without the Hebrew-Christian tradition, have their own character properly and fully revealed in relation to the work accomplished in Jesus. A promise which other disclosures of God convey, more certainly as they take definite shape, that they have within them more than they seem to be in themselves and their inter-relations, is both made more explicit in Jesus and afforded fulfilment.

This comes about moreover through the way Jesus provides a focus for the process of divine intervention as a whole, gathering up into His own life what has occurred religiously within and without it, drawing the whole as it were into Himself, and thereby establishing an identity of Himself as an individual with the impact of the transcendent upon us in all other ways. He comes before us thus, not as a man whose mind God has more than usually illumined and who finds God very near, a seer or a prophet, but as Himself Very God; and in His humiliations and suffering, endured without mitigation due to consciousness of the role He filled, we have the finality and fullness of God's giving of Himself and the means by which He ensures the triumph of His love in the hearts of men and the victory over all evil. The measure of God's concern to win us in this way to union with Himself affords us the key to the purpose for which we were made and our means of approach to other outstanding issues.

It does not by any means follow that major problems speedily dissolve before the understanding obtained in these ways. On the contrary they will remain a source of considerable tension. Unmerited and seemingly random and pointless suffering will continue to bewilder and tantalize the Christian. But he will not be altogether cast down by it, for he can confront it with his assurance, independently obtained, of the unlimited character of God's involvement in the world. It will, again, be very obscure to us how the triumph of the love of God bears on our supersession of the mortal lot we have now and the metamorphosis we may undergo in surviving death. It has not yet been disclosed what we shall be. We may speculate and may make some advances with this as with other questions, and it is well that the attempt be made. But the basis of our faith, in all such matters, is the disclosure of the unlimited concern of God to win us to Himself.

In this itself there is also much which eludes understanding and which we must accept on the basis of what we do understand and see to be the case, that is by faith. The difficulty is as much one of meaning as of truth, perhaps more so; for what can it mean for a man to be God? The recent preoccupation with meaning has particular relevance here. It will not do merely to cry out 'mystery'. The mystery must have some warrant, or we give very dangerous hostages to fortune, and what I have ventured to do is to indicate how this central Christian conception may begin to have meaning for us in the context of the process by which God makes Himself known to us. Consider it otherwise and you may not only find yourself doubting its truth, but not even able to give it any real meaning which may soften its seeming impossibility; you will not know properly what sort of claim to assess, and that is, I think, the usual position of the agnostic here.

The significance of particular Christian occurrences—

for example the apostolic witness or resurrection appearances—within the appropriate evidence as a whole does not concern us now. Nor need we consider the ramifications and difficulties of the doctrines which express the central Christian convictions, such as the doctrine of the Trinity. For to do that would be to embark on the work which the theologian must take over from the philosopher—without ceasing, one hopes, to be a philosopher, for this is one of the points *par excellence* where the co-operation between philosophers and theologians needs to be very close. All that requires to be said for our purpose is that our thinking on all such matters has to be fluid and open, notwithstanding the firmness of our initial conviction, and that we must neither overlook, nor be daunted by, the difficulties which are bound to present themselves with considerable force.

The difficulties need not cast us down, provided we renew the experience by which we find that the person who confronts us in the New Testament records, fragmentary and uncertain though these may be in some regards, is one with the supreme and mysterious reality whose impact men feel everywhere 'at sundry times and in diverse manners', in the enlivened religious experience. We do not yet see all things 'put under us', and in some respects not intended by the author of Hebrews we may never do so, 'but we do see Jesus, who was made a little lower than the angels for the suffering of death, crowned with glory and honour, that He by the grace of God should taste death for every man'.

This is where the work of some recent 'existentialist' theologians impinges on our theme. For they too have stressed the importance, for our Christology, of the enlivened present assurance. But they have also tended to isolate this from the historical evidence, and indeed to find the warrant for the latter in a present experience of God in Christ. There is much which I find extremely bewildering here, and I suspect that some of the writers in question draw unduly sceptical conclusions from recent Biblical scholarships and criticism, partly perhaps through neglect of distinctions such as I drew earlier between secular historical fact and 'religious fact'. I do not see how the 'Christ of faith' can be known except in properly knowing the 'Jesus of history', and if we neglect this we shall be apt to fall back, as only too many of our existentialist friends have done, on rigid dogmatism little in accord with the insistence on 'present experience'.

Our proper procedure in respect of the matter I have just been discussing, and also of difficult questions of the practical implications of Christian commitment in the world of today, may be made plainer in the following comparison. Consider two very different ways in which a map may be used. We may use a road map to motor about the country. This is a fairly straightforward mechanical business, most of all where there are frequent signposts. We plot the main centres on our route and look out for the places which link them. Provided we are reasonably alert we cannot go wrong, and a mistake is easily discovered and corrected. But to use a map in open country is a very different matter. The route on that map may be clear enough there also. We find we should continue straight ahead for a mile and then bear a little to the left up the slope of a hill and on to a valley beyond. But how do we know when a mile is covered in open country, perhaps with no distinct landmarks, how much to the left should we veer, and, worst of all, how does one keep one's direction on a curving and sloping hillside? Which of the various possibilities is the valley we are looking for? Anyone with the slightest knowledge of moorland or mountain walking, even on the mild scale possible in this country, will know these difficulties only too well, and will have learnt from disconcerting experience how easily one may go altogether away from one's course. Yet some seem to fare very much better than others and learn not to falter or make mistakes. I have been much aided myself, and duly impressed, by the uncanny sense of direction of a friend I have been fortunate enough to have as my companion on country excursions, and although he seemed to me to take a course which appeared at the time against all good sense, we always came out right in the end, and I could only marvel that what seemed all wrong to me turned out to be clearly right, and was obviously so to my friend all along.

Now this may be ascribed to a sixth sense which some of us have and others lack. But it is easy to make far too great a mystery of it all, as, let us say, of a 'woman's intuition'. My friend had an interest which I had not in the contours and configuration of the country-side, he did not just revel in it at random; and he had an interest in maps. He would make a point of identifying places on the map, while I treated the map as a bulky necessary evil to be consulted mainly when in difficulties. By consistent attention and practice and experience, my friend had acquired the knack of trans-lating a square inch of map into a square mile of open country and of discerning the lines of the countryside which totally eluded the unobservant.

Is there not a rough but instructive correspondence here with two ways in which we approach the Scriptures and other religious evidence? In its crudest form, the first is exemplified in attempts to settle religious controversies by quoting isolated verses of Scripture, or by seeking guidance or the solution to some moral dilemma by opening the Bible at random and noting the verse on which our eye or finger first alights; others hold the map upside down and interpret everything in the New Testament on the basis of the Old, or of arbitrarily selected parts of it; yet others elaborate theological notions in a purely *a priori* fashion, as if they were a set of formal abstract notions. All these let themselves be guided on the principle of the road map, as if the apprehension of truth in religion were a simple, mechanical matter which anyone could take up when he liked, and where one can be practically infallible. By contrast with this we have the person who acquires a sense of proportion and direction, a judgment arising from the habit of bringing the Scriptures to bear, as a formative influence, on life as a whole, of discerning their relevance by imbibing their spirit in the process of contending, with alerted faculties, with various intellectual and practical problems. This is not to ignore some very downright and specific and daunting things that we find in crucial parts of the Scriptures, or to make the latter imprecise or vague; but it is to enable the Scriptures to become a live and formative power in our developing experience. There is no infallibility here, although there may indeed be firmness of convictions and reverent heed to the hallowing of certain ethical principles by the religious situation in which they appear.

This last observation bears very closely on the question of the practicability of Christian ethics. Many recent theologians, impressed by the exacting character of Christian selflessness and having understood its requirements much better than some of their over-optimistic liberal predecessors, have thought it to be altogether beyond our reach in this world. Christian ideals are thus said, by Reinhold Niebuhr for example, to be 'impossible' ones. But we may take a less despairing view not only of our own hopes of conforming with these ideals, but also of their relevance in situations that seem to nullify them, if we think clearly about the authority of the person who taught them. After all, it was in connection with the exacting character of the claims He made upon His followers, in the case of the rich young ruler, that Jesus Himself observed that things not possible with men are possible with God.

At the same time, the way to be followed is not to be

discerned, least of all in the world as we find it today, without prayerful and often agonizing thought. Nor must we lose sight of the fact that the ethical judgments themselves have a part in our assessment of a situation as a religious one and in our discernment of religious authority; and this in its turn will happen only as the whole situation is made to yield its secret from within the wholeness of sanctified living.

It is when the Bible is allowed to address us in this way and become absorbed into the substance of our lives that we have the true existentialism and find in our Scriptures the proper foundation for dogma, and it is also when we make the Bible a part of ourselves in this fashion that we apprehend how the dominant figure within it encounters us in the present as Very God bringing His work of salvation to fruition.

CHAPTER 19

ENCOUNTER AND IMMEDIACY

The way for religion is not easy at present. Many things compete for the loyalties it used to elicit, most of all political movements such as nationalism. These stir men deeply and move them to devoted and unselfish service, they provide causes with which men readily identify themselves and for which they are prepared, indeed anxious, to make genuine and costing sacrifice. Movements of this sort provide a social force which is cohesive and at the same time allows considerable scope for ingenuity and resourcefulness. The quality of the movements which have this success is another matter, but it is hard to deny that, except as a feature of movements which are primarily political, religion has largely lost the appeal to whole-hearted enthusiasm and trust which should be pre-eminently its own. It is not at present a power to reckon with as in the past, least of all in the West; and it has rivals which seem more vigorous and prosperous.

There are many reasons for this and many new and exceptional problems created for religious folk in the modern world; and it would be a topic in itself to consider these carefully. There is however one aspect of the present situation which is of exceptional importance for the theme of this book and with which my thesis, if justified, should help us to cope.

This is the period of rapid and extensive change through which we are passing. To note this feature of contemporary life is commonplace. But it is all the same necessary for us to recall it and not overlook it at any point in seeking to apprehend or modify the contemporary attitude to religion. We may come to accept extensive transition and take it for granted without appreciating properly the effect it has on us unless, despite all its obviousness, we sometimes pause to consider it.

At the material level, the conditions under which we live seem to have been more radically altered within a few decades than over many centuries, perhaps millennia, in the past. Although these changes are the culmination (or intensification, for the end is not yet) of a process set in motion with the rise of modern science and much affecting men's minds in the past, yet the extent and rapidity of them in the present century involve so radical a break with previous conditions that there can be few parallels to them in history—perhaps these should be sought in pre-history in the first inventions and adaptations which gave to human life the form we know.

It is well within the experience of persons now living to have regarded an aeroplane with the utmost astonishment, sometimes with an almost incredulous wonder. Motor cars were a novelty before the First World War, telephones little used and radio barely known. All these came firmly and swiftly into the picture between the wars, and since then we have had extensive advances which drastically alter again the means of locomotion and communication. Some scientists regard the discoveries made in nuclear physics as equivalent in extent to the progress from the tom-tom to television. I do not know quite how to assess this sort of claim, but of the range and rapidity of newly gained advances in the control of physical powers and in general understanding, at the microscopic and macroscopic level alike, of our natural environment there can be not the slightest doubt.

Add to this the social and political upheavals of two world wars, and it is evident how important a feature of modern life is swift and extensive change.

It is no novelty, however, for change to induce a great deal of uncertainty and scepticism. Plato set himself to cope with agnosticism induced in that way in Greece in his time, and the tale has often been repeated since. Men's important beliefs, the beliefs by which they live, are largely drawn from their environment. This does not make these beliefs irrational or ill-considered. The proper directing of our attention, and the discipline of mind and character by which wisdom comes, depend on what we imbibe from our social surroundings and the impact of our neighbours upon us; and where there is little social stability the educational function of social conditions is retarded. Balanced judgment and the insight which comes with a fair perspective is difficult, novelties and curiosities have undue prestige, and bewilderment and despair ensue from the rapidity with which fashions oust one another and from the multiplicity of baffling problems created by new situations. All this and more is comprehended in the phrase 'the need for roots', which became widely current with the publication of Simone Weil's penetrating book of that title.

Not all is to be put to the debit side where change and upheaval are concerned. There are many counteracting factors and many ways in which the challenge to meet new and complicated situations stimulates original ideas and brings out exceptional traits of character. But where the upheaval is as complete as it is in many parts of the world today, scepticism and uncertainty are apt to prevail. This is well reflected in the anaemic character of much contemporary culture, in the excessive and sometimes frustrating determination of tough-minded thinkers to avoid anything which savours of idealism and elevated hope, and in the dull unstimulating state of religion in most lands, even where it is outwardly flourishing.

The situation is much aggravated in religion because there is here, in addition to the general need of sustaining present culture by making the past germinative within it, the more explicit dependence of belief on distinctive occurrences and on the effect of these on experience in general which I have been trying to exhibit. When the rupture with the past is sharp and the contrast between our present state and the past which ought to nourish us is extreme, apprehension of the form and substance of religiously significant history will be slight and uncertain. This seems to me to present the religious apologist with one of his hardest problems, and the drift from religion today must be ascribed in part to the lack of historical sense and of continuity with the past in an age when modes of life, and the contrivances and conditions by which life is sustained, are so novel and themselves unstable.

At the crude level this presents itself as inability to appreciate the relevance of insights and precepts derived from remote ages to our own stirring scientific times and our brave, if perilous, new world. The language of religion is strange and its substance is apt to be dismissed along with the superstitions which scientific understanding explodes. Part of the answer to this is to exhibit our indebtedness in literature and kindred modes of culture generally to the past, and the value for us of the cultural achievement of other ages very differently conditioned from our own. We do not dismiss Shakespeare and Homer because they addressed themselves to people lacking our amenities and problems. But these are negative considerations, and there can be no stemming the tide of unbelief and indifference unless we succeed in creating a proper historical sense and perspective and induce others to make the imaginative effort required to discover the past in its sustaining relevance to the present.

One condition of success in such an enterprise is to

create the social environment in which tradition may be rediscovered and perpetuated without becoming stale, and in which heed is naturally and spontaneously paid to the concerns and judgments that lie closest to religion. The problem of evangelism in short is much more a social problem than many realize, and it is the kind of social problem which calls for much resourcefulness and ingenuity as well as sympathy and determination.

It is likewise essential that the implications of any religious understanding we attain, as these become evident to us, should be heeded with the greatest possible earnestness, in deed as in word. The betrayal by Christians of their faith by reluctance to respond to its exacting practical claims is a major factor in their own lack of confidence and the apathy of others. This is also a subject in itself, and I can now only add the warning not to be diverted from exacting claims and difficult adjustments by too exclusive concern for other aspects of religious loyalty, the service of institutions for example. But the matter which arises most directly and expressly from the view I have outlined is that we must come to terms with the social and historical conditions of religious apprehension and cultivate the insight which is only obtained in association of ourselves with a live historical process. The doctrine of the church and of continuing Christian witness has its basis here.

Many will, however, find this course severe and its rewards not sufficiently precise and immediate. They hanker after seemingly more solid foundations of faith— a dogma presenting itself in its fullness with immediate authority, signs and wonders, directly inspired words and infallible institutions. Most of all perhaps reflective opinion today will present some hankering after assurances of the divine concern, and a contact with God, more direct than that which comes as the continuing in present experience of what God has wrought in ascertainable past history.

The last desire is very understandable, but we cannot set ourselves properly to the true tasks of spiritual regeneration until we disabuse ourselves of the allurements of this peculiar religious will o' the wisp. And to this end I should now like to add some further observations to what has already been said about immediacy in religion.

First, a word about the uneasiness that may be felt by those who are exceptionally conscious of the closeness of the presence of God and the importance this has had in religion. It may well be suspected that the outline I have given of the way we come to have a sense of personal encounter or communion in religious experience represents the process as much too sophisticated and reflective to conform with the immediacy or directness with which it is generally credited. The religious man, it will be urged, does not normally theorize about the nature of God and His dealings with us on the basis of an analysis of certain experiences and the patterns and sequences which they present. He is much more directly aware of the presence of God, and only occasionally aspires to philosophical reflection about this experience. In many cases of reflective religion, moreover, the main conclusions turn upon an alleged immediacy of encounter with the divine, much of the philosophy of religion having been prompted and given its direction by inspired and gifted mystics who, so the indictment may continue, make a special claim to immediate experience of God and contend, at least in some cases, that this is the indispensable core of all religions.

In reply I must first refer to the view advanced at the outset about the nature of God as a transcendent being, for, if that view is sound, it appears that the one thing in particular which is precluded for a finite creature is to have that unmediated contact with God which reduces the absolute mystery of His essential nature, and I have urged also that this finds very general support in religious declarations as typical and basic as any to which the allegedly mystical interpretations of religion may appeal.

It will however be more persuasive, and more relevant at this stage, to forswear these further variations on themes already presented and tackle the objections more directly by insisting that an experience which requires involved and sophisticated ideas for its analysis in a philosophical discussion does not thereby lose the naïve and unreflective character we might normally ascribe to it. The obvious parallel is our knowledge of one another, although it seems to me that our knowledge of the external world is not so unworthy of citation in the same connection as some contemporary philosophers assume. For it seems evident that some mediation is unavoidable in our awareness of other persons and that to indicate where precisely this lies and what the justification is for the assumptions we make in our normal communion with one another, and what inferential factors are implicit in this, requires a subtlety and power of abstract formulation which takes us far from the seeming directness and simplicity of ordinary experience. The ordinary man may no doubt be daunted by being told that his friends are inferred, and those who speak with Cook Wilson of immediate certainties here seem clearly to score heavily for that reason. But what appears simple and direct in normal experience, because the processes involved work so smoothly as to give that impression, need not be so in fact, and it is hard to see how any who give their minds to the subject, whatever the views to which they finally incline, can fail to find in the communion of persons with one another factors of much greater complexity than we appreciate in the course of such communion from moment to moment.

In precisely the same fashion our knowledge of the special relation in which we stand to the transcendent and the way we come thereby to translate the mystery and perfection of God as a Supreme Being, involved in the existence of conditioned or dependent being, into the specific and intimate details which commonly determine our worship, may have subtleties and complications which the total impression made upon us by the experience, and the assurances it produces, tend to obscure, and which require much skill and sophistication to uncover. This need not disconcert us any more than our friends need lose their significance to us if we find, on philosophical reflection, that they are 'inferred'.

Moreover, by the impressing into the ways and culture of society of the experiences which, in their sequences and accumulation, confirm and extend our conviction that the transcendent enters into personal relations with us, the experiences in which individuals are most acutely conscious of having communion of this sort acquire, at the time of their occurrence, a semblance of being self-contained and spontaneous which is greater in proportion to their dependence in fact on traditions and attitudes built up and sustained by the occurrence of similar experiences in the past and the way these are interwoven with other features of men's lives. The particular religious experience is thus recognized more easily and naturally for what it is, and the determination of it by events in the past is more subtle and unobtrusive. This is why the prophets speak so insistently and with a sense of an immediately inspired communication the familiar words 'Thus saith the Lord'. Few would claim now that declarations of this kind reflect some sort of verbal inspiration, although abnormal conditions and accompaniments of spiritual insight are not precluded by an understanding of prophecy along the lines outlined. But neither need we suppose that there is any 'I-Thou' relationship which dispenses with mediation through the events of our own lives and those of others and which does not depend on the subtle persistence of the past in the present. The very facts to which the insistence on the 'I-Thou' relation testifies are those which owe most to the aid which our experiences have from the cultural and social setting in which they occur.

A sense of immediacy may also be induced and sharpened when the new element in some religious illumination or occurrence takes a form which we may describe as a consequential one, that is the perception of certain implications of what has already come to be known in a religious way, for example the applicability of some ethical principle to a sphere of interest or activity where its relevance had not been previously perceived. This may come directly as ordinary moral insight but against the background of a general process in which the dominant feature is the enlightenment and direction provided by religion. In its identification with the religious process the moral insight conveys to our impression of the former whatever simplicity and directness it contains in itself, and in the same way other assurances and confidence obtained in the ordinary course of finite experience carry their own qualities into the impression we have of any total religious experience or situation of which they form a part. This also accounts for claims, made by those who seem most inspired religiously, which appear not consistent with the view I have offered of the building up over a period of the personal significance the transcendent may have for us.

Similar considerations help us to deal also with the problem of errancy in prophecy and revelation and with incompatibilities in claims advanced, with confidence and every appearance of sincerity, on the basis of allegedly divine disclosures. The reasons which dispose men generally to unreason and prejudice and dogmatism do not concern us as such in this book. But, granted that men are liable to err in matters of fact or in evaluations of things, and sometimes to persist in such errors in defiance of contrary evidence or without heeding it, we can well understand how the sanction of religion might seem to be extended to foolish and grave errors, when these come about, in the first place, in whatever ways such errors normally happen, but concern some alleged application or extension of notions in whose original production and development the distinctively religious processes described had a large share. Indeed, once initiated, we should expect erroneous and perverse attitudes to become more intractable in some regards because of the peculiar prestige that would attach to them in the general religious context in which they occur, although healthy and vigorous religion can in other ways, and by its more direct influence help us to safeguard against errors and be rid of them and of their predisposing causes.

We have also seen that religion is almost certain to be institutionalized and in that way to arouse enthusiasms and elicit loyalties other than those directly relevant to it as religion. The convictions produced in this way, and the systems of ideas by which religious experience is sustained and extended, are a fruitful source of disputations and errors such as those to which we are normally prone. There may thus arise in these ways also a sense of certainty and a devotion to a cause for which there is little justification, but which assume, for the agents themselves as well as for others, the semblance of unquestionable divine disclosure, so much do those appear in the general context of a communion of man with God in which the closeness of the relation is apt to obscure the element of mediation in it or hinder its being subjected to reflective analysis. The crank and the shortsighted bigot may therefore appear sometimes to have the same divine sanction as the genuine prophet, and the claim will not be altogether bogus, in as much as the crank as well as the prophet may be drawing in some measure, or at some removes, upon properly religious sources or be exhibiting attitudes whose general form has been determined by genuine or live religion. Indeed, the religious crank may well be having the sort of religious experience or illumination I have described, and be predisposed by temperament and history to have it more markedly and intensely than others. But he may yet make foolish and ill-founded claims on the basis of this experience because he brings to his understanding of it, and to its extension into other aspects of experience, misleading notions to which he has become committed independently and which may even intensify his dogmatism and inflame the passions by which dogmatic attitudes are often sustained. By contrast, one characteristic of the genuine prophet is that he combines with the intensity and vividness of any religious experience he has himself a sounder judgment than most persons about its relation to kindred experiences of his own or of other persons and the proper extension of these into further social and personal contexts. On the view I have advanced we may thus explain many aberrations of religion and much in the history of it which seems to offer the warrant of genuine divine disclosure for views or practices which are unacceptable or absurd; and we may do this without surrender of the notion of there being in the history of individuals and of society a process of divine disclosure and personal relationships of man and God which the continuing practices and traditions of society sustain and render, in course of time, ever more natural and unquestioned for those who find themselves in the appropriate setting and respond effectively to it.

These considerations accentuate for us also the importance of thought in the total life of religion, especially in times of cultural and intellectual advance. For it is by the effort to understand religious claims in terms of a process of revelation such as I have described and the integration of these claims, through renewal of religion in ourselves, with our cultural and social environment, that religion is developed and keeps its significance at various periods. The power which seemingly reactionary and bogus religious movements often have can also be more fairly judged in these terms, and it becomes possible to see how they can be beneficial while needing much pruning and correcting through reflection on their place in the general progress of religion.

Stress may also be further placed here on the importance of the social side of religion for its proper appreciation. For the correction and extension of religious insight was seen to turn on the right relating of certain religious occurrences to others in the pattern by which they are woven into the general life of society and the traditions and secondary activities by which this is sustained. Moreover the moment of wondering and stilled apprehension of finite facts as having an infinite or transcendent source, in deepening our sense of the unity of our natural environment, will intensify in the same way our sense of affinity and kinship with other persons; and the more our religious insight itself acquires the form of personal divine encounter and disclosure, the more will personal relationships as such be sanctified. Our social bonds will thus have the tightening of our bond with God.

This bears very closely on the intensely collectivist form of the early societies in which religion first came to birth. This, as I have stressed, must not be exaggerated to the point where the play of individual initiative and distinctive insight is overlooked. Nor must we forget that societies have always been composed of individuals. But as is also well known today, the individual in primitive communities is less aware of his distinctiveness than in later times and more subordinated to the community and the customs by which it is ruled. It follows that the context into which the insights of inspired individuals are woven, and the background from which the preconceptions that regulate those insights are derived, are affected throughout by collectivist notions and a deep sense of one's identity with a community. This is peculiarly helpful, at formative stages of the growth of religion, in sustaining the outlook or habit of mind which relates particular religious occurrences to others and coordinates them thus into a pattern which confirms them and extends their meaning. In so far as the sense of the personal dealing of God with men derives much of its spontaneity and apparent directness from this integration of religion within a particular social nexus, the habit of thinking in profoundly social or collectivist terms, and of merging oneself in the life of one's society, will have much to do with the first generation of the habit of mind which takes personal encounter with God for granted and discovers distinctive indications of it easily.

At the same time this initially helpful predisposition of mind leaves a heritage of grave complications and acute social and religious problems for later times. For when, in the advance of culture, it becomes necessary to shed the collectivism of early periods and appreciate better the importance of the individual, the collectivist habits and presuppositions which we have to discard will be found to be deeply ingrained, not only in our ordinary social attitudes, but in expressly religious dispositions and ways of thought. The supreme examples here are the notions of collective guilt and vicarious punishment, and one of the hardest problems of enlightened religious thinking is to get rid of these morally objectionable notions while retaining whatever deposit of religious experience in the past has been preserved in the religious formulation of them. It will aid us to do this wisely if we remember that the ideas to be discarded owe much of their force to conditions which were at one period helpful to religion.

In the same way we can understand better the course taken by various perversions of religion. The worst forms of these, as we saw, were those in which moral evil coalesced with idolatry. This has the consequence of setting up certain doctrinal reflections upon the total religious situation in which it occurs, and in the substance of these the peculiar requirements of morality, and especially the requirement of deliberate choice, tend to be obscured. But this distortion of moral truth is more easily accommodated to collectivist social attitudes than to the more enlightened procedures of later times, and as the collectivist attitude has in some measure the support of religion, through the help it has been to religion at a formative period, additional reinforcement is provided in these ways for religious and ethical assumptions which it requires much careful analysis for enlightened thinking to counter without detriment to features of the life of religion which it is vital to preserve.

Such considerations may lead to many adjustments in our own religious attitudes, and in making them we shall naturally have especial regard to the importance the individual has for enlightened ethical thinking. But in these and similar matters we shall be much helped to keep our balance and perspective by the consideration that the experience of God which the individual has, and by which the significance of the religious life of his society and its antecedents are disclosed to him, itself involves a consciousness of God as supreme and mysterious reality expressly illustrating the situation and circumstances in which God is thus known. That is, we do not become aware of God as present to us merely by appreciating something of significance in the past, but rather have the content of our present experience extended and made more precise as a personal encounter through the illumination which our present insistent awareness of God, and its more direct impact on our individual situation, bring to all the other elements which we assimilate into our total present experience. The present enlivened awareness of God displays for us the true character of all the items by which it itself is extended and enriched. But without such extension, sustained and given shape in the ways we have considered, the experience would remain more nebulous and ill-understood.

A new difficulty may however present itself here. Religion, we have seen, tends to reach out into the past and make the past peculiarly relevant and sustaining in the present, and it does this in a way which provides a new impetus to the further course of religion and its enrichment of life. But if religion is in this way, by its very nature and not by peculiar circumstances, a dynamic power in history, should we not expect all societies to display, in their religious life, a marked sense of historical process? And that, it may be argued, is not always forthcoming. It is only in some cultures and in some parts of the world that religion has carried with it a sense of divine disclosure and activity in history. Nor does the difference coincide closely with differences in degree of religious attainment. The religions of India, for example, show at certain periods a very high degree of insight and attainment, but they do not exhibit the same consciousness of religious destiny as the Hebrews had.

In reply, I maintain that the difference in question is largely due to historical differences of situation and circumstance upon which religion supervenes and by which it is affected. This can be exhibited more clearly perhaps in regard to primitive religions which seem to continue without sharp variation a round of religious ceremonial and practice from one generation to another. The obvious comment to make on such cases, from the point of view adopted in this study, is that there is not initially here any marked historical change or progress, and while religion must be considered to be infusing its peculiarly personal exchanges into the ebb and flow of living religious experience, it is not to be expected that this should induce the profound sense of religious destiny and clash of forces in a developing religious situation in the same way as where the enlivening of religion coincides with an attainment of that state of development in culture where history takes the form we recognize it to have for us and for peoples similarly placed to ourselves in the course of civilization.

It is where the stream of history quickens after the long sluggish periods of primitive ages that religion acquires its most notably religious character, and is thereby enabled also to make a more sure manifestation of what it most distinctively is in itself. But there is also to be found in Hebrew-Christian history a peculiar combination of secular and religious events which gives, to this stretch of history a role unique in the development of religion and a fulfilment of what religion is incipiently everywhere. It is the task of Christian witness and apology to exhibit this.

There is a finality in Christian truth in the sense that God has there provided the ultimate mode of His self-disclosure and the fullness of the means of reconciliation with Himself; but this truth may yet be variously appropriated as it elevates and dominates the changing and developing experiences of men, and in this process an exceptional part may well be played by the times in which we live. In one regard, as noted earlier, the prospect is bleak. Religion is undoubtedly at a low ebb, its successes are largely on the surface and the mass of the people in many lands have been estranged from the institutions and customs which nourished and informed their minds in religious matters. The aridity of thought and the enfeeblement of the imagination are grave hindrances, and we should be most unwise, if we are Christians, to assume that the victory over these is assured in our time—that is not the sort of easy optimism which Christian faith and history offer us. But if there should be a surmounting of the varied and confusing obstacles in the way, if true religion should be renewed in the present age, its triumphs will be distinctive and it will

shine with new splendours in extended modes of experience and understanding not yet subdued to religion or
charged with its power. The ability of religion to germinate within experience and so provide richer modes
of itself is one of the matters I have stressed, and it is
this germinative power of religion, elevating and trans-
forming experiences and never frustrating what is sound
and of merit in them, that we need most to stress when
we consider the relevance of an 'old story' to the novel
and rapidly changing circumstances of our time. The
mode in which Christianity is proper and appropriate
for today, and in which its truths become natural for
us and not artificial and unconvincing clichés, will
appear as the deposit of faith becomes a living force
in the world in which we live. The adequacy of faith
never fails to be evident in any circumstances, provided
faith is alive. The encounter with the living God in His
work once as a man among men, and yet present to us
now, adapts all that is within its compass to itself.

I have more than once referred to the Book of Revelation, not altogether by design to give it prominence and
yet not without a deep sense of its exceptional relevance
to our time and lot. It is a book written in circumstances
which have much in common with our own. When it was
composed there were grave political distress and uncertainty and severe persecutions, the 'great tribulation'
had begun, a great empire was losing its morale and
becoming more coldly and barbarously cruel, there were
wars and the threat of worse wars and their accompaniments of pestilence and want. In the midst of this the
early Christian communities were imperilled, not only
by hostility without, but also by much loss of character
and corruption of faith within; and it was in the exigencies and strains of these conditions, and the peril and
privation in which he himself was placed, that the author
of the Book of Revelation found himself raised to a new

sensitivity and pressed beyond the limits of normal apprehension. What his experience was like in all regards it may be impossible to tell; much, as we have seen, in the account we have of it can be reduced to a fairly common dimension in terms of the codes the initiates used. But, when all allowance has been made for this and cognate considerations, we are left with the impression of visions and discernment far beyond the normal terms of our existence; the sense of eternity, of Alpha and Omega, of first things and last things, runs through the whole, all appears in the light and strangeness and the stir and energy of a very different world from the one we normally inhabit, and whatever we judge this to be, its newness and splendour seem little in doubt. And yet this in itself is not the main and more lasting impression, it does not itself provide the theme of the book but its accompaniments and setting. The theme is that, in the midst of the confusion and newness, there is a throne, and on the throne, and alone able and worthy to open the seals of the book, is a Lamb as it were slain'. The writer was certainly near enough to the initial Christian occurrences to understand this, at the heart of it, as the life and death of the young man Jesus in Palestine. Those historical events, witnessed in records already given form and stability, afforded the key to all dominion and wisdom and glory, it was their light that made the rest resplendent, there was nothing they did not match or to which they were inadequate, all was made new because of them—a new heaven and a new earth.

The times in which we live are also stirring and strange, fraught with possibilities of terrible disaster and also with the means of entry into very new ways of living. What our amenities may be shortly, and what uses and abuses we shall find for them, only the experts can guess and that most uncertainly. But whatever the unprecedented lot into which we enter, however we conquer or are conquered by our environment, whatever new world we may inhabit beyond the present one and whatever we may find when we pass beyond our present existence, whatever adaptations we must make, there will always be possible, as it was for the first apostles, the vision of Jesus as the Lord of all life and its glory, provided we seek this humbly in the setting in which it was initially placed. It will match up to all change and all triumph, being itself the supreme triumph of God, for 'it pleased the Father that in Him all fullness should dwell'. This does not mean that all our difficulties may be ended, or that pain and evil may not continue to afflict us; these will surely continue to oppress us in some form in any foreseeable human existence and to set up their tensions for faith, and no one escapes 'the last enemy'. There will also persist at the heart of belief the strain and embarrassment of the reference to the incomprehensible, the mystery of God. We shall not even see all natural things 'put under us', but shall rather be much under their dominion. Nonetheless,

'Seeing we also are compassed about with so great a cloud of witnesses, let us lay aside every weight, and the sin which doth so easily beset us, and let us run with patience the race that is set before us, looking unto Jesus, the author and finisher of our faith; who for the joy that was set before him endured the Cross, despising the shame, and is set down at the right hand of the throne of God.'

For us today as of old this vision of Jesus is possible, if we diligently seek it where God ordained that it should be found, in the live and continuing witness to what Jesus was and did.

Index

Index of Proper Names

Subject Index

INDEX